A Monument to Education

Cultivating self control, truthfulness, and a right sense of honor since 1889.

BATTLE GROUND ACADEMY
A Monument to Education

C I N D Y G E N T R Y

HILLSBORO PRESS
Franklin, Tennessee

Tennessee Heritage Library
Bicentennial Collection

Copyright 1996 by Cindy Gentry

All rights reserved. Written permission must be secured from the publisher to use or reproduce any part of this book, except for brief quotations in critical reviews and articles.

Printed in the United States of America

00   99   98   97   96   5   4   3   2   1

Library of Congress Catalog Card Number: 96–75941

ISBN: 1–881576–65–5

Cover by Bozeman Design

Cover photos as follows: Top Row—Fleming Hall, circa 1911; Coverdale Hall (old gym), circa 1905; Peoples School, circa 1904. Bottom Row—Old Dormitory, circa 1922; Wall and Mooney School, circa 1889.

Published by
HILLSBORO PRESS
an imprint of
PROVIDENCE HOUSE PUBLISHERS
238 Seaboard Lane • Franklin, Tennessee 37067
800-321-5692

To all those who have unwaveringly believed in and generously contributed to Battle Ground Academy.

Because of you, the heritage continues.

Contents

Foreword	ix
Part I—1864–1899	3
Chapter One The Battle of Franklin	5
Chapter Two We Baptize Today—BGA	18
Chapter Three Wall and Mooney School	25
Part II—1900–1996	35
Chapter Four Mooney Moves—Peoples Arrives	37
Chapter Five The Fire—A Wicked Fate	46
Chapter Six Boarders—The First Dormitory	54
Chapter Seven The Tug-of-War	63
Chapter Eight All Out for Victory	72
Chapter Nine The Blizzard of 1951	81
Chapter Ten A Decade of Champions	90
Chapter Eleven Changing Times	101
Chapter Twelve Jubilation Celebration	109
Chapter Thirteen Building for Our Second Century	117
Part III—Class Composites	127
Appendices	221
A. Articles	223
B. Diploma and Dormitory	226
C. Commencement Day Announcement	227
D. Season Football Pass/Poster	228
E. Advertisement	229
F. Remembrances	230
Endnotes	231
Index	233

Foreword

The history of Battle Ground Academy is long and rich. There are thousands of persons whose lives have been deeply touched by traditions of Battle Ground Academy. It is expected that this book, BATTLE GROUND ACADEMY: A MONUMENT TO EDUCATION, will provide interesting information as well as rekindle warm memories with its outstanding, accurate compilation of pictures, stories, and happenings which have figured prominently into the proud history and rich heritage of our school.

We are indebted to Cindy Gentry of Franklin, wife of alumnus Allen Gentry (1970). Although she disclaims being a professional writer, she has added an exciting dimension through her vivid descriptions of many people, places, and stories which are well-known to the BGA community.

Begun in 1889, Battle Ground Academy is one of the state's oldest educational institutions. We are extremely proud of the heritage of BGA in Middle Tennessee, and, as we begin our 108th consecutive year of educating youth, each of us at BGA looks back at the past with pride and looks forward to the future with enthusiasm.

I hope you enjoy your copy of BATTLE GROUND ACADEMY: A MONUMENT TO EDUCATION. This is a book to be read, studied, enjoyed, and passed on for future reading.

Ronald H. Griffeth
Headmaster, 1996

A Monument to Education

Part I

1864–1899

CHAPTER ONE

The Battle of Franklin

The history of Battle Ground Academy could not be written without looking at the events that led to its naming. The circumstances that precede the Battle of Franklin are almost as important as that unforgettable day in November 1864 when Gen. John Bell Hood directed the Army of Tennessee into one of the bloodiest conflicts of the Civil War. Although the Battle of Franklin will go down in the history books as one of the least decisive battles of the war, it will long be remembered as some of the most grueling hours in our history. In order to fully understand the ramifications of the battle, one must first look at the fateful events just prior to that memorable day.

In July 1864, President Jefferson Davis replaced Gen. Joseph Johnston with Gen. John Bell Hood as the commander of the Army of Tennessee.

When Hood took over the Army of Tennessee he met with political factionalism due to heavy losses during the weeks of fighting around Atlanta. His predecessor, General Johnston, argued that Hood's combative tactics in Atlanta resulted in heavy losses, while Hood maintained that Johnston's losses from Dalton to Atlanta were great. For whatever reason, the Army of Tennessee could only put together 23,000 infantry by early September 1864 and Hood's dreams of a grand army faded as he realized the toll Atlanta had taken. Not only had he lost many men to battle or desertion, the men that remained were in low morale.[1]

John Bell Hood was thirty-three years old when he ordered the Army of Tennessee to make a frontal assault on the Federal troops entrenched just south of Franklin on November 30, 1864.

Even with the odds against him, Hood still envisioned an army that would mount an offensive and invade Tennessee. His plan called for taking Nashville back, moving on to Kentucky then swinging east and crossing the Cumberland Mountains in order to join Robert E. Lee's Army of Northern Virginia to beat Gen. Ulysses S. Grant's Army of the Potomac.[2] This plan was Hood's last attempt to parallel the war as it was when he was a hero. What Hood seemed to overlook was his shambles of an army and trying this maneuver in the dead of winter.

Hood's march northward meant crossing the Tennessee River which proved to be a problem due to flooding. The army finally crossed at Tuscumbia, Alabama, nearly one hundred miles west of the original point. The goal of Nashville met with early storms of snow and sleet as well as reports of a growing Federal strength in Middle Tennessee.[3] Gen. John M. Schofield commanded the Union forces that followed Hood's erratic northern movements. Ironically, Hood and Schofield graduated from the same class at West Point in 1853 and now they were destined to oppose each other on the field.[4]

As Hood's troops entered Middle Tennessee, his plan seemed to gain momentum. The Confederates were winning

W. A. Keesy, a soldier in the 64th Ohio, recalled the scene just prior to the battle: "Boldly on came the foe, the swords glistening and bayonets flashing."

the race and on November 29, Hood waited comfortably in Spring Hill just fifteen miles south of Franklin, expecting to deliver a convincing blow to the Union troops. What happened next is one of life's great mysteries. During the night 22,000 Union soldiers slipped past the resting Confederates and completely escaped Hood's grasp.

As the Federal troops moved toward the north they soon realized their hopes of reaching Nashville would be delayed. In Franklin there were two bridges that crossed the Harpeth River at the time and one had washed away while the other was severely damaged. Schofield thought the river would be too hard to cross with his seven-mile supply train. Schofield remained on the northern edge of town to supervise a means of crossing the river and left Gen. Jacob D. Cox with orders to set up a line of defense that would protect the river crossing and if he must, with his back to the Harpeth River, fight.[5]

Cox's division took position first in a line that formed a horseshoe with the Harpeth River to the rear. The line extended from the river and railroad cut near Lewisburg Pike across three major roads and continuing northward toward the river near the present day Hillsboro Road.

Cox set up headquarters in the house of Fountain Branch Carter just behind the main lines. At this time, Mr. Carter's household included his son Moscow, a Confederate colonel who was at home on parole, four grown daughters, a daughter-in-law, three families of young children and two servants.[6] Cox recalled, "I rode on with my staff to the house before me, which was on our left hand as we approached the town, and was partly hidden by a grove of trees a little way south of it. Rousing the family, they were told that we should have to make use of part of the house as temporary headquarters. They put their front sitting-room at our disposal,

John McAllister Schofield, a classmate of John Bell Hood at West Point, directed the Federal forces in the Battle of Franklin.

Following the Atlanta campaign, William T. Sherman sent Federal troops into Tennessee to stop a possible invasion, as he began his infamous march to the sea.

and, loosening sword belts and pistol holsters, we threw ourselves upon the floor to get a few minutes of greatly needed sleep."[7]

Outside the Carter house the Federal troops threw up an earthwork with a ditch in front. The works were topped with headlogs leaving a three-inch space for rifles. Osage orange trees as well as locust were cut and added to the defensive line. The field in front of these lines was basically open and level except for a locust grove just southwest of the house. If the Confederates did make a frontal attack, they would run across open fields firing at the well-defensed Federals.[8]

Meanwhile, Schofield remained behind the lines and directed a battery of three-inch rifled guns into Fort Granger to guard against an expected flanking movement. Fort Granger was built earlier in the war by the Federal troops when Franklin became Union occupied in the spring of 1863. From this position the Federals could command the railroad cut and the ground in front of Cox's division. The Federals were now ready to make a stand against Hood's army.[9]

Hood, now on a rampage following the blunder at Spring Hill, pushed his troops toward Franklin. As they marched, local citizens lined the road and shouted "Push on, boys, you will capture all the Yanks soon, they have just passed here on the dead run."[10] As Hood topped Winstead Hill, just two miles south of the Carter house, he surveyed a wall of blue coats entrenched on the outskirts of town. He was confident the enemy could not escape this time with the Harpeth River at their back.

When Confederate general Benjamin F. Cheatham viewed the Federal forces from Winstead Hill he told

A Monument to Education

The home of Fountain Branch Carter was secured as headquarters for the Federal army in the early morning hours on the day of the battle.

Hood: "I do not like the looks of this fight; the enemy has an excellent position and is well fortified."[11] Gen. Patrick Cleburne and Gen. Nathan Bedford Forrest suggested his cavalry could force Schofield from his works on the south bank with a flanking movement. But Hood made the ultimate decision and the stage was set for one of the bloodiest battles of the Civil War.

At four o'clock, November 30, 1864, the Army of Tennessee advanced 20,000 troops under a setting sun. Gen. A. P. Stewart's corps marched on the east side of the Columbia Pike and Gen. B. F. Cheatham's men marched on the west, except for the right flank under the command of Cleburne.[12] Hardin Figuers, a Franklin teenager at the time, describes the scene: "As the Confederate army began to file in between the two hills and to deploy right and left and take their positions in line, the Confederate bands began to play 'Dixie,' and a shout went up.... There was a moment of silence, and then the Federal band down near the gin house played 'Hail Columbia,' and the Federals replied with a vigorous shout of defiance.... The two

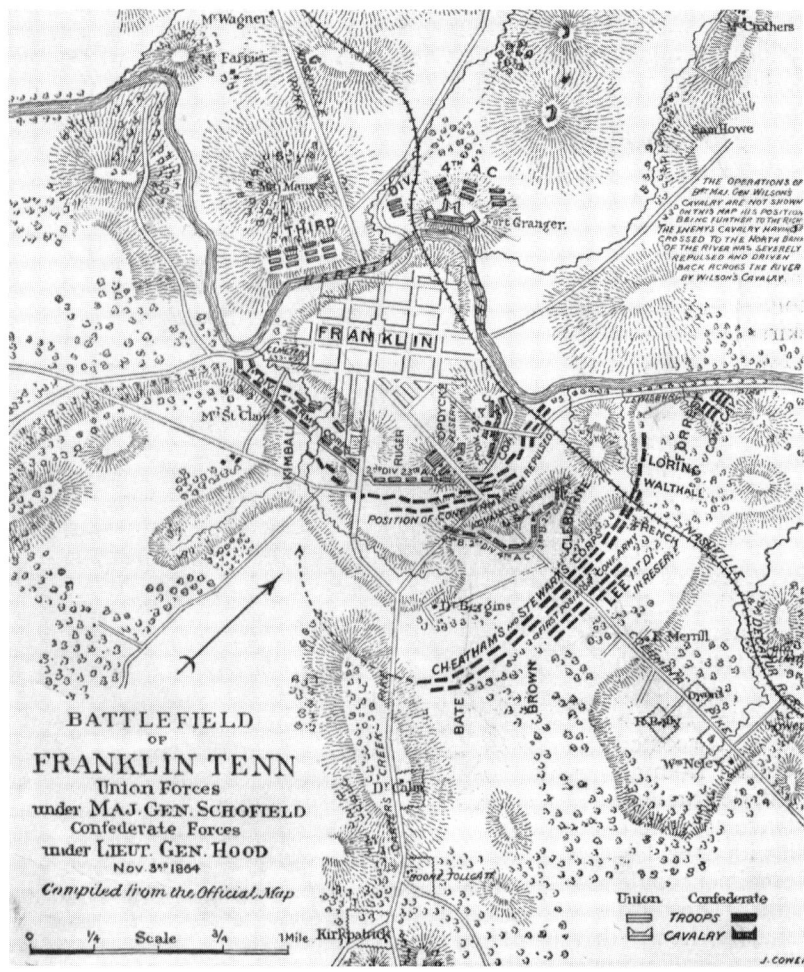

On November 30, 1864, around 4:00 P.M., Gen. John Bell Hood ordered a frontal assault on the Federal troops, despite the fact that many of his staff openly disagreed with the plan.

armies were in sight of each other; they were nearly two miles apart."[13]

The Confederate forces swept onto the battlefield in perfect alignment with colors flying.[14] For some reason, Wagner's advanced Federal troops did not immediately retreat as they were told to do in the case of a frontal assault. One of the men in Wagner's division later remembered: "They were coming on a run, emitting the shrill rebel charging yell and so close that my first impulse was to drop flat on the ground and let them charge over. I shouted to my company: 'Fall back! Fall back!' and gave an example of how to do it by turning

Winstead Hill lies less than two miles south of the Carter House. From this vantage point the Confederate commanders could plainly see the mass of Federal soldiers entrenched on the southern edge of Franklin and ready to fight.

and running for the breastworks. I had never heard bullets hiss with such a diabolical venom."[15]

As Wagner's soldiers ran for cover behind the main line, Cleburne and Brown's men followed so closely that the Federals in the main line dared not to shoot for fear of hitting their own men. Hundreds of Confederates poured through the opening made for Wagner's men. For awhile, hand to hand combat took place in the center of the Federal line around the Carter house. Confederate general Govan remembered "General Cleburne's object seemed to be to run in . . . with the fleeing Federals from Wagner's division. About that time General Cleburne's horse was killed. . . . I was very near him. . . . The impetus at which he was moving carried the horse forward after his death wound, and he fell almost in the ditch on the outside of the entrenchments. One of the couriers dismounted and gave him his horse, and while in the act of mounting, this second horse was killed by a cannon ball fired . . . from the gin-house."[16] Waving his cap, Cleburne progressed on foot to within forty yards of the enemy line and disappeared in a cloud of smoke. The great Irish general was shot near the heart and died still grasping his saber.

At this point, Union general Opydycke, whose men waited in reserve, began to move forward and fill in the gap at the Pike. His men quickly engaged in the hand-to-hand conflict that would eventually end in the closing of the gap and the capture of many Confederate soldiers. One of Opydycke's men recalled "At last the Confederates who were inside the works surrendered. We huddled them behind the cotton gin for safety. . . . Then began a series of charge after charge to break our lines."[17]

The men of Cleburne and Brown's divisions were pushed back to the main line of Federal works and beyond. Brown soon realized the toll taken on his men. He was seriously wounded and he lost all four of his brigade commanders. Gen. S. R. Gist and Gen. O. F. Strahl were killed while Gen. John C. Carter was mortally wounded. Also lost was Gen. G. W. Gordon who was taken prisoner.[18]

Of course, the fighting was not completely centered around the Carter house. Stewart's corps were fighting on the right with similar determination, but his entire line was

Early in the battle, Confederate soldiers managed to push behind the Federal line where hand-to-hand fighting took place.

A Monument to Education

Fountain Branch Carter's cotton gin sat across the road and southeast of the house. The gin was not destroyed despite the heavy fighting that took place around it.

being met by such a line of fire that they were overcome. A Federal soldier later remembered "Nine separate and distinct charges were made, each time men falling in every direction and each time being repulsed. In one of these charges, more desperate than any that followed, Gen. Adams rode up to our works."[19] It was during this fighting that Confederate general John Adams was killed.

As the sun set, the heavy fighting began to slow down. From that point until about nine o'clock that evening the Confederate officials knew little of what was going on. The fighting continued, but it seemed more like the fighting of individuals rather than that of an army.[20] One of Strahl's men recalled "After nightfall, . . . with but the light of the flashing guns, I could see only what passed directly under my own eyes. True, the moon was shining: but the dense smoke and dust [were] . . . like a heavy fog before the rising of the sun, only there was no promise of the fog disappearing. Our spirits were crushed. It was indeed the Valley of Death."[21]

Around eleven o'clock that evening Schofield ordered his men to move quietly toward a river crossing. One division would remain until all had passed then follow and burn the bridges. Schofield's army would move north and join forces with Thomas in Nashville. A Federal soldier said "As I passed the Carter house I saw the line of wounded, lying as they had been placed, and moaning most piteously. They did not seem to understand that the army had gone, and that soon they would fall into the hands of the enemy."[22]

Hood had not given up and ordered what was left of his troops to attack again the following morning, but sometime during the early morning hours, Hood was made aware of the Federal march into Nashville. As the sun rose over Franklin, Hood was finally able to view what he could not see the night before. After looking over the battlefield a Confederate soldier remembered "The dead, cold and stiff bodies were laying in every conceivable posture, all with ghastly faces and glassy eyes. Some lay with faces up and some with faces down. Some in a sitting attitude, braced with the dead bodies of their comrades. Some lay with two or three bodies on them."[23] In the end, there were eight thousand combined casualties, six thousand Confederate and two thousand Union.

Among the dead was young Capt. Tod Carter, the son of Fountain B. Carter whose house was in the midst of the battle. Tod joined the army with his brothers Moscow and Francis in May 1861. He had not returned home during the entire war and was excited at the thought of being so close as he marched with the Army of Tennessee in late November. Tod was an aide-de-camp to Gen. Thomas Benton Smith and not required to fight, but was heard to say "No power on earth can keep me out of this battle on my father's farm!"[24]

Young Carter mounted his horse Rosencrantz and led a charge in the center of Bate's Division on the west side of Columbia Pike. Near the enemies' earthworks he was struck nine times including once in the head. Rosencrantz lay dead just a few feet away. Word soon reached the family that Tod had been seriously injured and was still on the battlefield. His older brother Moscow immediately began a search but could not find him. Gen. Thomas Benton Smith later came to the house and directed the family to the spot where he lay. An unconscious Tod was carried by stretcher to his home and a surgeon removed the bullet, but he died two days later.

A young Tod Carter gallantly fought in the battle hoping to reach the home where he had not been for over three years.

The wounded soldiers were taken to the various "hospitals" around town. Carnton, the home of John McGavock, was one such hospital where field surgeons worked to save lives by the only means they knew how which in many cases meant the amputation of the injured

John and Caroline McGavock opened their home Carnton as a place for the Confederate soldiers to rest, recuperate, and die following the battle.

Almost 1500 Confederate soldiers lay to rest in a two-acre cemetery adjacent to the McGavock family plot.

limb. Blood stains can be seen today at this beautiful home where stories are told of a stack of amputated limbs as tall as the smokehouse. An estimated three hundred soldiers were tended to at Carnton alone following the battle.

The Confederate dead were soon buried in hastily dug graves on either side of Columbia Pike. Those that were identified were given a small plank on which their names were written. As the winter took its toll, some of the wooden markers began to disappear and used as firewood. John McGavock of Carnton donated two acres of land adjacent to his family cemetery for the slain soldiers. In April of 1866, the bodies were reinterred and buried as to the state they fought for. A large area was set aside for 225 unknown soldiers for a total of nearly 1500 Confederate soldiers. McGavock's wife Caroline kept a record of every soldier in a journal which is displayed in the house today.

A Monument to Education

The United Daughters of the Confederacy raised the funds to erect the Confederate Monument that stands in the center of Franklin's square. The statue was dedicated on November 30, 1899, to the delight of over ten thousand people who were in town for the event.

The Battle of Franklin may not have been as legendary as Shiloh or Gettysburg, but the struggle here is certainly noteworthy. In the years following the war, many efforts were placed on making a National Battlefield at Franklin. After many other such designations, Congress was not willing to fund another such project.[25] As time passed and the town grew, the battlefield was taken over by residences and early subdivisions. On November 30, 1899, the United Daughters of the Confederacy unveiled a thirty-seven-foot monument in the town square to memorialize those who fought and died on that fateful day.

CHAPTER TWO

We Baptize Today—BGA

When local citizens decided to start a school in Franklin, Tennessee, in 1889 to provide for their children the most current educational opportunities, they were following a long-established academic heritage. The first attempt at public education in Tennessee came in 1806 when 200,000 acres of land were set aside from which the income would be used for schools "forever."[26] There was some confusion in the beginning, but finally Harpeth Academy was opened in Williamson County in 1811. The first teacher was Presbyterian preacher Gideon Blackburn, and this school continued for many years under the leadership of such notables as James Otey, Andrew and Patrick Campbell, and Dr. J. P. Hanner. The school closed during the Civil War and never reopened. Andrew and Patrick Campbell later operated the Campbell School on West Main until the 1890s. Even today one can still see etched on a front window the names of two mischievous boys and the date March 11, 1895.[27]

Other early schools worth mentioning are the Franklin Female Institute and the Tennessee Female College. The Franklin Female Institute was established under an act of the Tennessee General Assembly of 1847. It was located where the Williamson County Public Library stands today and remained in operation as a girls' school until the Civil War. Following the war, boys and girls attended there until public schools became more prevalent after the turn of the

Andrew and Patrick Campbell opened the Campbell School after serving as principals at Harpeth Academy in Franklin.

century.[28] The Tennessee Female College opened in 1857 and sat in the block presently bordered by South Margin, Fourth Avenue, Church Street and Fifth Avenue. The college survived the Civil War and also remained in operation until the implementation of public schools. The original building burned in 1886 and was replaced by a beautiful Second Empire style structure which was torn down in 1916.[29]

During the summer of 1889, it became apparent that a new school would be added to this list of distinguished educational institutions. A group of local citizens decided to create a school that was "entirely non-sectarian; yet sound morals, good citizenship and Christianity will be its corner-stone." Every citizen was appealed to, to help the institution build a place to educate the boys at home. Could they have visualized the magnitude and impact this school would have one hundred years later? No doubt these visionaries were driven by the thought of excellent educational opportunities for their children. Little did they know how many generations would be attending the same school in the decades to come.

The setting for the school was carefully considered when the stockholders bought nearly six acres from Moscow Carter in a deed dated July 1889 for $1,140. The

The Franklin Female Institute was located where the Williamson County Public Library stands today. The building was demolished in 1905, just two years prior to the construction of the Franklin Grammar School which was added on to several times.

site was located across the road from the Carter house and a little to the south. The building site was almost exactly where the cotton gin stood during the Battle of Franklin. A newspaper article of the day states, "The ground has a history which will last as long as our institution of government lasts." The site was also considered because it was located near comfortable boarding houses which would be needed for out of town students.

The stockholders selected the following board of directors: William House, J. L. Parkes, V. W. Vaughn, Joseph B. Baugh, J. A. McFerrin, C. R. Berry and N. N. Cox. Cox served as president and Berry was the secretary and treasurer. Each of these men was "connected with the prosperity of Franklin and the county." The board immediately made plans to contract the building and the stockholders were assessed in June in order to pay for the land and begin work on the building. The structure would cost about ten thousand dollars to construct, and the directors decided about eight hundred dollars would be needed to place the school in first-class condition and keep it out of debt. Every citizen was appealed to, in order to help the school and build a place to "educate your children at home."

A Monument to Education

The Tennessee Female College held its first session in 1857 and was used as a Union hospital following the Battle of Franklin. This beautiful brick structure was built after 1886 when the original college burned.

Well-known teachers S. V. Wall and W. D. Mooney were asked to administer the school. They not only took charge, they agreed to move their entire student body from their school in Culleoka to Franklin. This included about forty boys who resided in different parts of the country. According to a local newspaper "their entire time and energy will be devoted to their business." Wall and Mooney taught with Sawney Webb at the Webb School in Culleoka before he relocated it in Bell Buckle in 1886. Both Wall and Mooney were regarded highly by Sawney Webb and each had been instilled with his beliefs and convictions.

Simeon Venable Wall was born in Williamson County on August 22, 1844. He was the son of Gen. John Brown Wall and Martha Wilson Wall who moved to Tennessee in 1810. At sixteen, he enlisted in the 80th Tennessee Regiment of the Confederate army. He served in the infantry for awhile, but was soon transferred to Forrest's cavalry where he served until the end of the war. Most of that time was spent as one of Forrest's private scouts and one of his last missions was to escort President Jefferson

Davis from Raleigh, North Carolina, to Dalton, Georgia, just prior to the president's capture and imprisonment.

Following the war, Wall entered college to extend his studies. He decided to enter the field of education where he quickly distinguished himself. He succeeded the Webb brothers at Culleoka in 1886 before moving to Franklin. He brought with him his wife of twenty-two years and ten children. He also brought a love of teaching and a desire to make Battle Ground Academy an educational institution of distinction. He tried to instill his religious beliefs into his students: "I will try to lead the boys that come to my school to Jesus and incite them to some feats of valor in His cause."

William Dromgoole Mooney was born in Huntsville, Alabama, on November 21, 1858, and was the oldest son of Rev. and Mrs. Wellborn Mooney. He attended prep school at the famous Webb School and graduated from Southwestern Presbyterian University with a B.A., an M.A., and he was the class valedictorian. His obituary speaks of his virtues: "He was an individual. His tongue could be sharp, his discipline firm. But he was the man the boys went to when trouble came their way. And he counselled them with a heart that was kind, a heart that loved youth."

Mooney's mind was versatile to say the least. He wrote both an arithmetic and an English grammar. He was a master of Latin and Greek as well as an athlete and a coach. His boys were physically sound and mentally alert. In a day when tobacco was used widely among males, Mooney vehemently opposed the use of alcohol and tobacco by his students and in a letter written to a prospective parent replied tersely "Cigarette fiends not wanted."

Although the school was chartered as Battle Ground Academy, it was more widely known as the Wall and Mooney School, following the custom to reflect the headmasters' names. When looking for students, Wall and Mooney wanted the best. An early catalog boasted: "If you wish to place your son in Vanderbilt University, Yale, Harvard, Princeton or some thorough college, then send

A Monument to Education

W. D. Mooney, left. S. V. Wall, right, joined in the formation of Battle Ground Academy or the Wall and Mooney School, as it was known at the time.

him to us and let us fit him for it. Our object is to furnish the elements of a solid education, and we try to cultivate self-control, truthfulness and a right sense of honor among our pupils."

On Saturday, October 5, 1889, Battle Ground Academy was dedicated with a speech delivered by Gen. William B. Bate, a veteran of the Battle of Franklin, former governor of Tennessee and U.S. senator. From Bate's speech:

> This building, in architectural form tasteful and useful, has been built by the free contributions of a patriotic, brave, and generous people—an educational monument, so to speak—in memory of that battle, which occurred years ago on this spot, and to that successful training of youth which is of the hopeful future. It is a memorial to the patriotism and heroism of those who, a quarter of century ago, fought and fell on this historic ground, as it also is a building dedicated to the public good where the gold-dust of knowledge from the hands of educators will be scattered over their budding intellects of the present and future generations. This cultured and generous people, proud of their lineage, their home, and their history, will see to it that this shall become a school where students will feel honored to have been graduated, not only in the branches of common English education, but in

Battle Ground Academy opened in 1889 as the Wall and Mooney School, as the schools were often named for their headmasters at this time. The beautiful brick building was built on the battlefield of Franklin near the site of Moscow Carter's cotton gin.

the Arts and Sciences, in the Greek and Latin, and modern languages. Its name, by which we baptize it today—Battle Ground Academy, and the site on which it is erected, are suggestive of those wonderful historic events in our country that had a cause as well as a consequence, and which most appropriately call for a brief reference on this occasion of its dedication.

On that momentous autumn day in 1889, the town of Franklin dedicated a school that would memorialize a period of history that many witnessed in order to provide hope for the current and future generations. They supported the school financially and in spirit, they sent their children with great dreams, and they were not disappointed. The school became, and has persistently remained, an integral part of Franklin. The quest for the best continues today as we look toward the next one hundred years of higher learning at Battle Ground Academy.

CHAPTER THREE

Wall and Mooney School

The first ten years at the Wall and Mooney School proved to be very eventful. A beautiful new brick building was constructed with ten thousand dollars raised through private donations in the community. It was scheduled to be completed by the first of September, but, due to delays, the first month of classes was held in the opera house above the post office on the northeast corner of the square. In the early days, the student body varied in size from 80 to 120. About 30 boys usually boarded in private homes in Franklin and classes met daily, even on Saturdays for those who needed extra help. A few outstanding young ladies were admitted to the school initially, though the majority were boys.

The first football team was organized in 1891. School uniforms, however, were not worn until 1894 when Mrs. Mooney recruited some of her friends to make them after securing an example from a college team to use as a pattern. For leg protection, heavy khaki canvas was used with built-in slits so that one-foot pieces of cane reeds could be inserted at one-inch intervals. Cotton batting was used to protect the knees, kidneys, and in the shoulder pads; and a canvas jacket was also worn over the jersey. Volunteers were plentiful for this project, especially among the young ladies of Franklin since each player had to be measured.

The early football schedules included colleges and universities such as Sewanee, Centre, and Cumberland,

An early tennis team poses in front of the original school building around 1899. Mr. W. D. Mooney is third from left.

because football was just coming of age and most high schools had not yet been introduced to the sport. The Wall and Mooney School not only played these teams, but more often than not, they won. It is reported that Mooney offered five hundred dollars to whoever could get Vanderbilt to play, though the challenge was never accepted. Wall and Mooney expected as much from their students on the field as in the classroom because they believed it produced a well-rounded student.

In 1893, the Chickasaw Nation sent twelve boys, who recently graduated from their reservation high school in Oklahoma, to Vanderbilt University in hopes they would return, educate others, and lead the tribal government. Upon arrival at Vanderbilt, Chancellor Kirkland informed the boys that all their requirements were acceptable except in Latin and Greek. He suggested they enroll at the Wall and Mooney School in Franklin for further studies.

As the boys made their way to Franklin, the people on the train learned of their situation and told them the

Pictured above are the young Chickasaw youths who attended Battle Ground Academy in 1894. From left to right: William T. Ward, Geo. W. Burris, William Bourland, Joe H. Goforth, T. B. McLish, Andrew Courtney, L. C. Burris, J. Boudinot Ream, and Jacob L. Thompson.

townspeople would be disappointed to see them in their street clothes. So the spirited boys decided to change into their ceremonial clothing and indulge the citizens of Franklin. Much to their surprise, most of the town turned out to see the Indian boys even thought the train did not arrive until midnight![30]

This was the second time in Franklin's history that local citizens welcomed members from the Chickasaw Nation. In 1830, President Andrew Jackson met with the Chickasaw chiefs and a treaty was signed which resulted in the removal of their people from Tennessee. The Chickasaws moved to the western lands on the other side of the Mississippi River and were followed by the Cherokee Indians in 1838 in the infamous "Trail of Tears."

> **WALL AND MOONEY'S SCHOOL.**
>
> S. V. WALL and W. D. MOONEY, A.M., Principals.
>
> This school, Battle Ground Academy, is located in one of the most beautiful and healthful sections of Middle Tennessee, eighteen miles south of Nashville on the L. & N. R. R. Our pupils enter Vanderbilt University on our certificate without examination.
>
> J. H. KIRKLAND, Chancellor of Vanderbilt University, says: "The academy of Messrs. Wall and Mooney is one of the very best training schools, so far as my knowledge extends, within the Southern states. The pupils they have prepared for Vanderbilt University have shown themselves not inferior in scholarship and thoroughness to those from any other school."
>
> CHARLES FORSTER SMITH, Ph.D., Prof. of Greek in Vanderbilt University for past twelve years, and Professor elect of Greek in the Wisconsin University, says: "In an experience of fifteen years as professor in Southern colleges, I have had no pupils better prepared than those which come to Vanderbilt University from Wall and Mooney's School. This great academy is steadily improving in thoroughness of instruction and excellence of equipment, rapidly growing in numbers, and has already few equals and no superiors within the range of my acquaintance."
>
> SEND FOR CATALOGUE.   .....S. V. WALL, FRANKLIN, TENN.
>
> Appeared in Confederate Veteran Magazine - 1894

This advertisement found in Confederate Veteran *magazine reflects the standards and practices of the school.*

The talks in Franklin continued over a few days and centered around the current sight of the Williamson County Public Library at Five Points and the Masonic Hall on Second Avenue.

During their years at the Battle Ground Academy, the Chickasaw boys participated in athletics and achieved academic success. Five of the boys graduated in 1895 and the remaining in 1896. The boys left their mark at the school and were fondly remembered for many years. Mooney later remarked, "If all Indian boys are as good students and as obedient as these twelve have been, I wish my entire school was composed of Indian boys."

S.V. Wall left the school in 1894 and moved to Texas where he founded the Wall College in Honey Grove. Mooney continued as the headmaster and the school was known for the next several years as the Mooney School. In a catalog from this time, Mooney explained, "Those who expect us to take raw lads and send them home finished scholars and polished gentlemen in the course of a few months, will be disappointed. But if you want him to be

The 1899 Mooney School gymnasium team.

thoroughly taught, if you want to impress him with how little he knows, instead of fostering his self-conceit and ignorance; if you really want him to do clean, honest work and be a clean, honest boy, then we want your boy."

The following story found in some miscellaneous papers pertaining to the early years of the school took place at the time when students boarded in private homes in Franklin. On one occasion, Mooney sent a student to live at a boarding house where several of his boys resided. The boy paid $250 and only needed to stay two weeks until another place was available. When the landlord refused to give the boy a refund, Mooney went to see the man on the boy's behalf.

As the story goes, the man refused Mooney too and began cursing. He caught Mooney's arm and got Mooney's right thumb in his mouth and would not turn loose. In the process of the fight, Mooney landed some heavy blows which broke the man's jaw and nose among other things. After the fight, Mooney got Tom Henderson to drive him to Vanderbilt hospital where his thumb had to be amputated. Mooney returned to class and finished the day while his adversary was put into the hospital for about two weeks. Needless to say, all Mooney boys were removed from that boarding house.

One year after the school opened, Mooney married Grace Reubelt of Henderson, Kentucky. The following extract from a letter he wrote to his soon-to-be wife expressed his conviction towards alcohol which remained with him throughout his life: "Am glad you enjoyed the candy, though if I had known the little champagnes were in the box, I fear I am too consistent a Prohibitionist to have sent them. You mustn't think me a crank, but 7 or 8 years ago, I had a terrible experience with liquor, and since then no drop of anything intoxicating has been tasted by me."

Mrs. Mooney was the student's friend and advisor, especially for those boarding who sometimes became homesick and in need of motherly love. The Mooney's first three children were girls and Mr. Mooney made it no secret that he wanted a son. When the students found out they were expecting a fourth child, a committee of some of the best students and athletes asked for a school holiday if the baby was a boy. As it turned out, the baby was the first of three sons and the holiday was granted.

H. C. Nichols graduated from the Mooney School in 1896, and, in his later years, remembered the school as vividly:

> I attended the Mooney School known as Battle Ground Academy in Franklin, Tennessee from 1893 through 1896. I guess the grounds occupied some twelve acres facing the Franklin and Columbia pike almost opposite Colonel Carter's residence. I recall an arbor tree in the front yard where we boys dug up Mini [sic] Balls and broken swords and rifles.
>
> There was enough ground to play shinny, similar to a form of golf and ice hockey where a puck is used. Mr. Mooney played with us at noon and insisted on fair play.

A Monument to Education

One day he was hit accidentally by a stick or ball in the face and quickly pulled out a hand mirror. Soon, he continued play.

We did not then have a real good baseball field and it was also too small for football, but we had football on vacant lots east and southeast of campus. Mr. Mooney was strictly opposed to cigarettes and a few of the boys would slip off and smoke. However, I don't think he caught anyone. Mr. Mooney taught Mathematics, Latin, Greek and the Bible. I judge he was about fifty years ahead of times in his methods of teaching and discipline.

Mr. Mooney taught Greek seven days a week. The regular school week was five days. Saturday mornings, he gave to the 'catch-ups' and to those who were capable of 'taking on' extra work. On Sunday morning the Bible was studied and the Greek testament was used. He had

The 1899 Mooney School baseball team.

the Latin class build a bridge over the River Rhine according to Caesar's specifications listed in, I think, Chapter 44 of the Third Book of Caesar.

He would send pupils in geometry to the black board to draw a circle, and if you had no string, you generally used your handkerchief; I made a compass out of two pieces of cane and a curved brass holder—one to hold chalk and one to hold a point. The boys made fun of it, but Mr. Mooney said it was clever and praised me for it.

The following is an example of a Mooney test:

1. Divide $39 among A, B, and C so that their parts shall be as 1/2, 1/3, and 1/4.
2. Find value of $5^2 \times 3 \div 15 + 9 - 2^2 + 17$.
3. Square of numbers from 1 to 25.

I. Prove 2 Δs congruent, if 2 $\angle$s and the included side are respectively equal.
II. Prove 2 Δs equal, if their 3 sides are respectively equal.
III. Synonyms for the following words:
   1. Declivity
   2. Ominous
   3. Presaging
   4. Transitory
   5. Glib
   6. Jaunty
IV. Write a brief letter to Mr. T. D. Crowe of Columbus, Ohio, asking him to quote you a price on a saddle horse; tell him just what you want as to size, gaits, color, age, breeding and price. Give him back references as to your standing.

Early graduates were often the winners of Vanderbilt entrance medals in Latin and Greek, the Founder's medal and other high honors. Mooney laid the groundwork early when accepting students to the school: "When your son enters our school, we ask that you send with him a

An early photograph found in the Battle Ground Academy archive entitled "The Foolish Five."

statement from his late teacher with regard to his character and scholarship. Because we read hundreds of pages every year from fond mothers telling us their sons have no bad habits and that they are clean in every way. Usually, we find that these boys are cigarette fiends and otherwise undesirable. These we get rid of as soon as possible. Good conduct and earnest work are necessary in this school."

According to information provided by Mooney's son W. D. Mooney Jr., N. F. Cheairs of the class of 1894 represented Vanderbilt in the Southern Intercollegiate Oratorical Association, winning the 1898 medal. Wallace Billington won the prize for the best entrance exam in the classics at Vanderbilt when he graduated in 1899. Former Mooney boy Millard Woodrow received the Law Scholarship as

The 1899 graduating class of the Mooney School. Front Row (Left to Right): Tom B. Matthews, Gerald Buchanan, B. T. Nolen, Woodlief Thomas. Second Row (L to R): J. C. "Indian" Smith, Mary Moss, Jim A. McFerrin, Patti Bolton, Fielding G. Gordon. Third Row (L to R): Unidentified, R. W. Billington, Jesse H. Gray, T. G. Pollard, Elva Davis, Theresa Mulley, F. H. Westfeldt, E. F. Schuler, Jesse Short, John Burchard.

well as the Cecil Rhodes Scholarship at Oxford. These are just a few examples of Mooney boys who went on to distinguish themselves at the college level. According to W. D. Mooney Jr., in the late 1890s, one-fourth of the undergraduate students at Vanderbilt and two-fifths of the graduate students were Mooney boys.

Whether called Battle Ground Academy or the Mooney School, the town of Franklin soon realized the impact of the school. Private citizens graciously opened their homes to boarders and merchants smiled when a holiday was granted. The traditions began and the town of Franklin would never be the same. The dreams of local citizens to provide their children with quality education became reality as the school flourished through its first ten years.

Part II

1900–1996

CHAPTER FOUR

Mooney Moves—Peoples Arrives

By the turn of the century, the Mooney school had become one of the most reputable college prep schools in the South. Students excelled in academics as well as athletics and most continued their educations at prestigious universities. The class of 1900 saw twenty-one members enroll at Vanderbilt when no other school had more than three. The 1900 catalog offered two scholarships, the first was to Vanderbilt for the best average in Latin and Greek, while the second was to Washington and Lee for the best record in Math and English. Other awards offered at this time included declamation, oratory and composition, the latter being sponsored by the *Review Appeal*.

The requirements for entering the Mooney School in 1900 included the following:

1. Ability to read English at sight and with a distinct utterance.
2. Ability to write a simple letter or composition correctly, a knowledge of the use of capital letters, elementary punctuation, possessives, and plurals.
3. Familiarity with the fundamental rules of arithmetic.
4. A fair knowledge of elementary history and geography.

At this time there were two debating societies which conducted a public debate at the end of each school year. The statement to be resolved in 1900 was "That the United

States government should own and operate its railroad." There was also a Young Men's Christian Association which produced a handbook, met weekly and sent one or two boys each year to summer Bible school.

In 1900, a group of BGA alumni decided to put together a football team and challenge the school's strong varsity team. The school accepted the challenge, but underestimated its opponents and never took the game seriously. Both teams fought hard and the ball was punted several times before the game ended in a 5-5 tie. The varsity team eagerly accepted the chance at a second game because they felt the alumni had been lucky and this time they would beat them by fifty points.

When it came time to play again, many of the alumni could not get excused from work since they had missed time recuperating from the first game. As it turned out, substitutes were called in and since most held daytime jobs, practice was held at night on the town square. In the second half, Tom Henderson of the alumni team punted seventeen times. One of the punts touched an opponent and went over the goal where an alumni fell on it for their only score. The varsity won this game 17-5 in another hard-fought game.

The 1900 varsity football team at the Mooney School was considered one of the best among prep schools at the time. They defeated Louisville, Indianapolis, Bowling Green, and the strong University of Nashville. Almost every member went on to Vanderbilt or Cumberland to become a star, including M. S. Bridges, Frank Kyle, Frank "Red" Smith, Booker Smizer, Ed Hamilton, Buford Mallery, and Brice Curd.

A *Purple and Green* school newspaper in 1901 related the following article which spoke of the tradition that already surrounded the school:

The Purple and Green *school newspaper.*

A Monument to Education

The faculty and student body unite in a feeling of gratification at the result of our last meet on the Vanderbilt track. The Franklin people always join us in the celebration and take great pride in our victories, though they never express any surprise when they hear the usual saying that "Mooney won." Four banners now grace the walls of the BGA, testifying the excellence of our work for as many consecutive years. As we placed our last trophy beside its predecessors, we felt that there must be a great deal in the atmosphere of these historic grounds to inspire the sons and grandsons of Confederate heroes with a buoyancy and strength to win in whatever they undertake. The same determination to conquer that overran the breastworks in 1864 and drove the enemy from Franklin, is still burning like a sacred incense on

The 1901 Mooney School track team displays championship banners from four consecutive years.

these grounds. The old ambitious spirit is still throbbing in the pulses of the Mooney boys. Its ideals unfold in the classrooms and outcrop upon the athletic field. The splendid vigor of brain and brawn is manifest alike in student and athlete. The careless, negative boy soon catches the inspiration of the place and develops a fiber worthy of these memorable grounds.

Many students boarded in private homes during this period and certain rules were set forth for this:

First—That I will keep no firearms in my possession.

Second—That I will not drink a drop of any intoxicant.

Third—That I will not visit the town or the railroad station without permission.

Fourth—That I will not be absent from my room at night, or receive any visitors at night.

Fifth—That I will play no game in my room at night, no cards at any time.

Sixth—That I will not call on any young lady without permission.

Supplement to the Purple and Green.

A supplement to the *Purple and Green* school newspaper, advertises "The Preparatory School Championship," a football game which was played on October 26, 1901, between the Mooney School and the Training High School of Indianapolis, Indiana. The Training School reigned as the 1900 and 1901 Middle West Champions with a student body of one thousand. The game was sponsored by the Vanderbilt University

A Monument to Education

Athletic Association and could be seen for the admission price of fifty cents. The Mooney School won the game with a score of 6-5 in a hard-fought battle where the only difference was an extra point.

James Nolner "Stein" Stone played football at BGA at the turn of the century. The skilled center went on to play at Vanderbilt from 1904–1907 where he gained prominence as a student athlete. He was also elected captain of the track team and played basketball at Vanderbilt. Stone received many honors during his college football career including All-Southern and All-American as well as being elected to the All-Time Vanderbilt football team.

The 1902 school year came to an abrupt halt when the building burned in the spring. Mooney decided that rather than rebuild here, he would move his school to Murfreesboro the following year. Local citizens realized the potential of Battle Ground Academy and a few interested individuals assembled in the office of Dr. K. S. Howlett to prepare a call for a community meeting to be held at the courthouse a few days later. The people of Franklin and

The school was rebuilt in 1903.

Local citizens raised the funds to construct a new school on the present campus in 1903 and just two years later a handsome gymnasium was erected.

Williamson County displayed great enthusiasm in supporting a movement to rebuild Battle Ground Academy.

Committees were quickly appointed and no time was spared. In just a few days the estimated sum needed was subscribed and the charter of incorporation was completed on July 8, 1902, by H. P. Fowlkes, K. S. Howlett, J. H. Henderson, Walter A. Roberts, D. E. McCorkle, and W. W. Faw. The board of directors consisted of the above six, plus: J. W. Harrison, German Marshall, C. H. Kinnard Sr., Enoch Brown Sr., George I. Matthews, L. W. Buford, Jesse E. Short, D. J. Kennedy, N. C. Perkins, William House, E. B. Cayce Jr., J. C. Eggleston, P. V. Channell, J. L. Parkes Sr., J. B. Lillie Jr., E. B. Campbell, J. H. Fisher, George H. Armistead Sr., J. H. Rolffs, J. C. Carothers, A. H. Ewing, and R. S. Owen.

Ten acres of land were purchased from John B. McEwen for ten thousand dollars on August 15, 1902. Located just

Majestic "Everbright," located on a rise just west of Battle Ground Academy, was used for classes when the original school building burned in 1902.

across the road and a little to the south from the original building site, the new building would house a library, office, and classrooms on the first floor and the second floor was composed of an eight-hundred-capacity auditorium. Battle Ground Academy was destined to remain one of the best educational opportunities available. The tradition of excellence did not cease even through a devastating fire that destroyed everything but the spirit, and the memories that could never die.

During the 1902–1903 school year, while the new building was under construction, classes met at Everbright Mansion which was located just up the hill. Everbright was a beautiful Greek Revival home built by John D. Bennett long before the Civil War. Richard and Rebecca Bostic (the daughter of Gov. Newton Cannon) moved into the house in the late 1840s and it was the scene of many extravagant parties thus the name Everbright due to the candles in the windows. Unfortunately, the house fell into disrepair and was torn down in 1937.[31]

The trustees hired James A. Peoples and Ernest Rees to run the school for one year with the understanding that brothers Hal and "Daddy" Peoples would come the following year after completing obligations at their respective schools. When they joined their brother at Battle Ground Academy, the school became known as the Peoples School. A 1902–1903 catalog reflects their philosophy: "We do not believe in short cuts. If youth is to win the mastery in this age of competition, he must be taught to go to the bottom of whatever he undertakes." James Peoples left a few months later to start the Peoples and Tucker School in Springfield, Tennessee, while BGA remained in the hands of his brothers.

R. G. "Daddy" Peoples became headmaster of Battle Ground Academy in 1903 and remained there until 1925.

The 1906 Peoples School baseball team—Front Row (Left to Right): Stanley Pullin, John Sherrill. Second Row (L to R): Hugh Channell, Allen Barnott, Floyd Blythe, Leonard Darnell. Third Row (L to R): David Blake, Will Morris, Tom Blake, Will Neely, Herman Moore.

Samuel Reynolds graduated from the Peoples School in 1909 and recalled that when he began school there in 1904, each day would begin at 8:00 A.M. with an assembly where roll was called and each student had to answer in person. This was followed by a Bible reading, prayer, announcements and sometimes Mr. Hal would speak. "He tried to inspire us to live uprightly and to aim at higher stations in life, materially and spiritually." He loved to talk about current events and the students quickly realized they could avoid a lecture by getting him started on a favorite topic.

A Monument to Education

In the fall of 1905, the beautiful maple trees that adorn the front lawn of the school were planted. During the spring of 1905, a new gymnasium was completed. At the time, a large pot-bellied stove, which sat at the north end of the building, heated the entire area. Today this building still stands and has been remodeled several times, most recently when the library was moved there.

A Battle Ground Academy postcard, circa 1909.

The first decade of the twentieth century brought great change for Battle Ground Academy. A devastating fire, the incorporation of a new school, and a change in headmasters would be enough to close the doors of most schools, but the determination was set. The town of Franklin rallied once again and aided the school because they knew what a positive addition it was to their town. Through it all, the school continued and prospered, learning in the face of adversity.

CHAPTER FIVE

The Fire—A Wicked Fate

The spring of 1910 witnessed another destructive fire on the grounds of Battle Ground Academy. According to the *Review Appeal*, March 3, 1910, a man passing the school shortly after 11:00 P.M. saw a blaze coming from the main building and ran to notify Prof. Hal Peoples. The following morning all that was left standing were the exterior walls. Lost in the fire were private papers, the office records, and a valuable library, all of which was insured for only $500. The building was insured for $7500 although it cost thousands more to build.

An article appearing just one week later in the *Review Appeal*, dated March 10, was headlined "Success Assured for Proposed Handsome New Academy Building." Already, over $7,300 of the needed $10,000 was subscribed. Once again, classes were moved to Everbright until the new building was complete. The students made resolutions to return and make Battle Ground Academy the school they remembered. The article also said Chancellor Kirkland of Vanderbilt University would be coming Saturday to motivate the students and the community in the rebuilding process.

The 1910 yearbook, the *Warrior*, contained a review of the year including the following statement: "After the fire there was much confusion for a few days, but the boys adapted themselves to the disadvantageous circumstances as well as could be hoped, and the work proceeded very well. Of course the girls are all right anywhere they are put."

A Monument to Education

When fire destroyed Battle Ground Academy for a second time in 1910, classes again met at Everbright.

The following poem was written by a Battle Ground Academy student and found in the 1910 annual:

"The Fire"

I.

Upon thy soil, Old Battle Ground,
Upon that rising, sacred mound,
Seven years ago and more
Men laid the brick, men built the floor,
A structure not a statue great,
Fraught with tapestries and date,
of great, heroic deeds to tell:
But where the youth may learn to spell—
    The Battle Ground Academy.

II.

Nor would a statue, grand and great,
Better the deeds commemorate
Than did those simple, clumsy walls,
Where lads and lassies read of the Gauls,
Where wrestled they with Math and Greek,
And learned of the Cherokee and Creek;
And awoke to find the world unfit
For boys and girls who have no grit,
    At the Battle Ground Academy.

III.

But on that fateful, winter night,
When the mist bedimmed the fearful sight,
The demon Fire crept through the door,
And spread his wicked flames the more;
Till through deserted hall and room,
Now o'er the very top they loom;
And send up many a fiery spark
To pierce the gloomy, utter dark,
    Our Battle Ground Academy.

IV.

Now only the crumbling walls are left,
Of windows, doors, and all bereft;
They tower in the vacant air,
Like a soldier bold, with now gray hair,
With shoulders bent, by age begirt,
Who stood the fire, but not unhurt,
Yet may another still more great
Rise soon from thy wicked fate;
    Old Battle Ground Academy.

—"Sal" (Charles Long, 1910)

The 1909–1910 football team did not look promising as many players graduated and it looked to be a rebuilding year. The year end annual recalled:

> When Coach Bateman called for volunteers to appear for football practice, about twenty-five (25) candidates responded to the call, among who were three of the 1908 squad—Cody, Sikes, and Hatcher, and Brown, sub. The rest was not only new but raw material, only one of whom had ever participated in a game. At first prospects for a good team looked slim, but under excellent coaching and hard practice, the cloud soon began to disappear, and by the first game a husky bunch had been rounded up, who were able to compete with the best prep teams.

By September 1911, the new building was ready for classes. Today, this is the main administration building,

The current Fleming Hall was built in 1911 when Battle Ground Academy was known as the Peoples School.

named Fleming Hall in honor of Sam Fleming who graduated from Battle Ground Academy in 1924. Some of the materials used in the new building include the bricks, cornerstones and the foundation of the old building that were spared in the fire. Once again, the students and faculty pulled together to prove their school was strong and would persevere.

The excitement of starting the school year in the new building soon turned to gloom with the death of Hal Peoples in September 1912. Greer "Daddy" Peoples continued administratively as headmaster for several years, during a period when the headmaster ran the school as a proprietorship. He was charged with maintaining the grounds and the property as well as paying all expenses so that whatever was left over would be his compensation.

"Daddy" Peoples believed greatly in trust and honor as is displayed in a booklet he published about the school: "Our school is conducted upon the honor system. No boy can ever be trustworthy without being trusted." He also promoted competition in the classroom. A classic teaching technique of his was called "trapping" where students would line up on a bench and he would begin drilling them randomly about various subjects. The person who answered correctly would "trap" or move ahead of those who did not have the right answer. In the end, the student at the head of the class would be given a star which was proudly pasted in his book.

The following poem about "Daddy" Peoples is found in the 1910 *Warrior*:

"Daddy"

I.

You are old, Daddy Peoples, the young man cried,
And pleasures with youth pass away;
But still you delight in Pipkin-boys' fall;
Now, tell us the reason, I pray.

II.

In the days of my youth, Daddy Peoples cried,
I knew a poor lad of his make,
Who grew too important for this little earth;
I love "Pip" for memory's sake.

III.

You are old, Daddy Peoples, the young man cried,
You've the sight of a far-seeing sage;
Our boys sleep in chapel whenever you speak,
Why this disrespect for your age?

IV.

Since my earliest days, Daddy Peoples replies,
I've sought to draw youths from their sin;
But, alas! they all sleep with busy accord
When I speak of the spirit within.

Prior to graduation in 1911, Josh Cody attended Battle Ground Academy and lived across the street from the school. Every morning before school started, he got up and milked his cow that stayed behind his house each night, then climbed on her back, rode her to pasture which was about a half mile out Columbia Pike, and then walked back to school. After a long day at school and sometimes practice, he would walk back to get her and ride her back to milk again. Cody was a great athlete at BGA as well as Vanderbilt where he became an All-American tackle and was eventually named to the National Football Hall of Fame. He later became the athletic director at Temple University. This story was found in a 1950s *Wildcat* and was contributed by an eyewitness alumnus.

A 1915 Peoples School catalog contains these pictures of a typical classroom (above) and the library full of books that were meant for use and not show (below).

    An invitation to the 1914 commencement exercises included a week of ongoing activities. The week began with the commencement sermon at the Methodist church followed the next day by a declamation contest. The oratorical contest was the next big event and the week finally came to an end with the commencement address. The class motto was "Esse Quam Vederi" and the class colors were maroon and white. The faculty included just four teachers; R. G. Peoples (principal), Daly Thompson (a 1910 graduate), J. H. Gordon and W. T. Dent.

    A catalog from this period lists the many attributes of the school. The location of the school was said to be "less than an hour's ride of Nashville by train, electric car or auto." Health and fresh air were a major concern at this time which was reflected by this statement, "When weather permits, our study hall is a five acre lawn, set in trees and carpeted with blue grass."

    The same catalog also boasted of the staff and the library.

The literary societies of the Peoples School provided invaluable training and practice in debate, public speaking, and parliamentary law.

Our teachers are all university men, with the best training and experience in their calling—men of sound scholarship and Christian character, understanding boys and the problems of life they are preparing these boys to solve. Our library contains over 1200 books suited to boys, carefully selected by the principal. They are meant for use, not show, and are in constant service.

At this time, two literary societies were at the school—the Sam Davis Literary Society and the Jefferson Society. The 1914 catalog emphasized the virtues of these groups.

The literary societies furnish invaluable training and practice in debate, public speaking and parliamentary law. For seven years the school has had a series of triangular debates with the Branham and Hughes School, the Columbia Military Academy and the Massey School, in which we have won nine out of fourteen debates.

The catalog concluded with a brief description of athletic opportunities available. "Our gymnasium and athletic field are not surpassed by those of any preparatory school in this section: The captain and two of the members of the Vanderbilt football team last year were graduates of our school."

"Daddy" Peoples dominated this decade with love and respect for his students. The school realized the significance of a strong relationship between the students and their teachers in order to develop mature, independent character. "Daddy's" assembly talks were intended to build the character of his students. Somedays he would speak an unusually long time and would without warning, dismiss the entire student body for the day. On one such occasion the students placed an advertisement in a local newspaper, "Card of Thanks: The boys of BGA wish to thank Mr. R. G. (Daddy) Peoples for the enjoyable holiday he gave them some time ago. This is to also let him know that they would like another in the near future."

In the early part of this decade it began to look as if the school would just be a memory. Another building burned and Hal Peoples died within a year and a half. The students were deeply affected and they learned one of life's greatest lessons. They did not give up and forget, that would be too easy. Instead, they resolved to take a stand, not because they had to, but because they wanted to. This kind of growth comes from within, and they all worked together to produce a stronger school.

CHAPTER SIX

Boarders—The First Dormitory

Battle Ground Academy saw many changes during the 1920s including those on the campus as well as in the world. The decade began with Americans full of elation over the recent war, yet ended very differently as the Great Depression approached. Many traditions were started during this period. The Greer and Plato literary societies were formed and the *Cannon Ball* annual made its first appearance. A new headmaster came on the scene and before the decade ended, BGA would be an all-boys school. The "roaring twenties" were exciting as well as changing times at Battle Ground Academy.

The *Battle Ground Breeze* was a school newspaper which covered all aspects of life at the school. The January 20 issue of 1920 contains many articles dealing with a student's school life. Best odds for the girls' basketball tryouts were as follows: Margaret McDaniel, Seval Jordan, and Anne Beasley as forwards, Susie Sugg and Florence Campbell as centers and Harriet Smithson, Mary Hoof, and Roberta Richardson as guards.

A student athletic association was formed in January 1920, to strengthen the athletic program both financially and in spirit. The students realized the teams were not getting enough support so everyone was asked to join for the cost of one dollar with a goal of the whole school joining. The money would go toward advertising and promoting athletics, and would be appropriated by the executive committee which consisted of a captain of each team, the yell leader, a coach, and a member of the faculty. Almost every boy and girl in the school was a member at the time the article was written.

Other interesting tidbits in the *Battle Ground Breeze* include:

BATTLE GROUND ACADEMY BEATS AMERICAN LEGION: The above headline may seem impossible, for the Germans couldn't do it. But we did. No, Geraldine, it was not with hand grenades or liquid gas; it was in the old game of basketball, 25-15.

Mr. Peoples asked his fourth history class what the United States got out of the war, and Matthew McDaniel promptly replied, "Cooties, influenza, and prohibition."

Wanted: School boys to join the United Loafers Union, whose sole purpose is to strike for an hour a day of school and no classes then. For further particulars see John Joyce, 520 Rabbit Track Alley, Franklin, Tennessee.

Wanted: Suggestions as to the best way to avoid Saturday school without studying. Anyone wishing to offer suggestions will please see Felix Truett, 1313 1/2 Snuff Avenue, Franklin.

One of the most memorable employees of the school began his work there in 1921. Elder William Henry Brown will be remembered by many former students as "Uncle Henry" as he was fondly called. As a general maintenance man, it was understood that anything that came under his jurisdiction would be done and done well. Uncle Henry remained at Battle Ground until 1948 when he retired due to health problems.

The Battle Ground Breeze *student newspaper.*

William Henry Brown, better known as "Uncle Henry."

The 1920 BGA girls' basketball team as pictured in the February issue of the Battle Ground Breeze. *Top Row (L to R)—Anne Beasley, unidentified, Genie Jordan, Carl Gardner (coach), Suzie Sugg, unidentified. Second Row (L to R): Mary Hooff, unidentified, Margaret McDaniel.*

Daddy Peoples knew how to handle students and understood the teenage life. In the 1923 school catalog he writes,

> But now he is beginning to put away childish things, childish virtues as well as childish defects, and to reach out toward manhood, with what manhood means. Not knowing with his own mind, he is peculiarly susceptible to the influence of the crowd.

Daddy Peoples could easily be addressing the students of today with this timeless message.

Daddy Peoples also knew just how much guidance a student needed in order to become a responsible adult.

Regarding the honor system, he felt "No boy can be trustworthy without being trusted." Yet he knew none of his students were so developed as to go without careful oversight. Every student was asked to take a written pledge of honor when taking the semi-annual exam. He also required the students to attend the church of their choice each Sunday and the first hour of each day was given to chapel exercises.

A catalog introducing the Peoples School during this period described the location of the school as being among the bluegrass hills of Middle Tennessee, "a land unequaled for beauty, healthfullness, fertility and variety of products. Pure freestone water brought by gravity from forested hills, nine miles away. No possible contamination. Abundance of outdoor sport and healthy recreation."

Boys' basketball team, 1924—Left to Right: Sam Fleming; Bob Jennings; Claude Thornton; Courtney Marshall; Bob Gracey; Albert Jordan; Coach, J. O. Davis.

Cut flowers and white tablecloths appeared everyday in the Peoples School dining room. (1924 Peoples School catalog).

Maxie Howlett attended BGA from 1921–1925 following a sister and two brothers who preceded her there. She was twelve years old when she had an interview with "Old Daddy" who said "if you can read and write, add, subtract, multiply and divide you are ready to attend BGA." She recalled,

> I lived a mile away and if my father was starting out to make housecalls, he would drive me to school picking up as many students along the way as his Model T would hold inside and on the running board. Otherwise, I would walk up the hill as most Franklin students did.

During the summer of 1924, Daddy Peoples resigned from BGA to take a position at Westminister College in Fullerton, Missouri. The board of directors decided to retain George I. Briggs to succeed him as headmaster. As an alumnus of the school, Briggs knew exactly what the school was all about and was ready to move progressively into the future. J. R. McCain, president of Agnes Scott College spoke of Briggs' virtues in a testimonial for the school.

A Monument to Education

Boarders' rooms were made to look as much like home as possible (1924 Peoples School catalog).

It gives me happiness to claim as a friend George I. Briggs, who is to take charge of Battle Ground Academy. He loves boys and knows how to win their confidence, and at the same time how to get them to work effectively. He is resourceful in making plans and untiring in carrying them out. He brings to his new work a fine record of achievement, and there is every reason to believe that he will do his finest work in this field.

As a daughter of George Briggs, Sarah Naylor grew up in the midst of Battle Ground Academy. She recalls her father would always invite a man to dine with them as a part of the interview. "You can learn more about a man if you have a meal with him. Table manners say a lot about a man," as her father would say. Briggs was a Bible scholar and would read a timeless message every night at dinner. Often he would act out scenes and demonstrate with fervor to the delight of his listeners.

Briggs' wife, the former Susie Lee Roberts, also played an important role at Battle Ground. The school needed a librarian so the Randolph Macon graduate went back to school to receive her library science degree and thus

George I. Briggs became the next headmaster of Battle Ground Academy in 1925 and remained there until his death in 1944.

became the school's first librarian. She also grew roses along the fence of their home and on Mother's Day every boy went to church with a red or white rose on his lapel. BGA was the center of the Briggs' lives and their devotion to the school fostered the school's popularity.

Chancellor J. H. Kirkland of Vanderbilt also testified as to the worthiness of BGA during this period:

> Battle Ground Academy has for many years been recognized as an accredited school of Vanderbilt University. The record of students entering from this school has been unusually good. In view of these facts, I do not hesitate to commend the school highly, and feel sure that the interests of pupils will be safeguarded by careful attention and skill of the teachers.

Briggs formed two literary societies at BGA in 1925. One society was the Greers in honor of Greer "Daddy" Peoples and the other society was named the Platos in honor of the Greek philosopher. Initially, the societies were strictly literary in nature, but as the years passed, the activities broadened to include athletics. One of the primary purposes of the two societies has been the development of a sense of fair play and good sportsmanship. This great tradition carries on today and is an integral part of the school.

The class of 1927 was moved to do something special for their school by establishing a yearbook "to carry the name Cannon Ball." The first *Cannon Ball* contained pictures of the school and each class as well as athletic teams and various organizations. The athletic teams of 1927 included football, basketball, baseball, track, and

This collage entitled "Campus Scenes" appears in the 1929–1930 Battle Ground Academy catalog.

midget basketball for the younger students. The football team of 1927 defeated team after team and it was not until the seventieth game of the season that they lost their chance for the state championship.

The 1928 basketball team was highly successful, beating everyone during the regular season by three to fifteen points. Castle Heights was the reigning state champion and when they came to play at BGA they led at halftime, but the blue and gold rallied to win 25-15. The Tennessee Interscholastic Athletic Association (T.I.A.A.) tournament at the end of the season pitted Battle Ground against Montgomery Bell Academy (MBA) in the semifinals. BGA lost, though Laird Holt made All-State at guard and won the loving cup for being the best sportsman in the tournament.

A key player on this team was senior Tom P. Henderson Jr. who also played baseball and football. He went on to be Vanderbilt's quarterback and in 1932 was named to the Grantland Rice All-American squad. He received nine letters in varsity sports at Vanderbilt. The year after Henderson graduated, Clarence Bradshaw "Pete" Gracey played football, basketball, baseball, and was on the track team. He was captain of the 1928 football team on which he played center. Gracey went on to play football at Vanderbilt too, and in 1932 was named an All-American.

Before Briggs became headmaster at BGA he had been working at the Baylor School in Chattanooga, an all-boys school. Even though he had daughters, he did not feel comfortable in the discipline of girls and began to phase out female students at BGA until the last class graduated in 1929. This policy remained in effect for fifty years until 1979 when BGA became coeducational once again.

The 1920s were exciting times at Battle Ground Academy. "Daddy" Peoples will long be remembered for his guiding hand and gentle understanding. His replacement, George I. Briggs, came on the scene with great aspirations for the already thriving school. Battle Ground Academy, with its rich heritage, was destined to grow in size and excellence. In a relatively short period of time, the school had risen to levels beyond the dreams of those who chartered it.

CHAPTER SEVEN

The Tug-of-War

Battle Ground Academy flourished during the 1930s under the direction of George Briggs. An early catalog lured students to the all-boys boarding school that was "non-military." The location of the school was advantageous because there were ten daily trains through Franklin, which was billed as one of the healthiest towns in the state, "where little sickness occurs." The school also offered day and night telephones as well as a telegraph system. The goal of the school in the early 1930s was to instill in their students "the principles of sound scholarship and to build within them those virtues which make for useful citizenship and honorable manhood."

The tuition for 1930 was $125 for day pupils and $650 for boarding students which included board, tuition, laundry and medical fees except operations. Boarding students were asked to bring such items as a Bible, dictionary, face towels, sheets, blankets, shirts, collars, underclothing, and toilet articles. One dollar per week was suggested for spending money.

The following is a daily schedule for the boarding students according to the 1930 catalog:

>   6:50 A.M.—Five minutes setting-up exercises
>   7:15 A.M.—Breakfast
>   8:00 A.M.—Inspection of Rooms
>   8:15 A.M.—School Begins

The "Shaded Portal" of Battle Ground Academy witnessed the evolution of many students in the 1930s.

11:00 A.M.—Chapel Begins
12:30 P.M.—Lunch
3:00 P.M.—School Ends
3:30–5:30 P.M.—Athletics and Recreation
6:15 P.M.—Dinner
7:15–9:15 P.M.—Study Hour
9:45 P.M.—Lights Out

The 1930 baseball team defeated Montgomery Bell Academy, Sewanee Military Academy, Columbia Military Academy, Branham and Hughes and Wallace and Duncan twice each and won the T.I.A.A. championship. According to the *Cannon Ball*, the outstanding players were: W. Gilmore, pitcher; "Granddad" Jordan, first base; Pennington, second base; and White, outfielder. Gilmore was the star of the season pitching ten games and winning nine. In ten games he struck out 158 men and in the "final game of the season against S.M.A. he struck out twenty-three men

The 1930 Battle Ground Academy T.I.A.A. championship baseball team.

to set a new world's record for prep schools."

The annual declamation contest was eagerly anticipated each year as students prepared to defend or refute a current issue. During the 1930s, Mrs. Pryor Lillie instructed the students and supervised the school contest. The speakers were divided into two sections according to their experience. The winner of the senior section represented BGA in the annual Mid-south Declamation Contest at Vanderbilt in the spring. For an idea of the type of topics that were covered, consider the following statements that were resolved in the late 1930s:

> 1936—Resolved: That a federal system of old age pensions should be established to provide adequate economic protection for the aged.

> 1937—Resolved: That Congress shall be empowered to fix minimum wages and maximum hours for industry.

> 1938—Resolved: That the Several States should adopt a Unicameral Form of Legislature.

> 1939—Resolved: That the United States should form an alliance with Great Britain.

The student newspaper, the Cannon Ball, *was first published in 1935.*

An article about the 1931 football team reflects the journalistic flare of this period:

One of the most exciting games of the season was played on Friday of the following week. Our squad of fighting demons journeyed down to Nashville to meet Montgomery Bell's notorious eleven. Our boys opened the game with ferocity and were marching down the field, when M.B.A. tightened down and got the ball on downs. The "Maroons" scored the first touchdown with a wide end run. We received, and Vaden, with the speed of Mercury, carried the ball for a touchdown. The score was tied. Things looked rosy, but M.B.A. did the same thing when they received. Then came the fatal moment when Captain Gracey got his ankle fractured, which caused him to be out for the rest of the season. He was greatly missed, but under the leadership of Hodges, who was Alternate Captain, the team fought on. The game ended with M.B.A., 13; B.G.A., 6.

In 1934, football great Carl Hinkle graduated from BGA where he was an All-State center. During his college football career at Vanderbilt, Hinkle lettered three years and as captain of the team in 1937, he achieved All-Southern, All-SEC and All-American honors. The same year, Hinkle was named SEC player of the year by the *Nashville Banner*. Hinkle was inducted into the prestigious National Football Hall of Fame in 1957.

After many years of competition in sports and debates, the Greers and Platos societies engaged in their first tug-of-war in 1935. The first tug-of-war was held at the "Big Harpeth River at the point where it runs under the bridge on the Nashville Pike" (or the current Franklin Road.) The Greers won the first event where "the crowd overflowed

A Monument to Education

the bridge and embankments and stretched in both directions down the pike." In the early days, the rope was paraded down Main Street and position was decided by the flip of a coin.

In 1938, at least two thousand came to witness this unique event and cheer on the students as they worked hard for position. Cameramen from three different newsreels—*Pathe, Universal,* and *News of the Day,* came to town to shoot the BGA boys as they struggled back and forth. It was a fairly quick battle that lasted only five minutes though all of the onlookers enjoyed the fun competition, especially watching the losers being dragged through the water. The Platos recorded their first ever win in this filmed tug-of-war.

This 1938 photograph of the tug-of-war is one of the earliest records of the event which began in 1935.

George Briggs often challenged the students to a marble game which he reportedly never lost. In 1938, the event was filmed for television and the "lucky" student was Gilliam Traughber.

The same year, Professor Briggs challenged the student body to a marble contest. He was an excellent player and for the eleventh year in a row, he promised the school a holiday if he was beat by a student. Freshman Gilliam Traughber represented the student body after winning a tournament with a field of fourteen fellow classmates.

Briggs and Traughber each started with fifteen marbles, but at the end of the two-hour battle, Briggs had all thirty. Briggs was so impressed with the boy's play that he granted the school a holiday the following day. It was rumored that he was so stiff from the battle that he did not feel much like teaching. The entire event was re-created a few days later when cameramen from *Pathe* and *Universal* newsreels came from Memphis.

An article in the 1937 *Cannon Ball* describes the inspiring teaching methods of Professor Briggs. "What would you do if you saw a hand dripping with blood writing some crazy words across your dining room wall?" He impressed the biblical story using everyday expressions to make his lessons more interesting for his students. His method of teaching was to explain a matter in such a way that it would not be forgotten. He often turned his class into an informal discussion which his students felt was far more important than anything the textbook could say.

This "All American" poster was used to advertise Battle Ground Academy during the late 1930s and 1940s.

An article in a 1937 *Cannon Ball* newsletter gives the figures on dining room consumption:

> Have you ever heard that B.G.A. stands for "Bacon, Grits, and Apples"? This is, in a way true, for here at Battle Ground, in one year, we eat a hundred large packages of grits, 1,032 pounds of bacon, and 280 pecks of apples! We got this straight from Mrs. Wilson.

The fifty-four boarding boys also consumed 70,000 rolls, 58,000 biscuits and nearly 3000 loaves of bread on which they used 100 gallons of syrup and 300 gallons of jelly. Other than bacon, they could put away 6 tons of meat as well as 1000 boxes of cereal. Dairy products consumed included 468 quarts of ice cream and 7,280 quarts of milk annually. Growing boys will eat!

During the 1930s a wide variety of sports were played at BGA. Traditional rivalries with area teams provided entertainment for the entire community. At a football game on November 23, 1933, BGA played MBA with over five thousand fans on hand. Of course, basketball, baseball, and track were mainstays at BGA, but other sports were also enjoyed during this time. Often, boxing and wrestling exhibitions took place during the halftime of basketball games. Softball was added to the schedule in 1936, and badminton and soccer were added in 1938. Swimming, golf, and tennis are minor sports that were played as well during this period. Younger students also participated in "midget" athletics, competing against local teams.

Freshmen were initiated during this time with the tiring responsibility of carrying a brick around for one week. Brick Week, as it was called, required the freshmen to carry the brick everywhere they went from Monday morning to Sunday night. If the brick was stolen, lost, or forgotten, the student was supposed to have a penalty imposed. Some boys decorated their bricks to compete for prizes. Upperclassmen sometimes demanded the freshmen buy them a cold drink downtown before they could be relieved of their brick.

A popular student during the late 1930s was Francisco A. Herrera from Cuba. He first learned of BGA through a *Cosmopolitan* magazine advertisement and decided to study and learn our language as well as our ways. Due to the 1933 revolution in Cuba, there were no schools open for two years. Frank studied for one year at home and also took violin lessons. When Frank returned to BGA after a summer at home, he introduced a new dance called the Congo to his fellow students. He kept the BGA boys updated with all the latest cultural differences and added a new dimension to their lives.

The 1930s at Battle Ground Academy were exciting times for students and teachers alike. Professor Briggs, a 1903 BGA graduate, came back with plans to move progressively into the future. New subjects were introduced and the best teachers were secured. Business law, college algebra, physiology, and sociology were added to the curriculum as well as a new physics lab. Area businessmen were brought in weekly to speak to the student body in order to introduce career opportunities. Briggs was proud of the school and tirelessly worked to bring in new students. He raised the standards and brought the school to a new plateau.

Frank Herrera was a popular student from Cuba in the late 1930s who intrigued the boys with his lifestyle.

CHAPTER EIGHT

All Out for Victory

The middle of this decade marked the fiftieth anniversary of the founding of Battle Ground Academy. Headmaster George Briggs was leading the school into an exciting future, preparing the students for college and life. The school offered a variety of courses during this period. Senior classes included English literature, American history, solid geometry, trigonometry, college algebra, Latin (Virgil), Greek (*Iliad*), and French II. The student-teacher ratio was about ten or twelve to one. Tragedies and triumphs lay ahead for the school as students awaited to hear from family and friends who were fighting for their country.

A group of Battle Ground alumni realized the need for an alumni association and met to discuss a plan. In May 1940, a formal meeting was held on campus and representatives from each class were present to celebrate the fiftieth anniversary of the school. During the meeting several men spoke of the history and tradition of the school, citing that at the present it was credited among the four or five highest—in the Southern Association for Schools and Colleges. Even Mr. Mooney returned and reminisced about the good old days. The meeting was adjourned after it was agreed to form an alumni association, electing a president and secretary.

Turney Ford was hired as head coach and athletic director in the fall of 1939. He had just graduated from Vanderbilt in the spring where he starred for three years in

A Monument to Education

football and baseball, also lettering two years in basketball. At BGA he taught economics, civics, geography and sociology. His first football season got off to a slow start, but he was pleased with his first year as he stated, "To me the season's high light has been the way in which the team came back after a bad start. The boys have worked hard all year and have shown fine spirit."

Not everyone is destined to play first string varsity, so in 1940, BGA introduced intramural teams. Every afternoon when the varsity teams practiced many boys were left with nothing to do, so Professor Robinson organized the boys into four teams and they competed in softball, soccer, basketball and their favorite, touch football. Some of the boys seemed to be a little self-conscious about their ability to play, yet still had fun with their fellow classmates.

Dorm life during the 1940s was monitored closely by the teachers as well as the house matron. Each year the school catalog outlined the activities of those who lived in the dorms, and each boy was to stick to the schedule or risk punishment. Before supper each weekday the boys were to participate in athletics or were given leisure time, and following supper, they were to study in their rooms or in the study hall if they had a deficient.

Friday night was open night for the dorm boys, with activities in the gym or the recreation room. They could ask to leave campus if their teachers decided their work was in good shape. On Saturday morning there would be school for those in need and Saturday afternoon could be spent as they desired. Saturday night was set aside to

Midway, top; Greystone, middle; and Westover, bottom. These three cottages served as home away from home for many boys during their years at Battle Ground Academy.

prepare for Monday's lessons. As for Sunday mornings, the students were urged to attend a church of their choice and Sunday night they would read passages from the Bible and each boy was required to write home.

Midway, Greystone, and Westover were the three homes near the campus used for dormitories. Greystone housed twelve to fourteen younger boys and Westover and Midway could accommodate around ten each. The house matron was to oversee the activities of the boys as well as offer advice when needed. If the matter was too large for the house mother, the teacher or Professor Briggs was summoned.

Though classes were in full swing, the students' minds would often wander to their friends and family fighting in the war and wonder if they were to soon be there. The school began the "All Out for Victory" program in which secondary schools prepared their students in the event they must join the war effort after graduation. The school started a calisthenics and drill program to prepare the boys, who were divided into three platoons according to size.

In the early 1940s, Battle Ground Academy joined the "All Out for Victory" program teaching the students the fundamentals of military training.

The following letter informed the parents of the school's plans to aid the country's defense:

To Parents:

In an effort to make a contribution to the program of National Defense, Battle Ground Academy has wisely, we think, made some plans in that direction. We feel that all parents will wholeheartedly endorse these plans.

At regular intervals we propose to give our boys under expert leadership a few fundamentals of military training. Some of these fundamentals include such items as close order drill, which teaches precision, familiarity with the rifle and its different positions, but more especially calisthenics or the physical training of our boys. The exercises will be in the open air and will include every part of the body. All boys will benefit by these exercises, not only in "feeling fit," but also in their carriage, posture, and general appearance. Other items connected with our program will be given from time to time.

The carrying out of these plans will in no wise disturb the main objective of the school—namely, thorough class-work. At all times we will put our main effort here, but we do feel that the boys will not only profit by the added program, but already they are showing that they enjoy it.

The main reason we are writing you is that you may know and appreciate the forward step that the school is taking. It is our belief that this will be considered by all a movement entirely proper and in keeping with the spirit of the present hour.

—The Faculty of Battle Ground Academy

The student body was outfitted with white pants, overseas caps, and white shirts with a BGA emblem. These uniforms were worn when drilling to present an

The Memorial of the BGA students who gave their lives in World War II.

appearance of neatness and uniformity. Drills occurred on Mondays and Thursdays, and lasted about forty-five minutes. Students were issued a "Victory Trainer" which was a wooden reproduction of a Springfield army rifle. The uniforms were later changed to a rich gray color and bore a BGA patch with red lettering.

The military drills continued until 1946 and proved to be very valuable to those who eventually served the country in war. The class of 1948 gave a bronze plaque to the school to memorialize those students who gave their lives during World War II. This plaque is located in the front hall of the administration building and lists thirteen alumni of Battle Ground Academy. The lives would be changed forever for those who lost friends as well as family during that challenging time in our country's history.

BGA received a devastating blow in May 1944, when Headmaster George Briggs passed away after a two-week illness due to a heart condition. He had been a guiding light to the school for nineteen years and his devotion to the school was unquestioned. He was loved by his boys because he loved them and had an understanding heart. He often said that his love for Battle Ground Academy was surpassed only by his love for his family. The 1944 senior class unanimously voted to give the school a portrait of their beloved headmaster to be hung in the library in a beautiful mahogany frame.

Following Briggs' death, the board of trustees appointed Glenn Eddington as interim headmaster and later hired him permanently. Eddington was a 1926 honors graduate of Davidson College. He returned to his hometown of Franklin the following fall to teach at BGA and complete graduate work at George Peabody College. He

A Monument to Education

was assistant headmaster and math teacher prior to Briggs' death. His first love was the classroom and he accepted the new job with reservations, knowing it would take him away from his students.

The 1944 football team was considered one of the best teams in the history of the school. According to the *Cannon Ball*, this was the first perfect record for the school and it was attributed to a number of factors: (1) a thorough coaching job by Coach J. B. Akin, (2) an unparalled team and school spirit, (3) the installation of the "T" formation, and (4) the fact that at all times

Glenn Eddington became the headmaster of Battle Ground Academy in 1944 upon the death of George Briggs. Eddington had been a math teacher at the school since 1926 and also served as assistant headmaster.

Willow Plunge was a favorite place for the boys of Battle Ground Academy to socialize in the 1920s.

there were eleven men working together as a unit. Capt. Ralph Spangler, alternate Mac Peebles, and most valuable player Fleming Williams led their team to an undefeated season in old uniforms given to them by Vanderbilt University.

In memory of Professor Briggs, the board of trustees decided to sponsor a drive to raise forty thousand dollars for a memorial gymnasium. The new one thousand-seat facility would house a basketball court flanked by locker rooms and showers, as well as a swimming pool and bowling alleys. This state of the art facility was greatly anticipated and after a few delays due to the weather, the inaugural games were played in March 1947.

Each spring during these years the students eagerly anticipated the opening of a local pool called Willow Plunge. This privately owned pool began as a spring-fed pond and its owner, C. H. Kinnard decided to make a concrete pool out of it. Initially it was one deep pool for diving, but a partition was later added to provide a shallow end for those who just wanted to wade. Willow Plunge was within walking distance from the school and BGA boys were usually well represented there.

The first bus BGA ever bought was in the spring 1947. The blue and silver giant measured over twenty-five feet long and seated twenty-eight passengers comfortably, and, if there were three boys to a seat, it would hold forty-two plus the driver. Equipped with luggage racks and a special deluxe heater, the cost of the bus was just over three thousand dollars. Battle Ground Academy was painted on every side so everyone knew where the proud shouting students were from.

In 1948, visitors to campus might think they were seeing double. During this year, there were three sets of twins enrolled at BGA. The oldest were Carroll and William

Three sets of twins attended BGA at the same time. Top Row (Left to Right): Carroll and William Jenkins. Second Row (L to R): Jimmy and Clifton Sedberry. Front Row (L to R): Bill and Bobby McArthur.

A Monument to Education

1949 Mid-south basketball champs: Front Row (Left to Right): Tom Lance, Jimmy Odum, Bill Cook, Bob Crenshaw, Frank Giles, Gerald Johnson, Jack Schmitt, Tom Robinson, Bill Isaacs, Bill Cobb, Charles Byron, Tyler Berry. Second Row (L to R): Jimmy Fristoe, Coach J. B. Akin, Howlson Wemyss.

Jenkins who were freshmen identical twins that dressed alike and enjoyed confusing the students and staff. Billy and Bobby McArthur were a little easier to differentiate as eighth graders, and the easiest to distinguish were seventh graders Clifton and Jimmy Sedberry. This was probably the first time in the school's history to have this many twins enrolled at the same time.

BGA hosted the Mid-south Basketball Tournament in late February 1949, in the relatively new George I. Briggs Gymnasium. Baylor, Columbia Military Academy, Castle Heights, Darlington, Georgia Military Academy (GMA), McCallie, Morgan, Sewanee Military, Notre Dame, St. Andrews, Tennessee Military, and Battle Ground Academy comprised the twelve teams vying for the title. McCallie was seeded first with BGA second, but the finals saw dark-horse GMA playing Battle Ground. BGA came away with their first Mid-south crown with Tom Robinson and Gerald "Mama" Johnson making the All Mid-south Team.

The 1949 baseball team walked through a tough schedule losing only one regular season game. Winning the Western Division, BGA now had to face Eastern Division

1949 Mid-south baseball champs.

champs McCallie of Chattanooga. The three-game series was taken to the limit as BGA emerged as the Mid-south Champion for the first time in the school's history. It was truly an amazing year as the school was declared Mid-south champs in basketball and baseball.

If one grows through adversity, the boys of Battle Ground Academy grew immeasurably during the 1940s. The loss of George Briggs as well as friends and family in the war made many of the young men mature beyond their years. On the other hand, BGA experienced success in the classroom and on the playing field. During the 1940s the boys of BGA learned many of life's lessons during an important time in their lives. Championship teams, a war overseas, drills with uniforms, the sudden death of a headmaster, and a new gymnasium all compromised a decade of constant change and constant coping for the boys on the hill.

CHAPTER NINE

The Blizzard of 1951

The 1950s were years of growth at Battle Ground Academy. The campus received many improvements, athletics moved in a new direction, and the students were feeling proud and ambitious following the war. The school's prominence in the world of education would be promoted by two new figures at the school and the tradition of excellence would flourish during the Eisenhower presidency.

Glenn Eddington made it no secret that he wanted to stay in the classroom, so he announced his resignation as headmaster in 1950 and took a position at the college level as a professor. The board of trustees turned to two men to lead the school into the future. Jonas Coverdale and Paul Redick were hired as co-managers, both coming from Castle Heights Military Academy (CHMA) in Lebanon. Coverdale served as president of the school and Redick took the position of headmaster.

Coverdale had been the headmaster of the CHMA junior high school since 1931 and Redick was CHMA's intramural director. A native of Nashville, Coverdale graduated from Hume-Fogg High School and attended Vanderbilt where he was captain of the 1923–1924 basketball team. Before going to Castle Heights, he was physical director for the Nashville YMCA for eight years. Coverdale owned and operated Camp Hy Lake, a summer camp near Queback, Tennessee. Redick graduated from Cumberland University and

Jonas Coverdale (left) became the president of Battle Ground Academy in 1950 after many years as the headmaster of the Castle Heights Military Academy Junior High. Paul Redick (right) came with Jonas Coverdale to Battle Ground Academy in 1950 to serve as headmaster of the school.

received his masters from Peabody. Prior to his years at Castle Heights, he was principal of the grammar school in Camden, Tennessee, and their high school coach.

In March 1951, BGA applied for membership in the Tennessee Secondary School Athletic Association. For several years, Coach Akin believed such a move from the Mid-south Athletic Association would benefit the school. Reasons for the change included "to develop its own athletic teams and players rather than solicit star athletes from other schools." In giving BGA boys the opportunity to play on varsity teams rather than be replaced by "one year students," more interest would be generated by playing local teams and it would be less expensive due to less traveling.

The blizzard of 1951 will long be remembered by locals, including the boys of BGA as one of the worst in history. Freezing rain damaged many of the trees on campus and classes were shortened due to the lack of heat. Only "Big Black Bessie" roared in the kitchen; even the dorm boys were without heat. The Church of Christ contributed its heated basement for the dorm boys and Redick opened his heated home so a few boys could sleep there. "Big Black Bessie" kept the kitchen going and not a meal was missed. Coverdale and Ralph Naylor took a few pictures as some of the boys pretended to be in a snowball fight.

A Monument to Education

The students of Battle Ground Academy enjoyed the blizzard of 1951.

In November 1952, some of the boys living in the dorm talked about how nice it would be to have a television. Dorm president Erwin McKee took a poll of the boys and everyone was in favor. Since the seniors would be leaving soon, each paid four dollars and everyone else paid five dollars. Sewell Electric helped by selling the seventeen-inch television at cost. The new television was enjoyed by students and teachers alike.

The 1953 catalog emphasized the importance of choosing the right school to prepare one's son for life.

> The selection of the proper preparatory school for your boy is of vital importance. These are the years when he is entering manhood and for the first time seeking his place in an adult world. His ideas and ideals are beginning to crystallize. For all his seeming self-sufficiency, he needs direction in developing and expressing his own individual personality.

When the boys of BGA decided to get into the spirit for an upcoming football game, the whole town was at risk. The following was found in a 1953 *Wildcat* newspaper.

> Then Thursday night rolled around, and IT happened. Clad in wading boots, bathrobes, oversized pants,

pajamas, and "long handles," and looking unnaturally weird in the end lights of the football field, IT assembled. . . . After a few yells, and speeches from Coach Akin and Brown, the boys heard a last minute briefing by Mr. Redick.

The "pajama parade" headed downtown, through the theater, hung "Mr. Hillsboro" (the opposing team) on the Western Union sign, sat and chanted on Main Street twice and returned to BGA. Apparently, this idea came from a Vanderbilt fraternity outing.

A summer edition of the *Wildcat* briefed the boys on what they would find when they returned to campus in the fall. Information was also included about the teachers' and students' lives during the summer break. The August 1953 edition relates that Mr. and Mrs. Bragg would be living in Westover in the fall with six or eight upperclassmen and

BGA students enjoyed weekends and summers at Camp Hy Lake which was owned by Jonas Coverdale.

that the new Redick's home was near completion. The Coverdales, Redicks, and Braggs spent a successful summer at Camp Hy Lake. Mr. Akin traveled for the school and helped spruce up the buildings. Mr. Naylor built a shed behind Mr. Akin's house and Mr. Smithson worked on his M.A. at Peabody College.

The students had a busy summer too. While most of the dorm boys returned home for the summer, the local boys kept very busy. A few boys attended a Boy Scout Jamboree in California, while others worked at or attended Camp Hy Lake. Several boys worked on area farms or attended summer school. Only a few managed to vacation all summer without working at all, and most found time to visit Willow Plunge and attend a party or two.

An underground newspaper sometimes surfaced during the 1950s called the *Hep Cat*. It was published "every once in a while" in a secret cave under Westover house. The paper fought for "less homework, longer breaks, more holidays (for teachers), less tests, senior privileges, more dances, BGA going co-ed," and much more. It attempted to sell "Crudential" insurance, drive the *Wildcat* out of business and report that "Battle Grand" won its first state championship in tiddlywinks. John Terrell sparked the "Wildsots" to their first state victory in the 457-year history of the school.

The "Spectator" was a regular feature of the *Wildcat* that kept a watchful eye on the faculty and students. The following excerpts reveal that lighter side of school life:

> Mr. Redick—Hudgins, you're late! You should've been here at 8:30.
>
> Mike—Why? What happened?
>
> Mrs. Evans—Joe, did you give the gold fish some fresh water?
>
> Joe—What's the use? They didn't drink what I gave them yesterday!

The Wildcat, student newspaper.

Dottie Frist—Kissing spreads germs, so it's stated.

Dick Boensch—Kiss me baby, I'm vaccinated!

Marylin—Darling, can you drive with one hand?

Bill—Yes, my love.

Marylin—Then wave to mama. She's in the car right behind us.

The additions and renovations to the Battle Ground campus during the 1950s were extensive. In 1951, a horseshoe drive was made between the current Fleming Hall, Peoples Hall, and Coverdale Hall, and the old road behind the administration building was closed. During this time, the two clay tennis courts were replaced with three lighted asphalt courts. The school bought Westover, the field beyond the Redick's, a field behind the gym, and the baseball field. No longer would dirt have to be hauled to the middle of the football field for a pitchers mound.

New stands were built for the football field in 1955 to accommodate the growing crowds. In 1957, a second floor was added to Coverdale Hall for dormitory rooms and a faculty apartment. The first floor contained a new kitchen, dining room, and lounge. A science wing was added to the administration building in 1958 with biology and chemistry labs. All the buildings were painted white for a uniform look and night lighting was added. The 1959 jamboree raised enough money to build a new track.

As expected, athletics played a big part in the life of most BGA students. Whether captain of the basketball team or member of the pep squad, everyone enjoyed the competition. The 1954 varsity football team held a 9-1 record and shared the Tennessee Valley Athletic Conference championship. The first bowl game BGA ever participated in ended in a tie with Tullahoma in the 1957 Butter Bowl in Pulaski, Tennessee. The next bowl appearance came just two years later when they tied again in the Butter Bowl, this time against Manchester.

This entire decade saw the football team coached by BGA Sports Hall of Fame member J. B. Akin. From the time Battle Ground Academy joined the Tennessee Secondary Schools Athletic Association (TSSAA) in 1951 until he retired from coaching in 1959, Akin's teams had winning seasons. He was honored when the football field was dedicated to him in 1958. Akin also coached basketball for many years, winning the district five times. He retired from coaching basketball in 1959.

Hal Smith, class of 1958, remembers Akin as a great teacher and how he even made the classroom competitive. Akin loved to play the "trapping" game with his Bible class students. This game was played by "Daddy" Peoples in the early part of this century and was still a favorite. Akin

Public speaking and debate teams have always played an important role in the students' development at Battle Ground Academy.

J. B. Akin, class of 1926, returned to BGA in the early 1940s and remained for thirty years.

would drill the students with biblical questions and if one missed the question, the next student to answer correctly would "trap" his classmate by moving ahead. If a student remained number one for two days, Akin added two points to his monthly grade. Akin will long be remembered for his love of the classroom as well as his love for athletics.

During the 1950s, many great teachers graced the classrooms of Battle Ground Academy. Those who remained for several years include Jonas Coverdale as president; Paul Redick, social science; J. B. Akin, natural science; Ralph Naylor, John Bragg, and Cannon Mayes, English; Carl Smithson, mathematics; Daly Thompson, Latin and Bible; Mrs. Pryor Lillie, public speaking; Betsy Redick, typing; Emma Haynes, housemother; and Mrs. James Buford, librarian.

In the spring 1959, Coverdale resigned his position as president in order to devote more time to Camp Hy Lake.

A Monument to Education

An aerial view of the BGA campus in the 1950s.

The position of president was retired with Coverdale and Paul Redick remained as headmaster. J. B. Akin became the business manager and athletic director. The transition was easy considering Redick's ongoing relationship with the school. Once again, the school was moving forward under the direction of new leadership.

Under the direction of Jonas Coverdale, Battle Ground Academy grew exceedingly. The campus enjoyed many improvements and athletics moved in a new direction as J. B. Akin dominated the decade as a coach. The whole town of Franklin benefited from the school and its reputation.

CHAPTER TEN

A Decade of Champions

Battle Ground Academy excelled in the classroom and on the playing field during the 1960s. This period will long be remembered for its legendary teachers, creative teaching and disciple techniques, and championship teams. The boys of BGA will never forget the speed tests of Carl Smithson and the eraser throwing accuracy of Harold Kennedy. The students of this era greatly appreciated their education when they entered college and found freshmen courses extremely easy due to the indepth education they received at the hands of such remarkable teachers. Many of these students also carried with them the experiences they gained through athletics, which, combined with their studies, produced highly successful adults.

In the fall of 1960, the BGA football team set their sights on the state championship Clinic Bowl. After defeating ten teams during the regular season, coach Ralph Brown's Wildcats received an offer from the Jaycees to appear in the eleventh annual bowl. Once the invitation was accepted, the student body kicked into high gear selling tickets which benefitted the physical therapy clinic at Vanderbilt for those in need. Father Ryan held the record for raising the most money at three thousand dollars. With that goal in mind, the BGA boys got to work and reached that mark in just two days. The day before the Clinic Bowl, over fourteen thousand dollars had been collected, and, needless to say, the Jaycees were delighted.

A Monument to Education

The next event to conquer was electing the Clinic Bowl Ball Queen who was picked by the school with the largest attendance at the dance. BGA won this too, choosing Barbara Beaman, a Harpeth Hall senior, as the event was televised by WSM-TV. The boys were on a roll with only one hurdle in the way of making a clean sweep of the Clinic Bowl festivities and that would be the game itself.

More than 28,000 fans came to witness the championship game on Thanksgiving Day. BGA's opponent was the number-one rated Isaac Litton High School of Nashville. The difference in the game proved to the BGA's superior tackling as they went on to win 13-0, and Charlie Trabue was awarded as the Outstanding Player of the game. The support of the game was overwhelming as even the Franklin High Band played for BGA during the game. The vow made at summer football camp as Hy Lake to win the state championship became a reality on Thanksgiving Day in 1960.

The Wildcat basketball team also achieved great success during the early 1960s. The 1960 squad was the first from a private school to play in a TSSAA state basketball tournament. Key players who helped the team advance to the sweet sixteen were seniors Buddy Benedict, Tom Fiveash,

The 1960 state championship team was coached by Ralph Brown, posted a 10-0 regular season record, and defeated Isaac Litton High School 13-0 in the Clinic Bowl.

and Terry Geshke. The 1962 Wildcat team also advanced to the state tournament after winning their district and region. Seniors Johnny Jewell, Duke Shackelford, Buster Shull, and Sid Tompkins led the team in 1962. The following year the BGA boys advanced all the way to the state tournament quarter-finals. This team was led by seniors Johnny Guffee, Bobby Morel, Bobby Schwartz, Walter Donaldson, and Frank Pinkerton. Bobby Schwartz was the first BGA boy to receive All-State honors. Each of these teams flourished under the enthusiastic spirit of coach Jimmy French.

On March 10, 1961, Battle Ground Academy was honored to have Princess Catherine Caradja of Romania speak to the student body. The princess escaped her homeland in 1952, and later made her way to the United States where she toured, speaking about the communistic rule that had taken over her county at the end of World War II. The Romanian homes were taken over by Russians, usually leaving just a single room in which to live. The listeners realized they were hearing firsthand the cost of communist domination. The princess impressed on her audience that America was the only hope of the Free World against communism.

A 1962 *Wildcat* reports seven new subjects added to the BGA curriculum. The new subjects were world history, taught by Mr. Ted Beach; economics, taught by Mr. Bo Stewart; physical science, taught by Mr. John Oxley; and mythology, taught by Mr. Don Patterson. Also added in the eighth grade were general science, taught by Coach Jimmy Gentry and introduction to algebra, taught by Coach Bill Brown. The additions were made due to ever-increasing college requirements.

Many students will remember the intensity of Carl Smithson's advanced math classes. A favorite teaching method of his was "chalk talk" in which every student was assigned an area of the chalkboard to work a problem. Smithson would state the problem and the chalk would fly. Of course no one wanted to be the last one working because he would make the student quote the rules which were embedded in his mind. Students will also remember the "wasp" which was the slip stick out of a slide rule. Smithson would sting unruly boys on the leg or on the palm of the hand. On one occasion, Smithson was in charge of study hall when he had to call down Bobby Lloyd who had lost a leg to cancer and wore a prosthesis. Smithson told Lloyd to pull his pants tight and when the "wasp" hit the leg there was only a thud. When Smithson realized he had hit the wooden leg he laughed so hard he fell out of his seat. After he composed himself again he said, "Alright, now give me the other leg."

Carl Smithson more than adequately prepared many boys for college with his advanced math classes.

Smithson's nickname "Goat" was received at Franklin High where he played football. Without a face mask on his helmet, he would tackle by butting the opposition and soon the name "Goat" was awarded him. The name remained with him through his days at BGA from 1952–1970. On one occasion some students decided to give Smithson a treat by leaving a real goat with hay and water in his classroom all weekend. Another time an alarm clock was left in his room with the timer set to disrupt class. When the alarm sounded Smithson promptly knocked the clock out the open window. Sometimes feared, always respected, "Goat" Smithson will long be remembered for his contributions to BGA.

A *Wildcat* editorial written by John Hampton in 1965 discussed the controversy of long hair. This was during a time when rock stars paraded their long locks and news photos showed demonstrating teenagers exhibiting an unkempt look. Hampton admitted that teenagers often rebel against authority and growing long hair was just one form of this. He said "a teenager thinks as an adult, but often acts as a child. He believes he should be treated as an adult and when his demands are not met he rebels." He finished the editorial by posing the question, "Is long hair worth the fleeting status it sometimes brings if it lowers the wearers worth in the eyes of most people? Is it worth it to you?"

Quizbusters

Quizbusters was more than a 30-minute, weekend afternoon, WLAC-TV local feature. For us at BGA it was an opportunity to prove our worth against all the public and private shcools in the Nasvhille area. It was a chance for the more scholarly, quick, members of our student body to capture the limelight.

The show fell in the mold of TV programming of that day. National quiz shows were popular and the syndicated *College Quizbowl* had developed a following.

With the help of several students we built a set that simulated the *Quizbuster Show*. Electric buzzers, lights, and a group of about two thousand ever-changing sample questions on 3x5 cards we thought mimicked those of the actual show.

Kenny Ward-Smith, Ed Kelly, Winston Grizzard, and Allen Cohen were BGA's first squad in 1963, the first year BGA participated. Week by week, BGA swept aside the competition to become grand champions.

In 1964, Kenny Ward-Smith was joined by Jack Wyattt, John Thompson, Phil Hollis, Gary Ghertner, and Eddy Benz. Talent, practice, and dedication again led to BGA winning the grand championship.

The final year, 1965, winning seemed BGA's destiny. First teamers, Bob Thompson, Remigius Shatas, Stephen Plonka, and Ken Phelps together with alternates, Hank Seaton, Bill McClanahan, and Pat Bray took the grand championship for the third year in a row.

The 1964 grand champion Quizbuster team.

There were many improvements to the BGA campus during the 1960s as a $100,000 expansion was begun during the first part of this decade. Four classrooms were added to the west side of Fleming Hall. The new study hall seated over one hundred and was complimented with new desks. On the third floor behind the study hall was the library that was furnished with new equipment. The second floor housed a bookstore, commissary, and recreation room while the first floor was a room for movies. The commissary was an institution in itself especially for boarders. Here they could buy everything from school supplies to ice cream and mints. A new lobby and an olympic size pool were added to the gym and dedicated in May 1965 with a speech delivered by Sam Fleming, class of 1924.

The life of a boarding student was much different than that of a day student, and, during the 1960s, the boarders enjoyed many great traditions and tried to create a few of their own. The boarders' week started Sunday evening with a coat and tie dinner at 6:00 P.M. A faculty member and their family would sit at a table with six students and the food was served family style as was breakfast each morning. The boarders shared great friendships and always took up for each other. Anytime there was something going on around the campus, the boarders were called to witness. On one occasion, Sutton O'Neil, a wheelchair-bound student with polio, crossed the entire length of the football field on his hands to the cheers of his friends. Another time, the boarders were summoned from their dinner in the cafeteria to watch Bobby Patterson break the state high jump record. At their home away from home, these boys bonded as a family and celebrated in each others success.

The boarders also initiated some traditions of their own. One such tradition was the annual party at the start of each school year where candy and cakes laced with Ex-Lax were offered to new boarders. Another popular occurrence was to slip out of the dorm after hours, just because they were not supposed to. On one such occasion, Jimmy Gentry who was in charge of securing the dorm for the evening, laid in the empty bed of an unsuspecting boarder and awaited his return.

Sometimes the boarders needed a place to recuperate from sickness or just needed some time alone. They usually found their way to the infirmary where Martha Smithson cared for them and guarded them with motherly love. Most boarders will remember their days at BGA with a smile. They will recall the camaraderie with other boarders and the respect of their teachers as well as the traditions of the school.

Tug-of-War Reinstated

In the late 1950s, fate seemed to have doomed the annual all-student BGA Tug-of-War. Earl's Fruit Stand had taken over the traditional tug site at the Harpeth River Bridge on Nashville Pike. The student body had grown. The rope, thought to be the largest size commercially available, was old and began to break and be retied from the strain of too many students. Mud balls led to mud wrestling as the students became disinterested. Faculty and administration were soon targeted. The mud battle resulted in the abolishment of the tug-of-war in 1959 until its revival in 1965.

The new Highway-96 West bridge across the West Harpeth would provide a splendid site with solid ground for the tuggers, and a long, high bridge for viewers. J. B. Akin said we could borrow the school's U.S. government surplus, early WW II rusty, Ford pickup truck to fetch the rope from the Nashville Bridge Company. Nashville Bridge's forklift hefted the one-thousand-pound rope onto an outlandish-looking rig we had made to hold the reel on our pickup. The pickup's tires ballooned under the weight but did not burst.

The rope survived a mandatory test to show that it would not break. The student body was even larger than it had been at the last tug, and the axiom was clear—"there would be no repeat of what happened last time."

But a more persuasive reason had to surface to get the administration's approval for the event—Nashville TV and press coverage. The tug was wholesome, and coverage would bring attention to the school in a favorable way. At first, only BGA librarian Libby Fryer was interested in the story. She called her friend, the executive producer of the national evening news *Huntley-Brinkley Show*, who commissioned his Nashville affiliate to cover the event for the network. Suddenly, each Nashville station and its network became interested. At school, the idea caught fire. Students and teachers organized to ensure the event would go smoothly. The administration acquiesced, and on May 17, 1965, one-half of the student body, the Platos, dragged the other half, the Greers, across the West Harpeth. A great event was alive again.

The annual tug-of-war which began in 1935 continued to be the highlight of competition between the Greers and Platos during the 1960s. (L to R) Plato Officers: Steve Chambers, Brother Campbell, Buzz Hamilton, Jimmy Rader. Greer Officers: Allen Anderson, Steve Hicks, John Moran.

The Key Club was chartered at BGA in December 1965 as an honorary service organization. The Kiwanis-sponsored club developed the following goals for its members: (1) to develop initiative and leadership, (2) to provide experience in living and working together, and (3) to prepare for useful citizenship. Early projects included caring for a needy family at Christmas, compiling a school directory, cleaning the Confederate cemetery, and adopting a military unit in Vietnam. Most students will remember the club's ongoing fundraiser of selling milk each day during the lunch period.

The tug-of-war was reinstated at BGA in May 1965 after a six-year absence as a disciplinary action. The revival of the long-standing tradition came from great student and alumni interest. This was the first year the tug-of-war was held at the bridge over the West Harpeth River on Highway-96 West. Although this is not the only annual rivalry between the Platos and the Greers, it certainly is the most popular. This annual event is still enjoyed today by the students of BGA.

The 1966 football team will long be remembered as possibly the best in BGA's history. Jimmy Gentry's first year as head coach saw key players returning from the team that tied Two Rivers in the Metro Bowl in 1965. Those players included Allen Anderson, Brother Campbell, Don Denbo, Harry Ford, Bobby Jackson, Ralph McCracken, Jack

The 1966 BGA football team celebrates after winning the state championship over Hartsville in the Tobacco Bowl.

Milam, Bill Pemberton, Jimmy Rader, Steve Robinson, and Capt. George Silvey. Gentry was assisted in coaching by his brother Bobby Gentry, a 1946 alumnus, and Bill Cherry, a 1959 alumnus. The team finished the regular season undefeated, outscoring their opponents 362-46 and with a defense that shutout five teams.

BGA met a strong Crossville team in the Hartsville Tobacco Bowl for the state championship game. Untied and unbeaten Crossville had allowed only twenty-six points all year. At the end of the first quarter the score was tied at seven. The turning point in the game was an incredible touchdown pass and reception from quarterback Brother Campbell to Robert Akin that ended the first half. BGA never looked back, winning the game 43-7, leaving no doubt who was the 1966 state champ. Other key players on the team included Logan Jackson, Buzzy Hamilton, Harry Blackburn, Bob Estes, and Johnny Hahn. Numerous players on this team were honored including George Silvey and Don Denbo who were named All-Americans.

The daily assemblies during this decade provided some of the most memorable experiences for the students as well as the teachers. At one assembly, native Williamson Countian Sam McGee, a member of the Grand Ole Opry,

Assemblies at BGA are recalled with fondness, such as the time when native Williamson Countian, Grand Ole Opry star Sam McGee (seated), played song after song.

played song after song at the students' insistence. Another assembly featured Archie Campbell, who was aided by student Jerry Church in the "Cockfight," where young Church stole the show. Once when the Harpeth Hall choral group came, the students decided not to applaud because the year before they were disciplined for clapping too much. After the fifth song, as the girls began to wonder if something was wrong, Mr. Redick and Mr. Akin started an ovation from the back of the room that moved slowly to the front, much to the girls' delight.

Students of the 1960s were instructed by great teachers, and lessons learned in the classroom prepared them for life. But many BGA students also remember what happened between classes more distinctly. Following are just a few examples of these memories. Students daily encountered A. J., Paul Redick's dog who lived across the street from the school and befriended everyone. The "smoke shack" was a small metal building near the football field where students with written permission could light up a cigarette. Students often irritated Dr. Joseph Green by pretending to step over a trip wire as they entered his class. One day he casually entered the room and stepped over the "wire" as the class erupted in laughter. A most impressionable sight was the day of Daly Thompson's funeral when all of the boarding students

A Monument to Education

J. B. Akin (left) succeeded Paul Redick as headmaster of BGA in 1968 after many years as a teacher at his alma mater. In 1969, John Bragg became the headmaster of BGA and J. B. Akin became president of the school.

walked downtown to the church for his service. The BGA and Franklin High School rivalry erupted in a near riot in 1968 following a basketball game where Franklin displayed a taunting banner.

In 1968, Paul Redick resigned as headmaster of BGA and J. B. Akin, class of 1926, succeeded him. Prior to returning to BGA, Akin was at Ashland City High School for five years. He came back to BGA in the early 1940s and during his tenure he taught all sciences as well as coached almost every sport for several years. Akin earned his B.A. from the University of Tennessee and his M.A. from Middle Tennessee State University.

The following year, Akin became the president of Battle Ground Academy and John Bragg was appointed headmaster. A native of McMinnville, Tennessee, Bragg attended Sewanee Military Academy where he played football and basketball, he served three and one-half years in the Pacific Theater of World War II then returned home to attend college. Bragg received his B.A. from the University of the South and completed his M.A. at Middle Tennessee State University. Bragg was the chairman of the English department at BGA for many years.

BGA was fortunate to have many highly trained and motivated teachers during the 1960s. Many of these teachers remained at the school for several years and are fondly remembered by alumni today. Among those teachers are Paul Redick, headmaster; Ralph Naylor, John Bragg, Boardman Stewart, Tony Cobb, and Danny Allen, English; Bobby Gentry, Carl Smithson, Billy Smith, Bill Brown, and Jimmy French, mathematics; J. B. Akin, Jimmy Gentry, John Oxley, Don Patterson, and William "Bunny" Akin; Daly Thompson, Latin; Billy Bradshaw, social studies; Mattie Lou Duke, speech; and Betsy Redick, typing.

Battle Ground Academy grew through many successful years during the 1960s. Championship football teams, campus additions, and new subjects created a sense of pride for the boys of BGA. During this time when teenagers were famous for defying authority, the students of BGA were reminded daily through tradition and disciplined instruction the importance of well-rounded education. An education cannot be found entirely in the classroom and the boys of BGA were blessed to encounter so many experiences by attending a school so rich in tradition.

CHAPTER ELEVEN

Changing Times

The decade beginning in 1970 marked a period when BGA would meet the demands of a changing society. In 1973, BGA discontinued boarding students, a practice that began with the conception of the school. By the end of the decade, girls were admitted to the school once again, fifty years later. With an open mind, BGA took the lead in exemplifying the role of private prep schools in a modern society.

The Fellowship of Christian Athletes gained many enthusiastic members during the 1970s. Established in 1964 at BGA, the FCA's purpose is to combine students' athletic ability with their desire to become a better Christian. The members were broken into huddle groups with an upperclassman presiding. Members gave chapel talks and competed against other chapters in sporting events. The Tennessee Chapter of the FCA is now directed by BGA alumnus Steve Robinson, class of 1967.

Grit day was celebrated during the 1970s with unusual flair. For fifty cents, students could come to school dressed (almost) anyway they liked. This provided a pleasant holiday from the day to day routine. The "biggest grit" award was given each year to a student and teacher who demonstrated unusual creativity in preparing their attire for the day. All proceeds benefited the school's social committee. This tradition is still practiced today with the winner eating real grits.

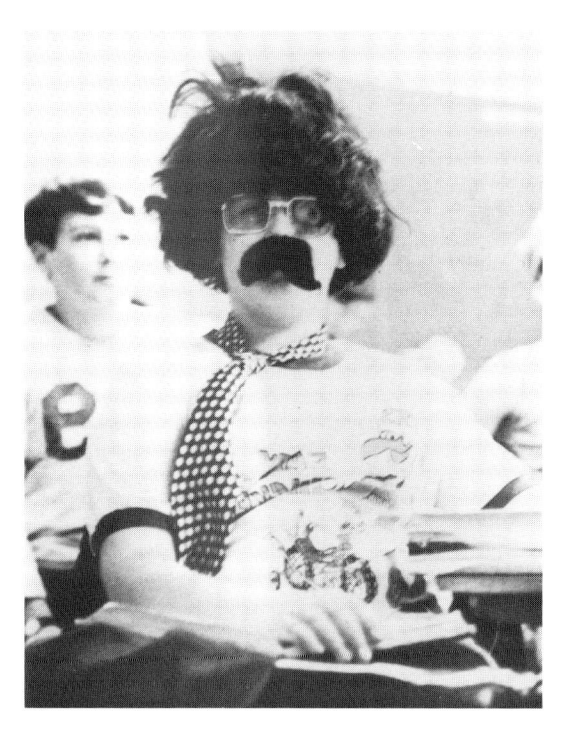

Grit Day is one day when the students can come to school dressed as they like, but the winner has to eat grits.

In the summer of 1971, the old dorm which had been built in 1923, was demolished to make way for a new building which would house the library, language department, and dining room. In its later years the old dorm housed underclassmen and contained four faculty apartments. The building served as home away from home for hundreds of BGA boys through the years. Boarders had their own language and learned to cope with such problems as waiting in line thirty minutes for the shower. The new building was to be complete by the 1972–1973 school year.

The Junior Classical League was established in the early 1970s to promote an awareness of classical literature, culture and civilization. In 1973, the members refurbished a two-year-old catapult and entered it in the National Catapult Contest in Indianapolis, Indiana. The students received television coverage from WSM-TV, WLAC-TV and NBC's *First Tuesday*.

BGA's 1972–1973 quiz team was invited to WSIX's *High School Challenge*. Capt. Danny Lorenzo and team members Gil Bubis, Jay Moench, and Larry Bubis practiced against the junior class and won 155-70 and later challenged the faculty. Bob Rauchle, Day Hollman, Dorothy Doggett, and Henry Seaton represented the teachers, beating the quiz team 225-210. At the actual competition, the BGA boys beat Murfreesboro Riverdale 195-120 then lost to Overton by five points following a one hundred point halftime lead.

In 1973, Battle Ground Academy discontinued boarding students on campus. As a final tribute to all who boarded, a final story will be shared. Thomas Woodall, class of 1973, related an incident that occurred in the late spring of 1972. Doug Jackson and Jimmy Graham boarded together in a room that overlooked the football field. During study hall one evening, Graham was studying in the cafeteria when Jackson and Woodall disassembled his bed and lowered it

The 1973 quiz team: (L to R): Jay Moench, Dan Lorenzo, Gil Bubis, Lenny Bubis.

by pieces on a rope out the window. They then reassembled it, completely made on the fifty yard line. When an exasperated Graham could not find his bed, witnesses were of little help. He finally looked out the window and saw it on the football field. Everyone let him worry a little about how to get the bed back in his room, then joined in to help.

During the 1970s, BGA football teams competed in four post-season bowl games. The 1971 team played in the

A catapult was built by some BGA students in the early 1970s and entered in a national contest.

Tobacco Bowl in Hartsville and lost 10-0 to Stratford. In 1972, the Wildcats lost to Warren County 17-14 in the Butter Bowl in Pulaski. The 1974 team also appeared in the Butter Bowl, winning 23-0 over Savannah. The final bowl appearance during this decade was again in the Butter Bowl in 1975 when BGA lost a close game 19-17 to Stratford. Each of these teams were coached by John Oxley and his highly capable staff.

Several basketball teams of the 1970s experienced success on the hardwoods. The 1972–1973 team completed the season with an incredible 22-3 record and a second-place finish in the district. The following year, the basketball team finished with an 18-7 standing, yet could not shake David Lipscomb High School as they lost both the district and the region championship games to this team. The Wildcats, however, advanced to the sub-state where they beat Hohenwald. BGA eventually lost to Happy Valley (ultimately the state championship winner) in overtime 41-39 in the semifinals of the state tournament.

The 1974–1975 basketball team, coached by Gary Smith, achieved great success with a 27-6 season. The Wildcats won the district, region and sub-state. They eventually lost 82-73 to Bolton, a Memphis team that had been rated number one all season. The following year, BGA moved up to the AAA league where they competed with larger schools in the state. The Wildcats still managed a 15-10 season, finishing second in the district and advancing to the region tournament. Here, they lost to Clarksville in the semifinals with Mark Barrett and Timmy Stewart named to the All-Region team.

The art department opened a studio in 1976 across Everbright Avenue in one of the houses owned by the school. The art house provided more space for creating and displaying the boy's work. Art teacher Linda Allen began the year with three-dimensional sculptures done in plaster, clay, wood, wire, plaster tape, styrofoam, or a combination. By the end of the decade, art would be a required subject for seventh and eighth graders. One project of the art students was designing and painting the front wall of the study hall in the spring of 1978.

The 1974–1975 basketball team: Front Row (L to R): Jay Luna, Ken Warren, Binks Lewis, Greg Gunnells, Rob Fesmire, Mark Heldman, Wayne Davis. Back Row (L to R): Mark Barrett, Mike Holland, Brad Williams, John Southwood, Maxwell Horkins, David Benson, Tim Stewart.

Soccer was reintroduced to BGA as a major sport in the fall of 1979. Soccer was played as an intramural sport many years ago at the school because other schools lacked teams to compete against. The school's first varsity soccer team, coached by Buzzy Fryer and Craig Porter, finished fifth in the state, a tremendous accomplishment for a first-year team. Jeff Anderson was a leading scorer for the team as they defeated and tied many teams with established programs. The final loss was by a narrow margin to Father Ryan in the first match of the state tournament.

For many years the assemblies at BGA have provided great learning opportunities as well as entertainment and lots of memories. Some of the most memorable assemblies during the 1970s include the Metro-Nashville K-9 Corps. Tandy Rice from Top Billing, the Space Flight Center from Huntsville, Arthur Murray's disco dancing, the "card-playing preacher" and Lester the owl from the Cumberland Museum.

The 1979 soccer team: First Row (L to R): Gary Curl, John Cartwright, David Gilmore, John Nance, Craig Wise, Billy King, Nick McCall, Don Searcy. Second Row (L to R): Doug King, Henry Wilson, Gary Parkes, Alistair Leslie, Jeff Anderson, Tommy Herbert, Vince Keene, Coach Fryer. Third Row (L to R): Jimmy Charron, George Tosh, Jim Davenport, Chris Ball, James Jennings, Rhea Garrett, Zack Jones, Ricky Price, Coach Porter.

BGA traditions play an important part in each student's life. The Greer/Plato rivalry has been a part of each boy's life for several decades culminating each year in a fiercely fought tug-of-war. Another annual tradition at BGA is the Jamboree fundraiser. Parents, students, and faculty donate various items, money, their time, and a lot of effort for the occasion. The Spanish Club under the leadership of David Hernandez set up a taco stand and the French Club sold various French cuisine. All of this food was on top of the massive amounts the parents dished out. Great food, a lively auction, and a raffled car were the highlights of the Jamboree during the 1970s.

As the decade came to a close, the boys of BGA experienced the biggest change of their prep school career. Girls

Disco dancing was demonstrated by the Arthur Murray Dance Studio for an assembly in the 1970s.

were added to the student body in 1979 in an effort to accommodate the demand for coeducational private education. Though the boys may have felt invaded at first, everyone was soon working together to make coeducation work for the best for everyone at BGA. Paige McClain, Jeanne Reindl, and Rhonda Trace were the only three girls accepted into the senior class in 1979. During their first year at BGA the girls in each class made a positive impact on the school by forming athletic teams and joining student organizations.

During the 1980s BGA was fortunate to have several highly motivated teachers who will long be remembered for their devotion to the students and the school. John

Parents make the annual Jamboree a great success as a fundraiser for the school. This car is one of many to be raffled during the many years of the Jamboree.

Bragg served as headmaster throughout the decade with J. B. Akin as president until his retirement in 1973. Numerous teachers made lasting impressions on BGA by teaching for several years during the 1970s; those include: Dorothy Lea, Dorothy Dogget, Don Snow, and Greg Kinman in the English Department; Bobby Gentry, John Herrmann, Gary Smith, Jim Webb, Larry McElroy, and Charles Wrenn in mathematics; John Oxley and Jimmy Gentry in the sciences; John Colmore, Doug Langston, Ronnie Prichard, and David Evans in social sciences; David Hernandez, Spanish; Lillian Stewart, French; Linda Allen, art; and Marcia Bowen, Latin. This fine group of teachers along with others who taught during this period are fondly remembered by many alumni today.

The decade of the 1970s was a time of adjustment for the world as well as the students at BGA. John Bragg guided the school through these years with tireless devotion. The students were destined to hold dear to the traditions that gave strength to Battle Ground Academy. The expectations for the future were bright as the school moved forward with a mission, and the addition of girls proved to be the spark the school needed to journey into the 1980s.

CHAPTER TWELVE

Jubilation Celebration

With the addition of girls in 1979, Battle Ground Academy's outlook for the 1980s took on a new dimension. The transition took place and the students soon felt comfortable with their new situation. Dr. Lucus Boyd joined the staff as principal, taking on administrative responsibilities while John Bragg continued as headmaster. The school flourished scholastically and athletically. New organizations were established and new teams were formed. Records were set and traditions continued as BGA concluded its first one hundred years. As the centennial celebration started, everyone soon realized the certainty of the next one hundred years of Battle Ground Academy.

The Key Club service organization was established in 1965 at BGA and prospered during the 1980s. Key Club members sponsored a basketball game pitting members of the senior class against members of the faculty. The fundraising game in 1981 raised five hundred dollars for Easter Seals. In 1983, the Key Club sold trees to aid the multiple sclerosis foundation and in 1986, members helped with the local CPS cancer run. Key Club members were required to have better than an eighty average to participate.

The girls of BGA wasted no time forming athletic teams and competing locally. During the first year the following girls' teams were organized: varsity swimming, middle school softball, and varsity tennis. Though each of these teams were young, they each gained experience on which

The 1980 girls' tennis team: First Row (L to R): Kim Hardin, Lori Herman, Lawrence Blank, Gina Bastone, Leigh McClain. Standing (L to R): Ellen More, Lean Chalfant, Kelly Baugh, Rhonda Trace, Sheila Alley, Becky Mayfield, Barbara Freeman, Mary Jane Cook, Beth Willoughby.

to build. The next year a middle school girls' basketball team was formed and the highlight of the season was a second-place finish in the David Lipscomb Invitational Tournament. Also added during the 1980–1981 school year were varsity girls' soccer, middle school girls' tennis and middle school girls' softball.

The first varsity girls' basketball team, coached by Jay Gore, was formed in 1982. This was also the first year for a varsity girls' soccer team, coached by Jody Jones and Lori Freeman. This team had a remarkable start by not losing a single game and tying Franklin twice. The 1983–1984 team finished second in the Middle Tennessee Girls' Soccer League and third in the state. Becky Drayton and Stacy

Girls' soccer got off to a great start in 1982 at Battle Ground Academy.

Burchett were named on the All-Tournament team.

The girls' athletic teams jumped into action and competed with the best across the state. The 1984–1985 varsity girls' tennis team won their region tournament with Alice Johnson named MVP. The 1985–1986 varsity girls' soccer team advanced to the state tournament and sophomore Stacy Burchett was given All-District, All-Region, and All-State honors. The 1985–1986 varsity girls' basketball team made it to the region for the first time. Stephanie Shouse and Alice Johnson won the doubles championship for the region in tennis in 1986. Girls' varsity soccer was sanctioned by the TSSAA during the 1986–1987 school year and they posted a 10-4 record. Girls' athletics were off to a great start and destined to play a major role throughout the state.

The 1981–1982 Forensic League excelled on a national level. This nationally sponsored league promotes interscholastic debate, oratory, extemporaneous speaking, and interpretation competition. Participants are judged in five areas: merit, honor, excellence, distinction, and double ruby. This year's team, sponsored by Vicki Lamb, ranked seventeenth in the nation among high school chapters. To be a member of the National Forensic League a student must have a certain number of forensic points which are obtained through competition.

The 1980s' BGA football teams played in five post-season bowl games. Each of these teams were coached by Don Vick and his skilled staff. BGA lost 14-9 to Mt. Pleasant in the 1981 Pioneer Bowl in Columbus. The next year, the Wildcats played Moore County in the Butter Bowl in Pulaski and won 28-7. In this game BGA faithful got one of their first glimpses of James Jewell passing to cousin John Jewell. This Jewell to Jewell combination would prove to be more exciting each year.[32]

James and John Jewell, who were cousins, created many memories for BGA's football faithful during the 1980s.

The 1983 football team played Huntland in the Bell Buckle Lion's Bowl in Cascade, Tennessee. The Wildcats won 42-16 with senior tailback Rodney Barrett breaking Stanley Gayles' record for rushing with 4,692 yards. The following year, BGA played at Franklin High School in the Kiwanis Bowl. Goodpasture beat the Wildcats 26-7 in Coach Vick's first clash with the school where he had been head coach prior to coming to BGA.[33]

BGA played in and won their first playoff appearance in 1985 with less than four minutes left in the game. James Jewell's pass to John Jewell on fourth and goal from the one, boosted the Wildcats to a 12-6 win over White House. BGA, however, lost the next game 42-22 to Goodpasture. The Jewell cousins left their mark on BGA, helping the team compile a 32-13 record. Throughout James' career, he completed 269 of 548 passes for 4,565 yards. He threw for 46 touchdowns and rushed for 7. Two-time All-State player John Jewell, caught 143 passes for 2,714 yards, with 32 touchdown receptions.

In 1986, BGA fell just one game short of competing in the state playoffs, so the Wildcats turned their sights on the Butter Bowl where they stormed to a 42-6 victory over Houston County. The tone for the game was set in the second play from scrimmage when quarterback Brandon Jones threw a 48-yard completion to George Jones who was stopped just short of an eventual touchdown on the two yard line.[34]

BGA produced several successful wrestlers during the 1980s. In 1982, Randy Uselton had a 37-2-1 record for the year and was the first BGA boy to win a state championship. Hal Abbott placed fourth in 1983 and second in 1984 at the state meet. Matt Ligon made it to the state tournament three times in his high school career. He finished fourth in 1985, second in 1986, and third in 1987 as a senior. He also set the record for the most wins in the state of Tennessee.

BGA was also fortunate to be the home of two extraordinary swimmers during the 1980s. Mark Dillard, class of 1983, won the state championship in the 200-meter backstroke four years in a row. He also held twelve southeastern swimming records. One of his times was compared with the best international times for a week and Dillard's was the fastest time in the world. Chas Morton, class of 1989, was a state championship swimmer his freshman year through his senior year. As a junior he was

Mark Dillard, class of 1983, state championship swimmer.

Chas Morton, class of 1989, state championship and Olympic Festival Gold Medalist swimmer.

a Gold Medalist in the Olympic Festival and named Tennessee's Athlete of the year by *U.S.A. Today*.

Wildcat basketball during the mid-1980s was dominated by the outstanding athletic ability of Barry Booker. As a sophomore in 1983, Booker aided the team's 7-6 winning record by averaging 17.5 points and 9 rebounds per game as well as being named to the All-State team. As a junior, Booker was considered a top college prospect and was named to the All-State team again as BGA finished with a 20-8 record. In 1985, All-American Booker led the Wildcats to a 27-5 record, winning the sub-state. Other key players on this skilled team were seniors Mark Puryear, Johnny Hughes, and Ric Chapman; and juniors John Davis, John Jewell, James Jewell, and Brad Jones. Gary Smith's excellent coaching was recognized as he was voted All-Metro coach of the year. Booker went on to

All-American Barry Booker, class of 1985.

be an outstanding player for Vanderbilt.

The students at BGA established a chapter of Students Against Driving Drunk during the 1983–1984 school year. In the first year the organization sponsored a meeting with other area schools with Robert Anastas, founder of SADD as the speaker. The BGA students encouraged other schools to form their own chapters in order to make a difference in the lives of others. They also sponsored a "Safety Dance" after a home basketball game. The group was interviewed by Franklin's channel three and WDCN, public television in Nashville.

The 1983–1984 school year was a memorable one for BGA's middle school sports. The boys' middle school basketball team came in second in the Harpeth Valley Athletic conference with Chad Jewell as the leading scorer and rebounder. The girls' middle school basketball team came in second in the Hillsboro Invitational Tournament and won the Sportsmanship Trophy too. Both boys' and girls' middle school soccer teams came in second in the HVAC, the boys touted a 9-2-1 record while the girls season finished 4-2.

The Honor Council has played an important role in maintaining high virtues among the student body at BGA. Six senior members are chosen by the faculty and the student body each year based on their leadership ability and character. When the Honor Code is violated, the Honor Council meets to review the case and recommends the appropriate action to the administration. This system helps to preserve high standards of morality, integrity, and honor through the understanding of their peers.

During the 1980s, the students at BGA were fortunate to have innovative teachers who wanted to make a difference. Those who taught for a majority of the decade include: John Bragg as headmaster; Lucus Boyd as principal; Larry McElroy, Barry Sensing, and Gary Smith,

A "Students Against Driving Drunk" chapter was formed at BGA in 1984 with the following founding officers (L to R): Chris Cone, publicity; Chuck Brown, president; Elizabeth Brown, vice president; John Jewell, treasurer; Tiffany Hall, secretary.

BGA statue inscribed with a poem written by Dr. Robert Foote, a 1962 alumnus.

mathematics; Robert Walker, Laurel Eason, Sharon Anderson, Don Snow, and Jody Jones, English; Dennis Gibson and Judy Davis, science; Doug Langston and Tom Gilman, social studies; Carol Lea-Mord, art; David Hernandez, Spanish; Lillian Stewart, French; Gloria Robinson, speech and theater; Dorothy Doggett, guidance; Margaret Hickey, dietician; and Tom Warren, librarian.

As the decade came to a close, plans were made for a massive celebration of the school's one hundredth anniversary. The year's festivities were called "Jubilation Celebration" and everyone joined in the fun. The school's entire student body appeared on *Good Morning America*. Headmaster John Bragg stood in front of the group in the quadrangle and introduced the school as the students joined in, "Good Morning, America!" The anniversary was the theme of the homecoming parade as Grand Marshall Bill Hall of WSMV led the festive parade through Franklin.

For posterity, the school buried a time capsule containing BGA memorabilia in the quadrangle of the school and the plaque states that it may be opened May 26, 2089. The time capsule is located just behind a statue that was created for the anniversary celebration. The statue, titled "The Discussion" depicts a young man and a young woman on their quest for knowledge. The year culminated with the graduation exercises where ex-speaker of the house, Tip O'Neill addressed the 1989 seniors.

Battle Ground Academy has accomplished what few schools can even dream about. One hundred years of college prep education through wars and a depression, and still going strong. Conscientious young men and women learning, making decisions, and forming organizations were all a part of a school that enjoyed a strong heritage. As the school celebrated one hundred years of education, the future appeared on the horizon.

CHAPTER THIRTEEN

Building for Our Second Century

Though the decade is not complete, BGA has already experienced championship athletic teams and excellence in the classroom. As the county grows, BGA has been forced to expand its facility in order to meet the demands. In the past few years, BGA has risen to a new plateau and the popularity of the school has reached new heights. In keeping with its heritage, board members have taken steps to insure the prosperity of the school as they look toward the year 2000 and beyond. Currently, the school promotes the total student academically, athletically, and morally.

The decade began with the retirement of Headmaster John Bragg who had dedicated forty years of his life to Battle Ground Academy. When Bragg came to BGA he taught English and Spanish and served as chairman of the English department. He became assistant headmaster in 1959 and selected headmaster in 1969. Bragg was succeeded in a long line of prestigious headmasters by Dr. Ronald Griffeth. He received his B.A., M.A., as well as his doctorate from the University of Georgia. Before coming to BGA, Griffeth served as headmaster of Deerfield-Windsor School in Albany, Georgia. His duties include managing finances, supervision of all personal, administration, curriculum planning, and alumni/public relations.

Two new organizations were formed at BGA in 1990. Larry McElroy formed Mu Alpha Theta for students in

Dr. Griffeth came to BGA as headmaster in 1990 and continues to serve today.

grades ten through twelve who exhibited strength in mathematics. To be a member, students must have better than an 85 average if in honors math, or an average of 94 or above if in standard math classes. The members sponsor the Mu Room to help students having trouble. Another organization that formed during this school year was the history club. Paul Gasparini sponsored this group, as president Brian Whitaker conducted a project endorsed by the Williamson County Historical Society. The students cataloged and dated Civil War articles from the school's collection.

The speech team has always been one of the strongest assets of BGA. During the early 1990s the speech team represented the school in national tournaments and in 1990 was ranked in the top thirty in the nation. Coach Gloria Robinson led the team to win the National Forensic League (NFL) Sweepstakes. Robinson was the NFL chairperson and the Tennessee High School Speech and Drama League president. Later, the team was coached by Sandra Davis and Charles Oakes who kept up the winning tradition. Chase Wrenn won the state tournament in the 1991–1992 school year and Hal Vincent came in second. The 1993–1994 team took first place at the NFL National Qualifying tournament for Tennessee.

A new program formed at BGA during the 1991–1992 school year. The Insight Program involved seniors, juniors and later sophomores, who took a pledge to be positive role models. Also called peer facilitators, each member took a pledge not to drink alcohol. Each facilitator was assigned a group of students from the sixth, seventh, eighth, or ninth grade to meet with at regular intervals. Members also attended class parties and went on field trips. Facilitators earned one-half credit on their transcripts for participating.

Two organizations to promote creativity were organized during the 1980s. The *Quadrangle* and *Centennial* flourished in the early 1990s as students worked together to produce publications for the school. The *Quadrangle* was created as a "vehicle for creativity" in prose, poetry, art, and photography. Putting together a magazine also aided the students in advertising, solicitation, criticism, layout, editing, and production. The *Centennial* was founded in the spring of 1989. The student paper contains articles covering sports, music, and literature as well as many other aspects of student life.

In 1992, BGA athletics moved their competition to the single A level in the TSSAA. The football team completed a winning season even though two key players were sidelined due to injuries. The following year, BGA posted an incredible 14-0 regular season and was the first BGA squad to make it to the state championship game in a playoff system. The team lost a heartbreaker 10-13 to Oneida in the 1992 Clinic Bowl. Midstate coach-of-the-year Kurt Page led the Wildcats through a year of wide open offense which provided an exciting season for BGA faithful.

The 1993 football season was expected to be another thriller as many players returned. Again, they swept through the regular season and won the district and the region. In the second round of the state playoffs, BGA encountered Greenback and jumped to a 21-0 lead, but Greenback came away victorious. One loss does not make a season and BGA was definitely on the winning track.

The 1992–1993 basketball team saw five starters returning and expected a winning season. Brandon Wood, Seth Pettus, Alex Gregg, Jeff VanLandingham, and O. J. Fleming led the

The Quadrangle *was created as a "vehicle for creativity" in prose, poetry, art, and photography.*

The Centennial

Established 1989
BGA's Official Student Newspaper

November 1994 — November 1994

A Century Of Pigskin
By Jeff Russell

In 1894, the headmaster of BGA, W.D. Mooney, brought football to Franklin. Battle Ground Academy was the first college-preparatory school in the South to play football. Mr. Mooney had seen the game played in the Northeast, and he recognized that it would do well at B.G.A.

In 1901, B.G.A. earned their first championship against the Manual Training School of Indianapolis. The team won by the score of six to five at Vanderbilt's Dudley Field. The early uniforms were constructed by several local women out of heavy khaki canvas. Cotton was inserted into the uniforms for knee, shoulder, and kidney pads. Each uniform was custom made for each player. The team played in the school's colors of purple and green behind the present-day Boys' and Girls' Club on Columbia Avenue.

B.G.A. teams have been in many other championship games since 1901. In 1944, B.G.A. had its first undefeated and untied record in school history. Under the coaching of James B. Akin, the team finished their season 8-0-0. In 1960, the team won its first ever state championship. The Wildcats plastered Cumberland County, 33 to 0, in the Clinic Bowl to win the state title and remain undefeated and untied. Six years later, the Wildcats repeated their 1960 performance and, again, won the state title by defeating Stratford, 14 to 7. In 1992, the Wildcats were looking for their third state championship and entered the Clinic Bowl with a record of 14 and 0 against Oneida. However, B.G.A. lost that game by the score of 13 to 10.

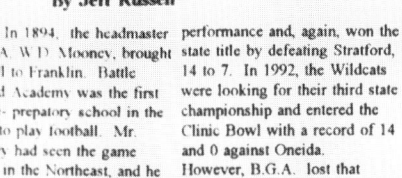

B.G.A.'s appearances in bowl games have not been rare. They have appeared in six Butter Bowls, two Tobacco Bowls, one Lions' Bowl, one Rebel Bowl, one Metro Bowl, one Kiwanis Bowl, and one Pioneer Bowl, to go along with the three appearances in state championship games. The school's overall bowl record is 8-5-3.

Football has long been a tradition at B.G.A. From its beginnings in 1894 to the present team, the Wildcats have always fielded competitive teams. With the first century of gridiron competition coming to a close, B.G.A. continues its tradition of exellence in the sport of football.

Editors: Chevonne Wrenn and Matt Schroer
Business Managers: Adam Reynolds and Pual Smith
Faculty Sponsors: David Hernandez and Don Snow

Strangers Among Us
By Corrie Davis
cont'd p. 2

On the week of October 9, 1994, the SACS committee visited BGA and the week was a success! The Southern Association of Colleges and Schools in an organization that accredits schools and gives a diploma from BGA it's prestige. The student body and faculty alike, have heard a lot lately that this group of teachers and administrators from 15 to 18 different schools, said a lot of "good things" about the students and faculty, but what did they really say?

Dr. Griffith informed *The Centennial* that the committee was very impressed with the attitudes of the faculty. SACS got a general good feeling on campus and they appreciated the hospitality and warmth they received form the students. The SACS committee was generally impressed with the accessibility of the teachers and the effort that they put forth to help the students. Dr. Griffith sees that as a crucial part of what BGA is about, helping students when they need assistance, he is very proud of the teachers. SACS thinks that Battle Ground Academy has great teaching, and that the student faculty ratio is great. SACS was very impressed with the students and parents because they were very courteous, friendly, open and above all well-mannered -- WAY TO GO WILDCATS!!!! The SACS committee encouraged BGA to prepare for the split of the High School and Middle School (hopefully this should happen in 1996). They encouraged the faculty to plan for the coordination of the two schools, so that BGA can avoid having two different worlds, High School and Middle School.

About the food...Since the SACS committee is mad up of faculty from other school, they understand the problem that BGA is having with the food. They have the same cafeteria problems as we do, it is very hard to cook for 500 people a day, and have the food taste good. They encouraged the faculty to continue trying to resolve the problem, and suggested getting a committee together to aid in this proceed. There was a meeting on Tuesday, November 1, for parents to discuss how to solve our food dilemma. Hopefully students encouraged their parents to attend this imperative meeting and they expressed some feasible ideas about how to fix the food.

Mr. Gibson said that the SACS committee was impressed with what the science department can accomplish with their adequate facilities. They suggested a new teacher to take the load off of the hard working science teachers that we already have

The computer lab, as BGA is already aware, is state of the art and offers courses that will help students in the real world.

One of the members of the visiting committee, Gordon Mathis, a former BGA history teacher,

The 1994 BGA Homecoming Court with Queen Alice Leonard.

BGA's official student newspaper.

team through an undefeated regular season. As they entered the post-season playoffs, the Wildcats head coach Gary Smith began to realize his twenty-six years of coaching could finally see an undefeated season. The team made it to the state championship game where they dominated, beating Cascade 79-56. Coach Smith and Coach William Belliford guided the 1993 Wildcats through a perfect season (33-0) that will never be forgotten.

The following year, four returning senior starters meant high expectations for the Wildcats. Alex Gregg, O. J. Fleming, Seth Pettus, and Jeff VanLandingham sparked the Wildcats to a rare undefeated regular season for the second year in a row. The squad again entered the state championship playoffs with hopes of a repeat. They had no trouble beating Chattanooga Christian and Oneida (which was a 1992 Clinic Bowl rematch). Then came the championship game against Goodpasture, a rematch of the region finals which BGA lost by five points. Down by four with under a minute to play, BGA clawed back to force overtime. In overtime the Wildcats never trailed, winning 65-62, back-to-back state championships.

The 1993 BGA basketball team celebrates after winning the state championship game.

The 1994 Wildcat basketball team displays two fingers after winning back-to-back state championships.

Other BGA students excelled in athletics during the early 1990s. Stephen Harvey won the state wrestling championship at 140 pounds in 1993. He was named "Wrestler of the Year," and achieved over one hundred wins in his career. The 1993 golf team was second in the state as junior, Michael Trailov led the team to a 13-1 record. The same year, senior Scott Perkinson won the state in shot put, throwing 50 feet, 6 inches as well as the discuss with a 162-foot, 5 1/4-inch throw. He also finished fifth in the 110 meter hurdles. Nineteen ninety-three was a year for many champions at BGA.

BGA lost one of its most beloved teachers in December 1994. David Hernandez taught Spanish for twenty-three years at Battle Ground Academy. He fled his native Cuba to live in a free country where he would no longer suffer from communist imprisonment. Dorothy Doggett, a colleague of Hernandez' remembers him as follows:

The halls of BGA will echo with his heavy Cuban accent in stern but caring admonition and in irrepressible, soul-deep laughter as long as there are ears that remember and hearts that love this unique, warm, funny, wise, learned and lovable teacher. And they are myriad.[48]

Every school bestows medals and honors on graduating seniors and these awards are commonly memorials to various alumnus and patrons of the school. The following awards are currently given to deserving students as listed in the 1994 *Cannon Ball*.

The Pinkerton Watch is awarded annually to the senior who, in the opinion of the faculty, has proved to be the best all-around student of the senior class.

The Bill Ross Award, sponsored by the mother of the late Bill Ross, is awarded by the vote of students in grades nine through twelve to the most deserving member of the senior class. Criteria: befriending those who needed a friend, helping those who needed help, and understanding those who needed to be understood; always acting quickly without need of recognition and humbly without thought of self.

The Durwood Sies Leadership Award is given by Durwood Sies, a 1940 graduate of BGA. It is given to the senior who, in the judgment of the faculty, exhibits the most outstanding leadership.

The Paul Guffee Award is given by a former BGA headmaster and his wife, Mr. and Mrs. Paul Redick, in memory of the late Paul Guffee, a 1961 graduate of BGA, who was an outstanding student-athlete. It goes to the senior who, in the judgment of the faculty, exhibits excellence in scholarship, athletics, and all other phases of school life.

As Battle Ground Academy looked to the future, it was apparent that with the current popularity of the school and its tremendous growth, plans to expand would be imminent. Enrollment increased from 347 students in 1990–1991 to 520 in 1994–1995. Due to the location of the campus and no potential for growth, the board of trustees decided it would be in the best interest of the school to move.

David Hernandez, a native of Cuba, joined the BGA staff in the early 1970s as a Spanish teacher and remained there until his death in 1994.

The new North Campus of BGA will reflect many of the traditional details of the original campus. The academic complex will carry on the theme of the quadrangle and will be flanked by athletic fields. Battle Ground Academy remains focused on academic excellence as the school boldly plans for its second century.

Realizing the value of the heritage of the original campus, it was decided to move the upper school to a new location and keep the historic campus for a middle school. The board of trustees adopted a long-range plan and in 1993, announced a plan to address the immediate goals.

The initial step called for upgrading and maintaining the present campus which would be called the South Campus. Two public streets were closed to provide a consolidated

Historic Glen Echo located on North Campus.

Artist rendering of the library/media center on the new North Campus.

campus with a safer atmosphere. Once the upper school moves, the South Campus can offer spacious facilities for 220 middle school students in grades sixth through eighth. A new road will allow students to be dropped off in front of Fleming Hall and Peoples Hall. The cohesiveness of the South Campus will afford the middle school students with improved learning opportunities in a historic setting.

The board decided about fifty acres would be required for the purposes of the upper school. In 1994, the school purchased the historic property, Glen Echo, an 1830s' house which includes fifty-five acres. This property is located on Ernest Rice Road, just northwest of the Mack Hatcher Bypass and the Franklin Road intersection. The North Campus will enhance historic Glen Echo with compatible buildings that will house state-of-the-art classrooms, laboratories, and furnishings to meet the needs of college-bound students. The master plan calls for a library and media center, student center, academic classroom/lab facility, historic Glen Echo residence, sports/fitness center, and a performing arts center as well as athletic fields. The continual educational mission of Battle Ground Academy has given birth to an exciting and expanding future. When Battle Ground Academy was founded in 1889 with S. V. Wall and W. D. Mooney as its leaders, the mission statement was quite simple: "If you wish to place your son

Entrance to site of the new North Campus. (Summer 1994)

in Vanderbilt University, Yale, Harvard, Princeton or some thorough college, then send him to us and let us fit him for it." As the school moves into a second century of higher education, BGA can boast that graduating classes have a one hundred percent placement rate in four-year colleges. Battle Ground Academy has been a leader in college prep education in the southeast for over one hundred years. The heritage of Battle Ground Academy is a culmination of the lives of each person to ever walk on the historic campus. Every student, faculty member, parent or friend of the school has contributed in some way to the legacy of this great institution. The picturesque campus and tree-covered lawn are constant reminders of the prominence of Battle Ground Academy in the community and the state. Yet, BGA is not content with resting on past laurels. The school's expansion is a prime example of their quest to develop the best academic atmosphere possible for the growth of each student. Battle Ground Academy's enduring tradition of academic and athletic excellence continues with a new spirit as the school moves into its second century.

PART III
Class Composites

A Monument to Education

1893 Senior Class and Faculty

Top Row (Left to Right): A. W. Watkins, T. R. Peebles, W. R. Barnhill, J. R. Moran. **Second Row (L to R):** T. P. Wall, H. R. Reid, S. V. Wall Jr., R. M. Buford, S. D. Dodson. **Bottom Row (L to R):** T. P. Flippen, R. P. Hollinshead, E. L. Roberts, H. H. Lane Jr. **Not Pictured:** M. J. Anderson.

1899 Senior Class and Faculty—p. 130 (top)

Top Row (Left to Right): Unidentified, R. W. Billington, Jesse H. Gray, T. G. Pollard, Elva Davis, Theresa Mulley, F. H. Westfeldt, E. F. Shuler, Jesse Short, John Burchard. **Second Row (L to R):** J. C. "Indian" Smith, Mary Moss, Jim A. McFerrin, Pattie Bolton, Fielding G. Gordon. **Bottom Row (L to R):** Tom B. Matthews, Gerald Buchanan, B. T. Nolen, Woodlief Thomas.

1903 Senior Class and Faculty—p. 130 (bottom)

Top Row (Left to Right): William Perkins Cannon, Spence Thomas. **Bottom Row (L to R):** George I. Briggs, Phil Kennedy, Farrell Buford.

1906 Senior Class and Faculty—p. 131

Top Row (Left to Right): Herman Moore, Putnam, Greer Peoples, Frank Aydelott, Ben Brown, Holmes Anderson, Hal Peoples. **Second Row (L to R):** Jerry Hampton, Will Neely, John Sherril, Russell Gray, Joe Ryland, Will Jefferson, Stone Reynolds, Lucien Smith. **Bottom Row (L to R):** Walker Martin, James Jones, Janet Pierce, Bertha Fleming, David Blake, Clarence Pierce.

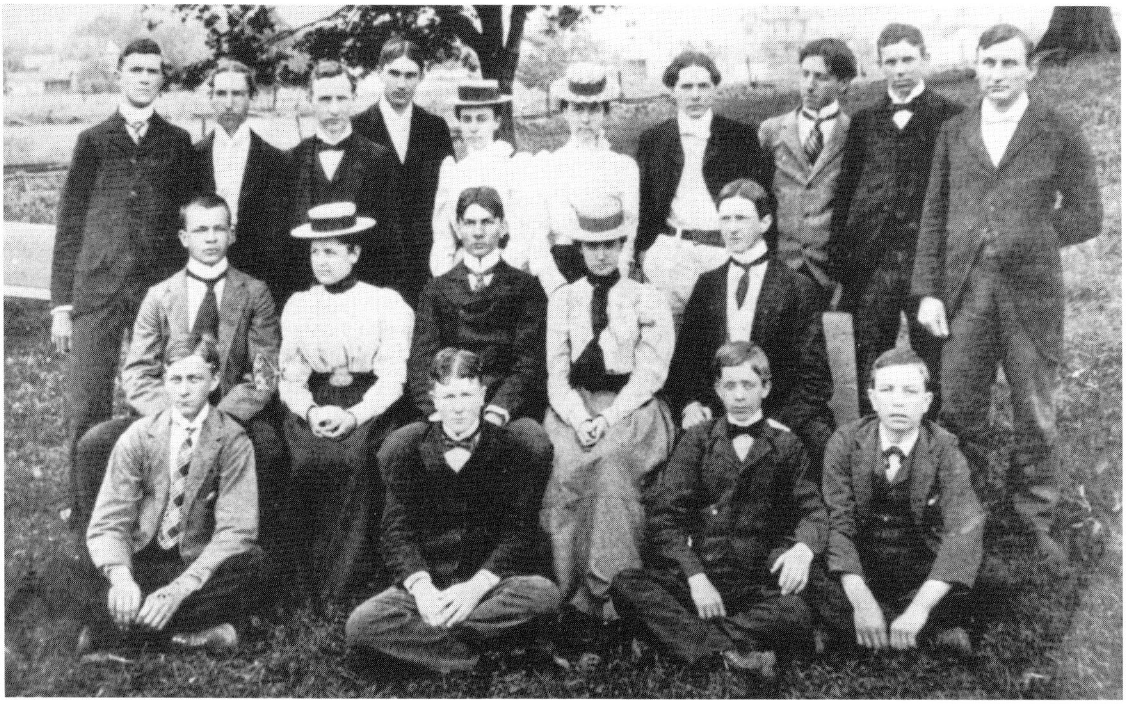

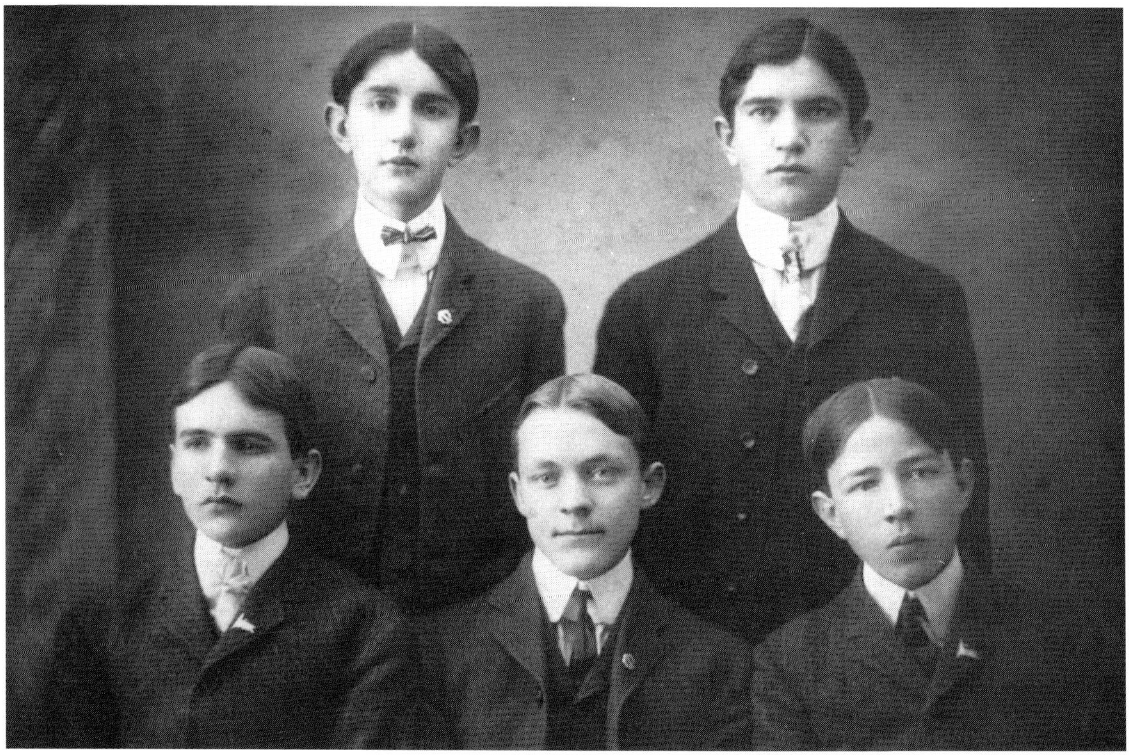

1907 Senior Class and Faculty—p. 132

Top Row (Left to Right): H. S. Reynolds, N. N. Polk. **Second Row (L to R):** R. H. Denham, W. T. Dent, C. B. Braun, A. Barnett. **Third Row (L to R):** J. C. Taylor, Lois Flemming, Mamie Denham, Josephine McPherson, D. C. Davis. **Fourth Row (L to R):** W. A. Sanders, J. L. Smith, W. W. Courtney, J. S. Pullen, A. E. McClanahan. **Fifth Row (L to R):** J. H. Anderson, M. M. Morelock. **Bottom Row (L to R):** R. H. Peoples, W. K. Greene, R. G. Peoples.

1908 Senior Class and Faculty—p. 133

Top Row (Left to Right): G. H. Armistead Jr., A. B. Paschall, J. M. Bickley, O. M. Sorrels. **Second Row (L to R):** H. J. Paulk, J. E. Ring, A. B. Fleming, W. H. Klyce. **Third Row (L to R):** L. D. Darnell, G. T. Reid, Arminta Darnell, Irene Caudle, Fannie Loo Davis, W. P. Meacham. **Fourth Row (L to R):** J. G. Sowell, A. M. Patterson. **Bottom Row (L to R):** R. H. Peoples, I. M. Stainback, R. G. Peoples.

1909 Senior Class and Faculty—p. 134

Top Row (Left to Right): Marvin R. Rose, John E. Amis, Richard S. Reynolds. **Second Row (L to R):** Irvine B. Early, Irma Redford, Fitzgerald R. Caudle, Ida McAlpin, Cowan D. Stephenson. **Bottom Row (L to R):** W. G. Logan, R. H. Peoples, R. G. Peoples, K. McAlpin.

PEOPLES SCHOOL.
FRANKLIN
H.S. REYNOLDS TENN.
N.H. POLK, ALA.
R.H. DENHAM TENN
W.T. DENT, TENN.
C.B. BRAUN KY.
A. BARNETT KY.
L.J.C. TAYLOR TENN
LOIS FLEMMING, TENN
MAMIE DENHAM TENN
JOSEPHINE McPHERSON TENN
D.C. DAVIS TENN
PRES'T
W.A. SANDERS TENN
J.L. SMITH MISS
W.W. COURTNEY TENN
J.S. PULLEN KY.
A.E. McCLANAHAN TENN
J.H. ANDERSON TENN
R.H. PEOPLES B.A.
W.K. GREENE B.C.
R.G. PEOPLES B.A.
FACULTY
SENIOR CLASS — 1907.
CALVERT BROS.

A Monument to Education

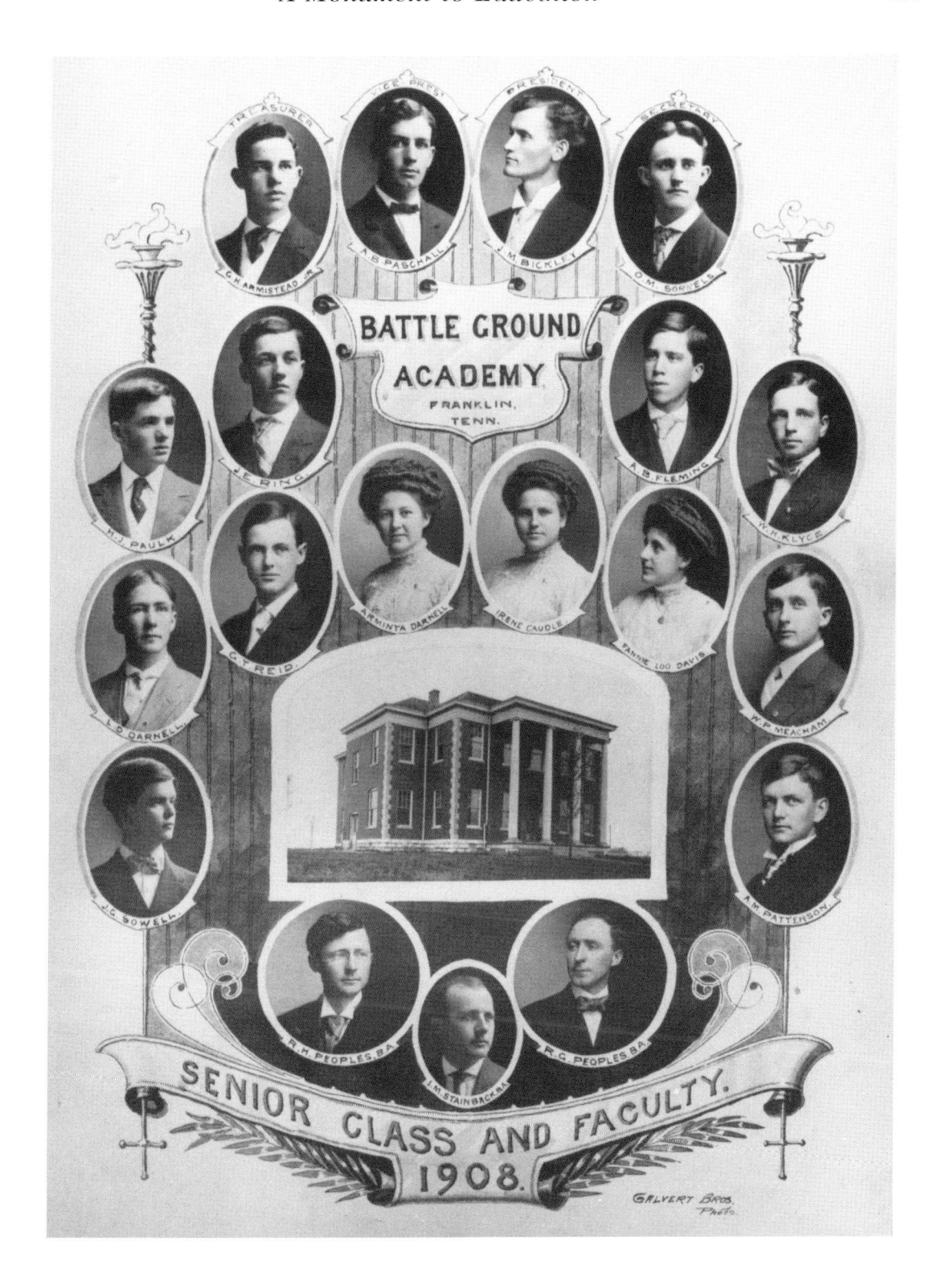

BATTLE GROUND ACADEMY
SECRETARY.
PRESIDENT.
TREASURER.
MARVIN R. ROSE
JOHN E. AMIS.
RICHARD S. REYNOLDS.
IRMA REDFORD
FITZGERALD R. CAUDLE.
IDA MC ALPIN
IRVINE B. EARLY
COWAN D. STEPHENSON.
W.G. LOGAN.
R.H. PEOPLES B.A.
R.G. PEOPLES B.A.
K. MC ALPIN.
SENIOR 1909 CLASS AND FACULTY.

A Monument to Education

1910 Senior Class and Faculty

Top Row (Left to Right): S. John House, Marion Davis, Daly Thompson, Miss Willie James Mallory, R. Bridgforth Wilburn, J. Wallace Tanner, Enoch Brown. **Second Row (L to R):** John G. Reams, Carroll E. Buchanan, E. M. Pipkin, C. H. Bateman, Edward M. Carter, Geo. A. Hatcher, Fred Haueter, Chas. A. Long. **Third Row (L to R):** Gus. A. Davis, R. H. Peoples, R. G. Peoples, Howard R. Carter. **Bottom Row (L to R):** Edgar B. Anderson, William L. Padgett.

1911 Senior Class and Faculty

Top Row (Left to Right): C. W. Barrier, R. H. Peoples, R. G. Peoples, C. H. Bateman. **Second Row (L to R):** Kernan Faw, Mary Elizabeth Steele, Katie Cotton, Mattie P. Cotton, Mary Chriesman, Elsie Steele. **Third Row (L to R):** J. W. Glaze, R. W. House, Willie R. Hatcher, R. C. Walker, C. E. Buchanan, G. P. Shannon, T. H. Elliot, J. W. Lovell, Henry Pointer Jr., S. C. Dunbar. **Bottom Row (L to R):** Orren Davis, H. P. Fowlkes, J. C. Cody, Parkes Armistead, E. B. Anderson, J. W. Gannaway, A. T. Sikes, James Keith.

A Monument to Education

1912 Senior Class and Faculty

Top Row (Left to Right): H. G. Rooker, J. A. Nunn, H. B. Rozelle, D. G. Seward. **Second Row (L to R):** W. H. McLean, Cynthia Hatcher, M. G. Rucker, Jessie M. Pierce, O. M. Shelby, Agnes Daniels, M. M. Smith, R. E. Lowe. **Third Row (L to R):** Virginia R. Howlett, D. M. Robison, R. H. Bell, Margaret W. Faw. **Bottom Row (L to R):** C. W. Barrier, R. H. Peoples, R. G. Peoples, D. W. Morrison.

1913 Senior Class and Faculty

Top Row (Left to Right): W. H. Kittrell, Elizabeth Cody, W. D. Paschall, W. A. McCullough, Marguerite Dozier, W. J. Hughes. **Second Row (L to R):** H. N. Reams, N. S. Ring, Rush Worley, Mary Davis, C. H. Brown, M. M. Smith. **Third Row (L to R):** C. E. Downum, Frances McAlpine, Rebekah Fleming, A. G. Shelby. **Fourth Row (L to R):** J. C. Covington, Gillis Steele, Annie Cotton, L. H. Armistead, Helen Anderson, Emily Beasley, T. W. Pointer. **Bottom Row (L to R):** Lawson Clary, J. H. Anderson, R. H. Peoples, R. G. Peoples, Carroll Buchanan.

1914 Senior Class and Faculty

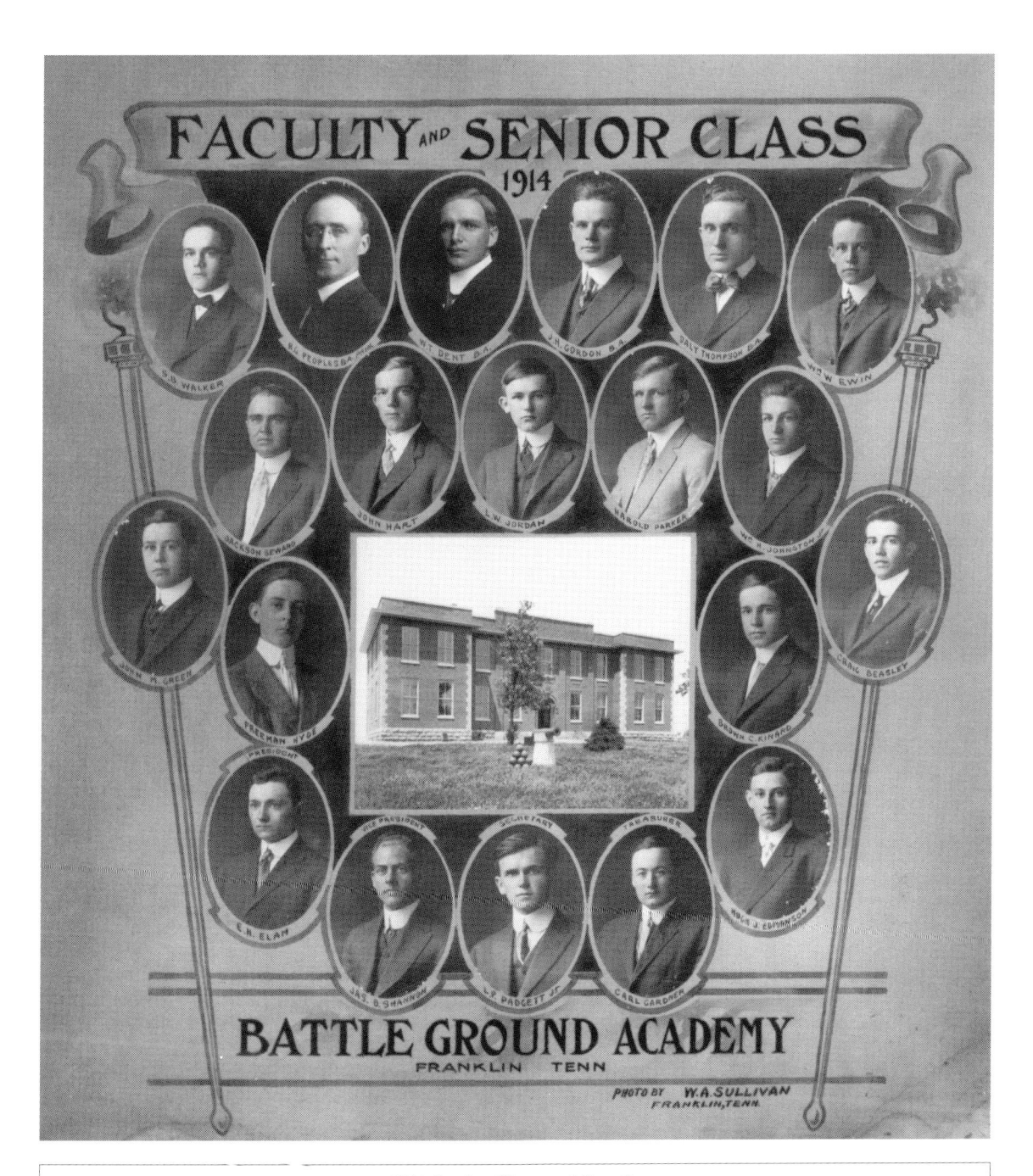

Top Row (Left to Right): S. B. Walker, R. G. Peoples, W. T. Dent, J. H. Gordon, Daly Thompson, Wm. W. Ewin.
Second Row (L to R): John M. Green, Jackson Seward, John Hart, L. W. Jordan, Harold Parker, Wm. H. Johnston Jr., Craig Beasley. **Third Row (L to R):** Freeman Hyde, Brown C. Kinard. **Bottom Row (L to R):** E. H. Elam, Jas. B. Shannon, L. P. Padgett Jr., Carl Gardner, Hugh J. Edmonson.

1915 Senior Class and Faculty

Top Row (Left to Right): Gerald Summers, Haynes Cotton, Louise Armistead, W. D. Sugg, Zellner English, Ewing Marshall, James Russell, Willis Jones. **Bottom Row (L to R):** Wilburn Beasley, D. M. Robison, W. T. Dent, R. G. Peoples, Daly Thompson, Robert Jordan.

1916 Senior Class and Faculty

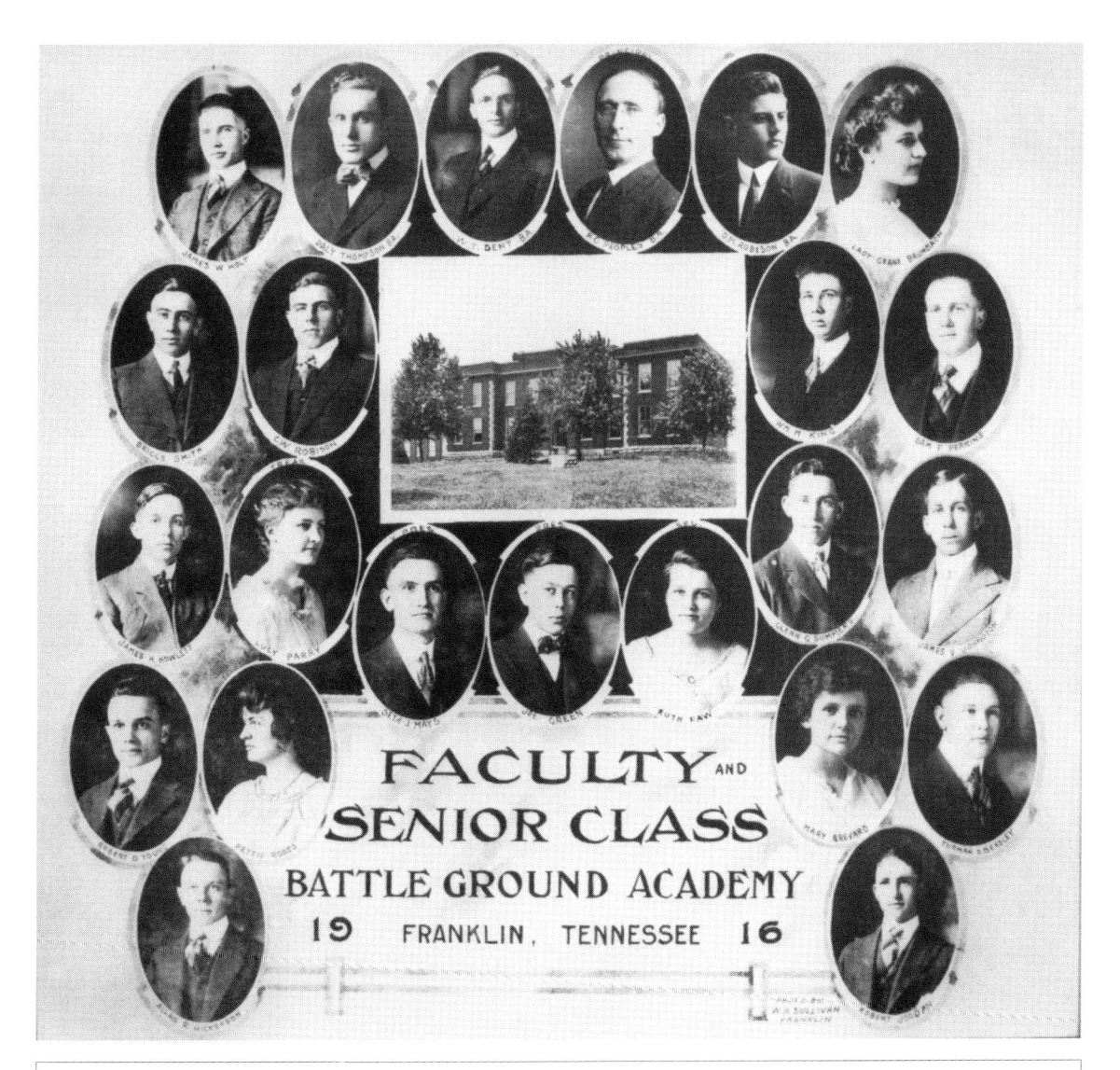

Top Row (Left to Right): James W. Holt, Daly Thompson, W. T. Dent, R. G. Peoples, D. M. Robison, Lady Geane Brumbach. **Second Row (L to R):** Briggs Smith, C. W. Robison, Wm. M. King, Sam F. Perkins. **Third Row (L to R):** James H. Howlett, Lucy Parry, Seth J. Mays, Joe Green, Ruth Faw, Glenn G. Summers, James V. Johnston. **Fourth Row (L to R):** Robert O. Young, Pattie Rodes, Mary Brevard, Turman O. Beasley. **Bottom Row (L to R):** Allan R. Hickerson, Robert Jordan.

1917 Senior Class and Faculty

Top Row (Left to Right): Frances Shannon, Leonard P. Bond, Geo. B. Jackson, R. G. Peoples, W. T. Dent, Carl Pinkerton, Thaniel P. Dozier. **Second Row (L to R):** Lela Abernathy Page, Elizabeth House, Dorothy Breese, Daly Thompson, Bessie Lillie, Susie Lee Grigsby, Annie Ogilvie. **Third Row (L to R):** Earle Davis, Albert W. Hardison, Marshall Cook, Roy Thompson. **Bottom Row (L to R):** Mary Frances Jefferson, John Neely.

A Monument to Education

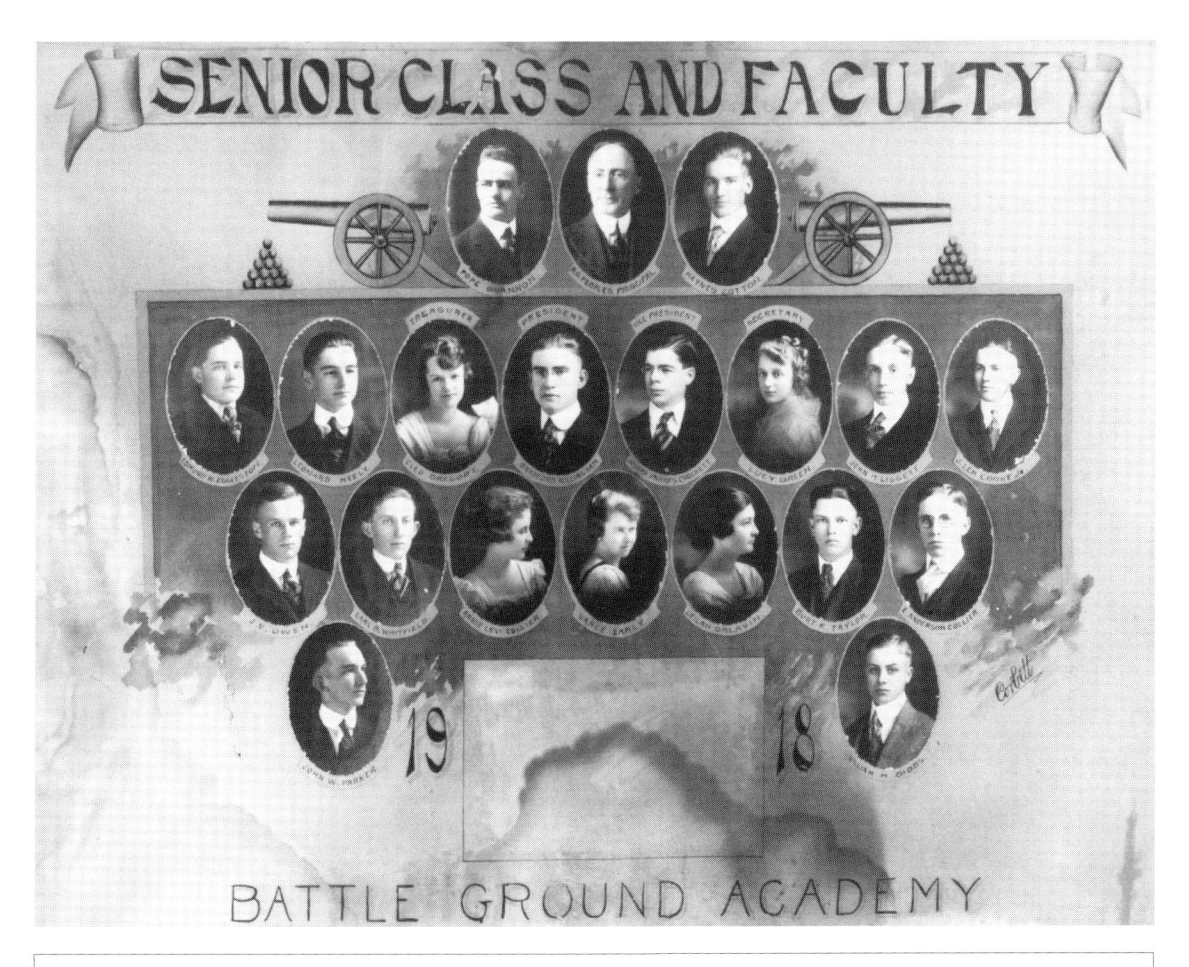

1918 Senior Class and Faculty

Top Row (Left to Right): Pope Shannon, R. G. Peoples, Haynes Cotton. **Second Row (L to R):** Edmund W. Eggleston, Leonard Neely, Cleo Gregory, Bradford Willingham, Joseph Parkes Crockett, Lucy Green, John M. Liggett, J. Lem Cooke Jr. **Third Row (L to R):** J. V. Owen, Earl B. Whitfield, Annie Levi Collier, Vance Early, Leilah Galavin, Burt F. Taylor, E. Anderson Collier. **Bottom Row (L to R):** John W. Parker, William M. Gibbs.

1919 Senior Class and Faculty

Top Row (Left to Right): R. G. Peoples. **Second Row (L to R):** T. H. Cotton, G. I. Briggs. **Third Row (L to R):** Anna Hall McDougall, Margaret Marshall, Miss Cynthia Hatcher, Jean Reid Shannon, Elizabeth Newell. **Fourth Row (L to R):** Harriette M Baugh, James Leslie Buford, John Sugg, Sarah G. Polk. **Fifth Row (L to R):** G. Eric Mount, Alfred English, Eugene M. Regen, Allan Battle Rodes, William E. Mitchell. **Sixth Row (L to R):** Helen Clay, H. H. Horton, Fred T. Peebles, Rebekah Lyle Ewing. **Seventh Row (L to R):** Jack Anderson, Graham Armistead, Elizabeth Grigsby, Robert W. McLemore, Roberta Wikle. **Bottom Row (L to R):** Mary Farr Denton.

A Monument to Education

1920 Senior Class and Faculty

Top Row (Left to Right): Robert Holt, D. P. Langford, R. G. Peoples, Carl Gardner, Minnie Brevard. **Second Row (L to R):** Eleanor McFadden, Frances Gordon Buford. **Bottom Row (L to R):** Louisa Crockett, Matthew F. McDaniel, Beasley Overbey, Elizabeth Faw.

1921 Senior Class and Faculty

Top Row (Left to Right): Elbridge E. Anderson, Margaret McDaniel, J. O. Mills, R. G. Peoples, J. O. Davis, Herbert Crockett, Kirk Bowman. **Second Row (L to R):** Robert R. Horton, Florence Meacheam, Mary Ruth Smith, John M. Hardison. **Bottom Row (L to R):** Jack Pinkerton, Kirby S. Howlett, Helen Davis, Jennie Fleming, Marion Green, James H. Campbell, Albert S. Hatcher.

A Monument to Education

147

1922 Senior Class and Faculty

Top Row (Left to Right): Turner Meacheam, Susie C. Sugg, Nichol Britt, Prof. R. G. Peoples, Rush Worley, Joe Bowman, Genie Jordan, Daniel H. Roberts. **Second Row (L to R):** Mary M. Hooff, Marbel Smith, A. W. Beasley, J. O. Davis, Evelyn Buford, Elizabeth Matthews. **Bottom Row (L to R):** John Joyce, Alma Johnson, Elizabeth Neely, Donald Mitchell.

1923 Senior Class and Faculty

Top Row (Left to Right): Justin Ewell, Sarah Faw, Nat House, L. W. Jordan, R. G. Peoples, J. O. Davis Jr., Emery Godwin, Mickie Fleming, Philip Parham. **Second Row (L to R):** Sam G. Webb, Nela Ree Black, James Smith, Irving Luna, Hilary R. Crockett Jr., Rebecca Cooke, Ira Foster, Rachel Anderson, Bruce Thomas White. **Bottom Row (L to R):** Frank Owen, Malcolm Gibbs, Frank Tucker, Curtis Green, Lowell Boaz, Murphy Holt.

A Monument to Education

1924 Senior Class and Faculty

Top Row (Left to Right): John F. Long, M. C. Simpson, J. O. Davis Jr., Herbert L. McCall. **Second Row (L to R):** James G. Browne, Stewart Campbell, Sarah Anne Beasley, Dan German Jr., Asa Watson Jr., Charles W. Wikle. **Third Row (L to R):** Walter P. Cotton, Kathryn Alice Hatcher, Margaret Owen Davis, R. G. Peoples, Sarah McGavock Roberts, Lucille Temple Tulloss, Fred V. Parkes. **Fourth Row (L to R):** Albert D. Jordan Jr., Martha Lou Owen, Cecil Derwent Jones, Samuel M. Fleming Jr., George A. Reynolds, Mary Alise Whitfield, William L. Hooff Jr. **Bottom Row (L to R):** Russell Burke, Joseph C. Eggleston Jr.

1925 Senior Class and Faculty

Top Row (Left to Right): Theodore R. Lillie, Everett H. Bales, Buford Manley, J. D. Whitfield Jr., James Findlay Hudgens, Courtney Kennedy Marshall, Harrison Haywood Green, Mayes Hume Jr., George C. Paschall Jr., Kennedy Gibbs, William Henry Moss. **Second Row (L to R):** Thomas Bond, Martha Hatcher, Maxie Perry Howlett, Sarah E. Jackson, Lula Mai Boaz, Samuel H. Compton. **Third Row (L to R):** Helen Hogin Jordan, Mary Sam Tulloss, M. C. Simpson, R. G. Peoples, A. C. Fant, Margaret Frances Jennings, Raymond S. Whitfield. **Bottom Row (L to R):** Howell W. McPherson, Herald Breining, Gaston Buford, William Francis Gray Jr.

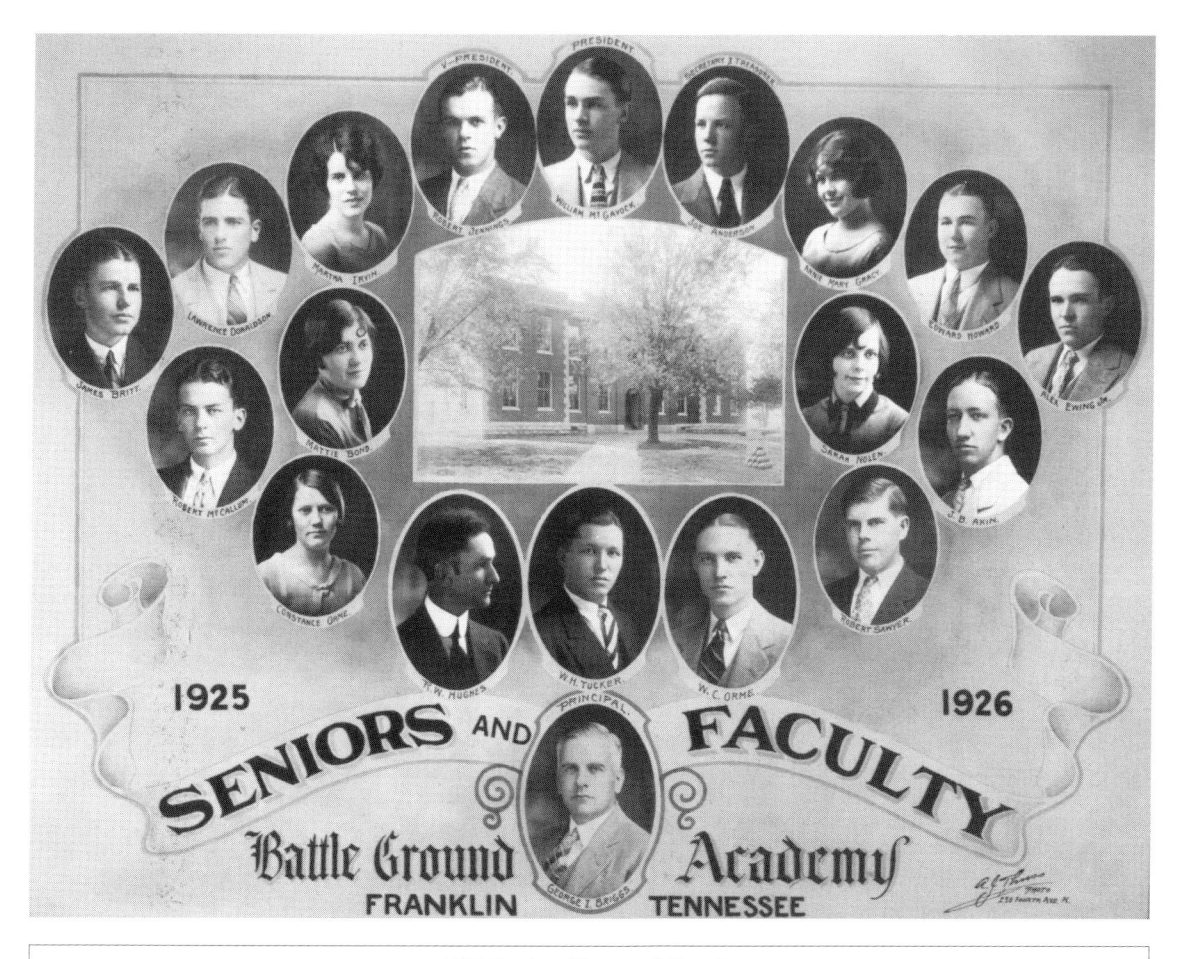

1926 Senior Class and Faculty

Top Row (Left to Right): James Britt, Lawrence Donaldson, Martha Irvin, Robert Jennings, William McGavock, Joe Anderson, Annie Mary Gracy, Edward Howard, Alex Ewing Jr. **Second Row (L to R):** Robert McCallum, Mattie Bond, Sarah Nolen, J. B. Akin. **Third Row (L to R):** Constance Orme, R. W. Hughes, W. H. Tucker, W. C. Orme, Robert Sawyer. **Bottom Row (L to R):** George I. Briggs.

1927 Senior Class and Faculty

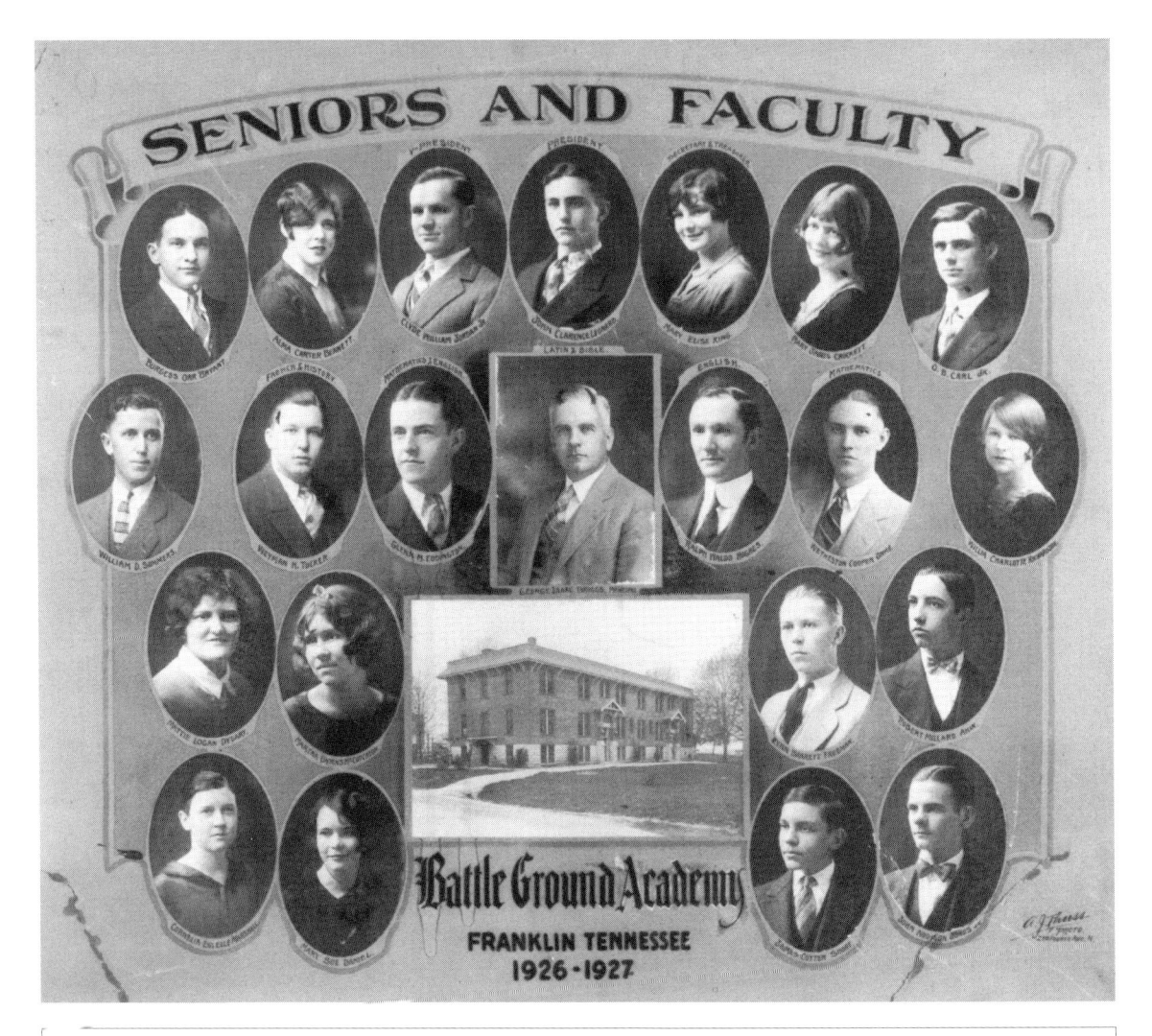

Top Row (Left to Right): Burgess Orr Bryant, Alma Carter Bennett, Clyde William Jordan Jr., John Clarence Leonard, Mary Elise King, Mary J. Crockett, O. B. Carl Jr. **Second Row (L to R):** William D. Summers, Weyman H. Tucker, Glenn M. Eddington, George Isaac Briggs, Ralph Waldo Hughes, Wetheston Cooper Orme, Willia Charlotte Richardson. **Third Row (L to R):** Mattie Logan Dysart, Martha Byrns McCutcheon, Lynn Barrett Freeman, Robert Millard Akin. **Bottom Row (L to R):** Cornelia Estelle Marshall, Mary Sue Daniel, James Cotton Short, John Addison Jones Jr.

A Monument to Education

1928 Senior Class and Faculty

Top Row (Left to Right): Margaret Frances Tucker, J. M. Farrell, R. W. Hughes, G. I. Briggs, G. M. Eddington, J. L. Buford, Henry Ashworth. **Second Row (L to R):** Horace Riggs Harwell, Martha Elizabeth Farnsworth, Alice Gertrude Irvin, Jack Monroe Lockhart, Benjamin Collins Redman, Edna Porter Maury, William Fleming Franklin. **Bottom Row (L to R):** Laird Holt, John Vane Overton, John Bell Regen, Abner Wryland Alley.

1929 Senior Class and Faculty

Top Row (Left to Right): Elizabeth Carothers, Jettie Ashworth, Elizabeth Hawkins, Clarence Gracey, W. T. Gilmore, Frances Bruce, Patti McLemore. **Second Row (L to R):** Joe Pinkerton, Byrom Pennington, Ben Redman, James Haynes, James Gilmore, Thomas Gregory, Warren Gray, Norval Martin. **Bottom Row (L to R):** Jake Martin, William Lyon, Vassar Parker, Otey Briggs, Calder Willingham, Frank Miller, Paul Guffee, R. V. Akin.

1930 Senior Class and Faculty

Top Row (Left to Right): James P. Hume, John T. Church, Nance B. Jordan, Claiborne H. Kinnard Jr., Stephen D. Catron. **Second Row (L to R):** William G. Austin, William S. Jones Jr., John A. Ware, Andrew D. Gillespie Jr., Stephen G. Cliffe, Harry J. Guffee, William McD. Moore. **Third Row (L to R):** Hamp E. Thomas, Ben E. Waller, Clem E. McGlocklin Jr., George I. Briggs, Edward W. Seay, Springer M. Gibson, Fulton M. Greer. **Bottom Row (L to R):** William M. Regen, William W. Davidson, Robert E. Kell, Glenn M. Eddington.

1931 Senior Class and Faculty

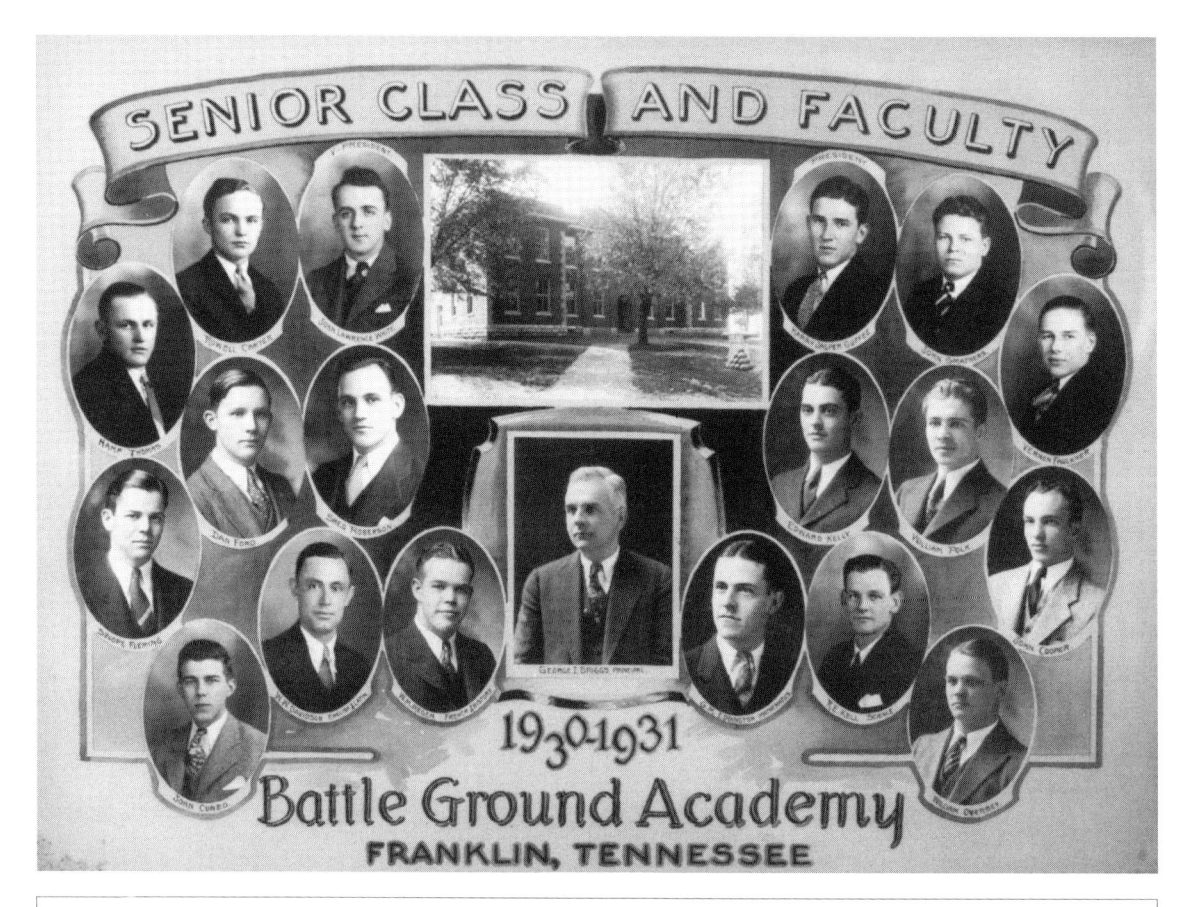

Top Row (Left to Right): Hamp Thomas, Rowell Carter, John Lawrence White, Harry Jasper Guffee, John Smathers, Vernon Faulkner. **Second Row (L to R):** Swope Fleming, Dan Ford, Shed Roberson, Edward Kelly, William Polk, John Cooper. **Bottom Row (L to R):** John Cuneo, W. W. Davidson, W. M. Regen, George I. Briggs, G. M. Eddington, R. E. Kell, William Overbey.

A Monument to Education

1932 Senior Class and Faculty

Top Row (Left to Right): Melvin Farnsworth, Wendell Mayes, William W. Davidson, William M. Regen, George I. Briggs, Robert E. Kell, Glenn M. Eddington, Joseph Wilson, Kelly Dysart. **Second Row (L to R):** Edward Warren, Arthur Parks, William Huddleston, Pete Stegall, Bert Ervin, Ernest Edmondson, Hartwell Beasley, Vernon Faulkner. **Third Row (L to R):** John Vaden, John Jordan Jr., C. S. Burns, Dan Ford, Eugene Patterson Jr., Albert Murray, George Brown, Harold Edwards. **Bottom Row (L to R):** James Akin, Edward Cole, James Jones, Walter Brown, Edgar Ball, Richard Hayworth.

1933 Senior Class and Faculty

Top Row (Left to Right): Guy Alexander, William Jones, W. A. Bryant, W. M. Regen, George I. Briggs, G. M. Eddington, R. E. Kell, Willard Throop, Frank Davis. **Second Row (L to R):** Amis Kinnard, William Daniel, Charles Haffner, John Clayton, Hugh Gracey, Newton White, Fred Millington, Robert Moseley, Eugene Bryan. **Third Row (L to R):** Robert Phipps, Robert Garner, Bill Cave, George Brown, Elvis Hunter, Tom Welch, William Marlin, Kermit Holland Harold Edwards, Gene Henry. **Fourth Row (L to R):** James Houk, Clyde Miller, Edward Roscoe, Steve Murrey. **Bottom Row (L to R):** C. S. Burns, Clarence Cooke.

A Monument to Education

1934 Senior Class and Faculty

Top Row (Left to Right): W. M. Regen, G. M. Eddington, George I. Briggs, Paul Hug, W. Alton Bryant. **Second Row (L to R):** Roy Alley, Wilbur Boswell. **Third Row (L to R):** Johnny Bratton, Milton Woodard, Billy Love, John Durrett, North Miller, W. T. Robison. **Fourth Row (L to R):** Clark Cortner, Robert Garner, Giles Vaughan, Edward Steele, Carl Hinkle, Ernest Cody, Welch Caton, Leon Sweeney, Vance Burke. **Bottom Row (L to R):** Clark Tippens, John Walton, G. T. Curry, Tildon Pete Borders, Faxon Small Jr., Charles Haffner, Leslie Buchman.

1935 Senior Class and Faculty

Top Row (Left to Right): Paul Hug, G. M. Eddington, Geo. I. Briggs, R. E. Kell, W. A. Bryant. **Second Row (L to R):** Kenneth Noojin, Bill Hume, Allen Steele, Jimmy Brown, William Pitner, J. D. Motlow Jr., Edward Jones. **Third Row (L to R):** Bill Tippens, Curtis Moody Jr., Dave Alexander, Edward May, Billy Love, Neil Ervin, Gus Miller, Sam Parks, Glenn Turner. **Fourth Row (L to R):** Ben Throop, J. O. Walker Jr. **Bottom Row (L to R):** Jack Lee III, Frank Evins.

A Monument to Education

1936 Senior Class and Faculty

Top Row (Left to Right): Lionel Sweeney, Richard N. Harris, Nance Jordan, G. M. Eddington, George I. Briggs, Kelly V. Woodham, W. Alton Bryant, Harry Bryan Jr., Kernan Akin Jr. **Second Row (L to R):** Nathan J. McMullen, Bramlett Tulloss Jr., Curtis Moody Jr., Jack Moore, Felix G. Buchanan, Charles M. Kent Jr., William Hume, Dick German Jr., J. D. Motlow Jr. **Third Row (L to R):** Lent Rice, John M. King, Jack Lee III, Waitt Rue, James E. Woodard, Henry Cannon, Esmond Hillard, W. C. Moncrief Jr., Gordon H. Sawyer, Ted Buckley. **Bottom Row (L to R):** Gus Moran Jr., Charles McKinney, W. Mac Wemyss, William H. Shull.

1937 Senior Class and Faculty

Top Row (Left to Right): William Eudailey, J. M. Tolbert, G. M. Eddington, George I. Briggs, Nance Jordan, G. R. Buford, Bill Baker. **Second Row (L to R):** John Still, Willis Postlethwaite, Harrison Rue, Tom T. Floyd, Early Myatt, J. B. Smithson, Capers Andrews. **Third Row (L to R):** Bouldin McWilliams, Jack Church, Joe Pursell, M. D. Ingram, Kenneth Thompson, James Akin, Bill Culbreath. **Bottom Row (L to R):** Harry Thweatt, Edwin Mason.

A Monument to Education

1938 Senior Class and Faculty

Top Row (Left to Right): Jimmy Akin, Bob Allen, A. W. Smith, George I. Briggs, G. R. Buford, Pete Lucas, Bob Weaver. **Second Row (L to R):** Tom Robinson, Wood Taylor, Crocket Cook, James Tolbert, Nance Jordan, Kirby Primm, Oren Richardson, Shelly Ellett. **Third Row (L to R):** Milton Tate, Wells Stanley, Graham Mitchell, G. M. Eddington, Leroy Sugg, Paul Mishler, Grady Stapp. **Fourth Row (L to R):** Billy Ashworth, Laddie Cowie, Arthur Huie, Bob Black, Albert Bauman, Burt Craig, Billy Jamison. **Fifth Row (L to R):** Will Reese Mullens, Claude Gordon, Harrison Rue, Bob Bratton, Milton Price, Harry Hill. **Bottom Row (L to R):** Kenneth Grantham, Jesse Walling, Frank Herrera, Frank North.

164   BATTLE GROUND ACADEMY

1939 Senior Class and Faculty

Top Row (Left to Right): Milton Tate, Billy Robertson, Leonard Brittain Jr., George I. Briggs, Frank Herrera, Pete Lucas, Bob Weaver. **Second Row (L to R):** Bill Moss Jr., Mack Hatcher, James E. Poindexter, Nance Jordan, G. M. Eddington, G. R. Buford, W. T. Robison, C. K. McLemore, Jim Patton Jr. **Third Row (L to R):** Red Driskill, Harold Meacham Jr., Harold Pace Albert Thomas, John Ridley, Nathan Osborne Jr., Buck Cannon, Frank North, Ben Gant, Campbell Haffner, James East. **Fourth Row (L to R):** Marshall Meacham, Bobby Yarbrough, Paul Ogilive, Dan Gentry, Jim Bennett, Weldon, Carruth, Cooper Scruggs, Donald Smith. **Bottom Row (L to R):** Billy Rose, Bob Bratton, Joe Jones, Mack King, Mike Nolan, James Goldman.

1940 Senior Class and Faculty

Top Row (Left to Right): J. W. Largen, Archie Lobb, G. M. Eddington, Geo. I. Briggs, Turney Ford, Jim Hobgood, Peter Askew. **Second Row (L to R):** Lewis Hagler, Sam Tate, W. T. Robison, Sam W. Newell Jr., G. R. Buford, Elkton Pitts, Willis Willey. **Third Row (L to R):** William Billington, Lawrence Cooper, Julio Deschamps, Rufus Ross, Leonard H. Armistead Jr., Lewis Bibb, Joe Holliday Jr., Mack Osburn, Charles Murdock. **Bottom Row (L to R):** Jimmy Chapman, J. B. Simmons Jr., Jim Short, John Hoskins, Milton Meacham, Durwood Sies Jr., L. A. Sands Jr., John Paterson, Walter Green.

166 BATTLE GROUND ACADEMY

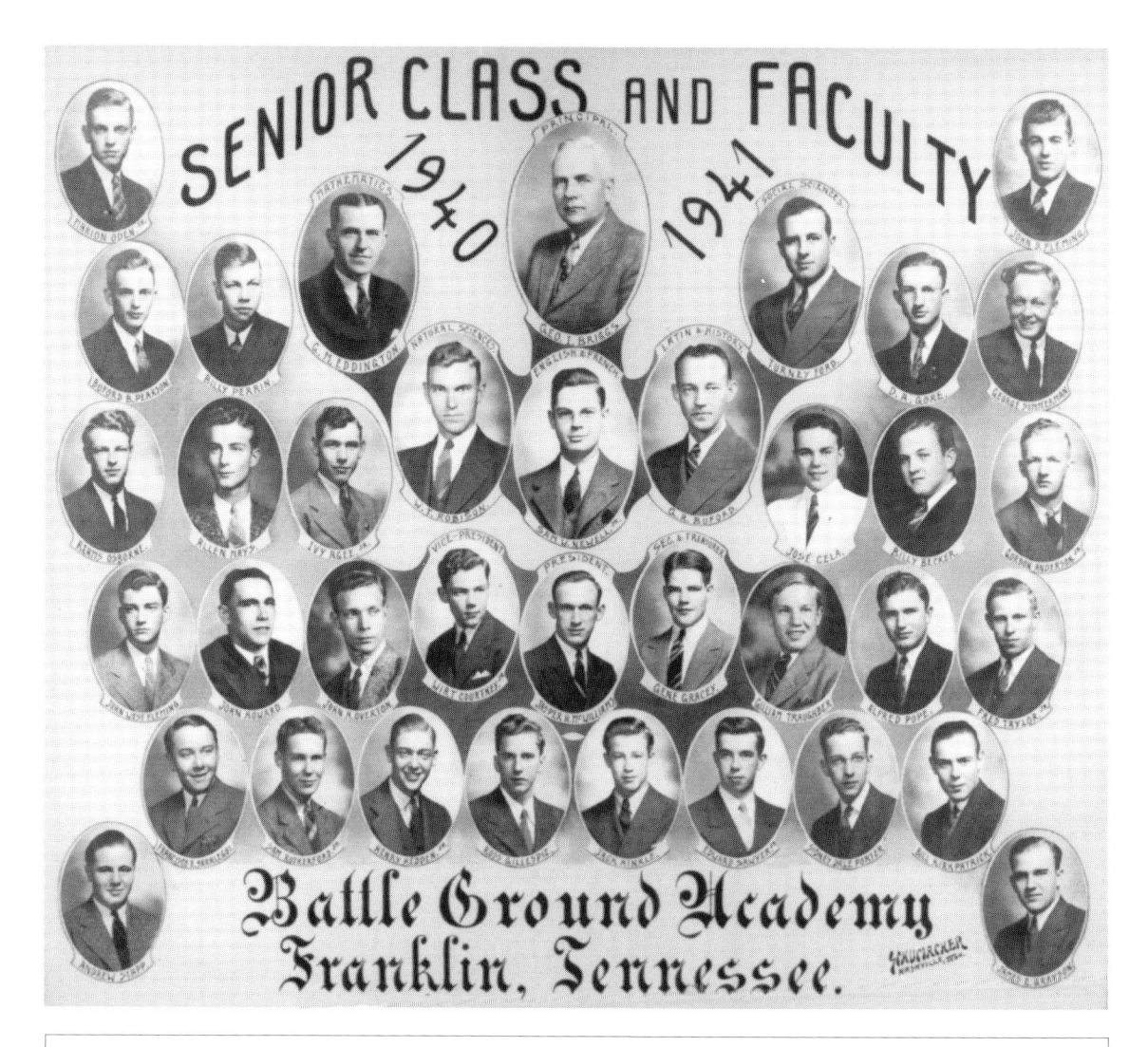

1941 Senior Class and Faculty

Top Row (Left to Right): Marion Oden Jr., Geo. I. Briggs, John D. Fleming. **Second Row (L to R):** Buford B. Pearson, Billy Perrin, G. M. Eddington, Turney Ford, D. A. Gore, George Simmerman. **Third Row (L to R):** Reams Osborne, Allen Mays, Ivy Agee Jr., W. T. Robison, Sam W. Newell Jr., G. R. Buford, José Cela, Billy Becker, Gordon Anderson Jr. **Fourth Row (L to R):** John West Fleming, John Howard, John H. Overton, Wirt Courtney Jr., Jasper H. McWilliams, Gene Gracey, Gilliam Traughber, Alfred Pope, Fred Taylor Jr. **Fifth Row (L to R):** Francisco R. Saralegui, Sam Rutherford Jr., Henry Hedden Jr., Ross Gillespie, Jack Hinkle, Edward Sawyer Jr., Sidney Dale Porter, Bill Kirkpatrick. **Bottom Row (L to R):** Andrew Stapp, James E. Grayson.

1942 Senior Class and Faculty

Top Row (Left to Right): Dick Bryson, Stone Reynolds, Ted Davis, Turney Ford, George I. Briggs, G. L. Mitchell, Jack Marquess, Bill Gale, Fred L. Kelley. **Second Row (L to R):** Tommy Lyons, James Caton, G. M. Eddington, Francis A. Bass, Orville White, John Warren, Jimmy Hill. **Third Row (L to R):** George McElveen, Sonny Wilson, Frank Donelson, Hunter Armistead, Bill Harlin, Francis Coombs, Chandler Ward. **Bottom Row (L to R):** Clay Waites, Ellis Johnson, Sandy Brown, Bill Black, N. Y. Walker, Fred Taylor Jr., Stanley Trezevant, Powell Covington, Billy Ormes.

168 BATTLE GROUND ACADEMY

1943 Senior Class and Faculty

Top Row (Left to Right): Charles Hamilton, Wallis Beasley, J. B. Akin, George I. Briggs, G. M. Eddington, O. F. White, Ira Jones, Shelton Blythe. **Second Row (L to R):** Ned Douglas, Milton Lea, Bill Ross, Richard Courtney, Spencer Holt Jr. **Third Row (L to R):** Charles Kelley, Carrol Turner Jr., Tom Harlin, Bobby Kelton. **Fourth Row (L to R):** Henry Williams, Bettis Montague, John Underwood Jr., Frank Kaye, Frank Puryear, L. M. Kirkpatrick, Rufus Branch, Bert Parrish, Bruce Nicholson. **Bottom Row (L to R):** Leroy Hardison, Bill Dabbs, Gene Ward, Frank Davies Jr., Brown Cannon, Clennie Pinkston, Bill Light, Cherry Easley, Charles Grayson.

A Monument to Education 169

1944 Senior Class and Faculty

Top Row (Left to Right): Murray Wallace, Jimmy Isaacs, I. L. Jones, J. B. Akin, George I. Briggs, G. M. Eddington, O. F. White, Charles G. Phelps Jr., Bobby Short, Jack King. **Second Row (L to R):** Bob Harris, George M. Wampler, Jesse Colton, Billy Jackson, Cecil Oliver Jr., T. H. Alexander, Norvel Walker, W. L. Pannell Jr., Edwin D. Gray Jr. **Third Row (L to R):** J. A. Hardison, Alva Jefferson, David Haney, Marshall Walker, Billy Maiden, Buddy Kite, Jimmy Sawyer, Alex Wilson Jr., Jim Savage, Sinclair Daniel. **Bottom Row (L to R):** Joe Palacio, Lile Smith, Phil Davis, Leon J. DeBrohun, Charley Stanley, Milton Wauford, Jimmy Graves, Richard Otis Doyel, Jack Reynolds, Billy Henry.

1945 Senior Class and Faculty

Top Row (Left to Right): P. H. Wade Jr., J. B. Akin, Glenn M. Eddington, Orville F. White, J. C. Raburn, M. C. Harris. **Second Row (L to R):** Ferrell Alexander Jr., Eugene Abercrombie, Billy Cook, Bob Hedden, Sam Reeks Jr., Felix Carvajal, Billy Dinges, Ben Fennel Jr. **Third Row (L to R):** Bob Garrett, Lewis Goodwin, Carl Grantham Jr., John Green Jr., Allan Hardison, Bill Hedden, Harold Huff, Henderson King Jr. **Bottom Row (L to R):** Ralph Spangler Jr., Billy Smyer Jr., Oscar Simpson Jr., Billy Sawyer, James Lillie, Mac Peebles Jr., Jack Pinkerton, Ed Reynolds, Fleming Williams Jr.

A Monument to Education

1946 Senior Class and Faculty

Top Row (Left to Right): Felix Govantes, G. R. Buford, R. E. Naylor, J. B. Akin, Glenn M. Eddington, Orville F. White, P. H. Wade Jr., T. O. Pinkerton, Anthony P. Shupe. **Second Row (L to R):** Sam Moran Jr., Clem Blackburn. **Third Row (L to R):** Bobby Gentry, Robin Courtney, Gordon McDaniel Jr. **Fourth Row (L to R):** William Cleland, Core English, Rodger Cotton, Jim Moore, William Brittain, William L. Hoge, Bryan Pace, Bob Bradford, R. W. Wood Jr., John L. Webb. **Fifth Row (L to R):** Dick Burrow, George E. Davis, David Harris, Shannon Montgomery, Edmond Phillips, Harvey Pride, Winston Ligon, Richard McKeel Jr. **Bottom Row (L to R):** William McCord, Jack Lunn, Jimmy Robertson, Dan Puryear, Bill Dykes, Sam Ragsdale, Albert Jordan III.

1947 Senior Class and Faculty

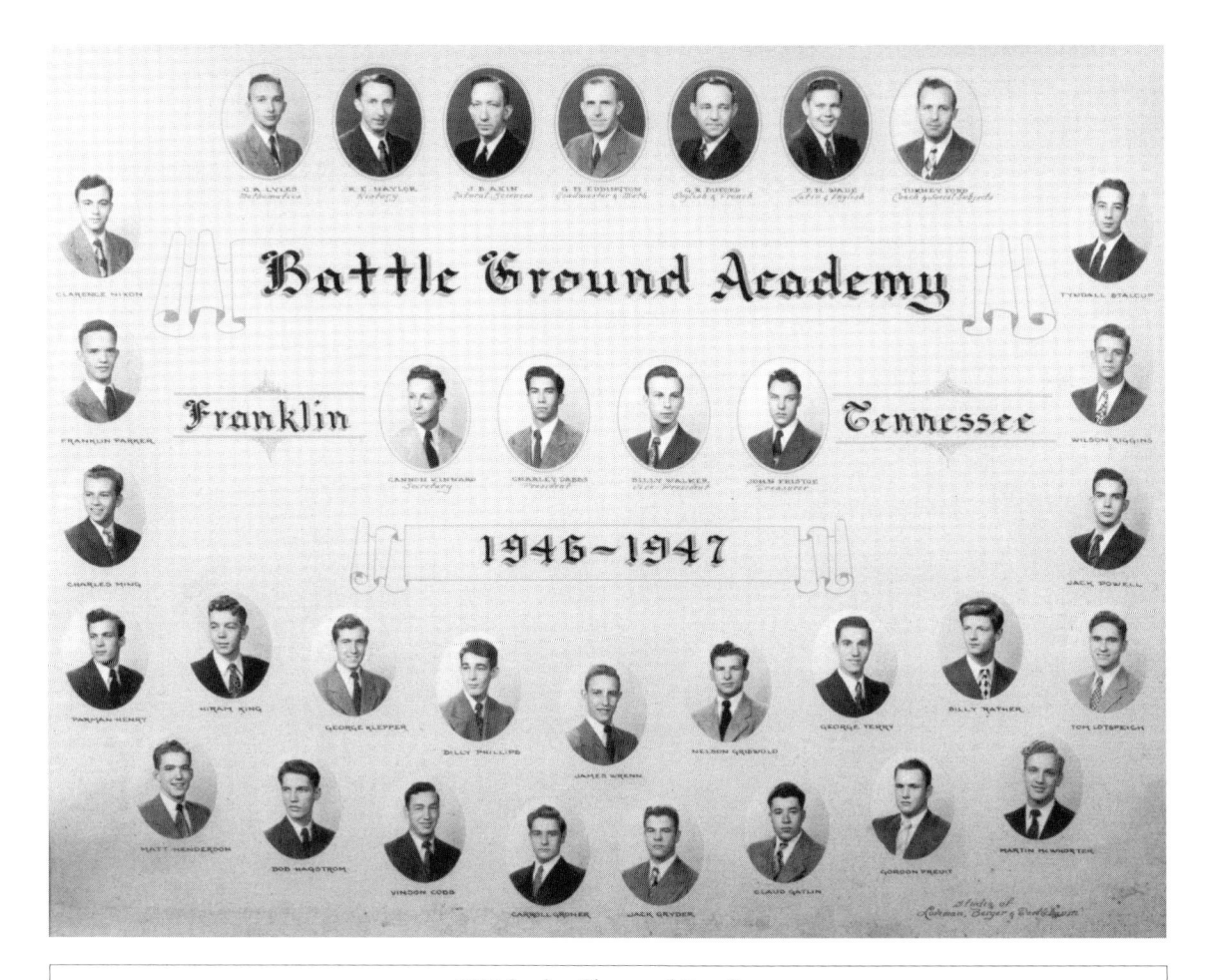

Top Row (Left to Right): G. A. Lyles, R. E. Naylor, J. B. Akin, G. M. Eddington, G. R. Buford, P. H. Wade, Turney Ford. **Second Row (L to R):** Clarence Nixon, Tyndall Stalcup. **Third Row (L to R):** Franklin Parker, Cannon Kinnard, Charley Dabbs, Billy Walker, John Fristoe, Wilson Riggins. **Fourth Row (L to R):** Charles Ming, Jack Powell. **Fifth Row (L to R):** Parman Henry, Hiram King, George Klepper, Billy Phillips, James Wrenn, Nelson Griswold, George Terry, Billy Rather, Tom Lotspeich. **Bottom Row (L to R):** Matt Henderson, Bob Hagstrom, Vinson Cobb, Carroll Groner, Jack Gryder, Claud Gatlin, Gordon Preuit, Martin McWhorter.

A Monument to Education

1948 Senior Class and Faculty

Top Row (Left to Right): P. H. Wade Jr., J. B. Akin, R. F. Harmes, G. M. Eddington, R. E. Naylor, G. R. Buford.
Second Row (L to R): Dudley J. Pewitt, Jake Stringer, Jimmie Smith Jr., James Lofton, Bobby Carter, Frank T. Akin, James P. Redford, Jerry W. Dillard, John S. Beasley. **Third Row (L to R):** Paul Thomas Butts, Herman Sawyer, Tommy Lance, William J. Stalcup, Alex Harlin, Bill Doak, Orlando Suarez, William O. Gorden, Ralph Montague Hughes Jr. **Bottom Row (L to R):** Jerry Farris Hamra, Billy Rather, Henry Fuller, David Puryear, William C. Pennington, George Flanigan, Kenneday M. Gibbs, James Kilpatrick Bennett, Douglas C. Seward Jr.

1949 Senior Class and Faculty

Top Row (Left to Right): P. H. Wade Jr., J. B. Akin, G. M. Eddington, G. R. Buford, J. E. Fisher, R. E. Naylor.
Second Row (L to R): William E. Hood, William E. Isaacs, Tommy Robinson, Tommy Lance, Edwin O. Eggert, Tyler Berry III, Joe C. Eggleston, Jack Church, James R. Cooper, George W. White, Herbert V. Sanders Jr. **Third Row (L to R):** Chas. E. Byron III, Howlson Wemyss, Robert Chapman, Robert Dulaney, Jack Schmitt, Bill Kelly, James E. Barney, Howard H. Garrett, W. T. Ewell, Jack Kinnard, Cordell Blankenship. **Fourth Row (L to R):** James W. Lyon, Charles Dulaney, Joe Percy Jennette, Eddie Gross, Kirtley Hill, Robert R. Thompson, Greeley H. Roddy, Jimmy Tomlin. **Fifth Row (L to R):** Walter T. Kinnard, Travis McCall, Wilson C. Williams Jr., James E. Houseal II, Harold Scott, Jimmy Jacobs, Billy Cook, Richard Moore. **Bottom Row (L to R):** Walter W. Ogilvie Jr., Andrew G. Shockley, Thomas D. Warren, Gerald L. Johnson, Eugene R. Howard Jr., Glenn Eddigton Jr., Samuel A. Brown Jr., J. Morton Rhyne, Alfredo Hernandez, States Rights Finley.

1950 Senior Class and Faculty

Top Row (Left to Right): P. H. Wade Jr., G. R. Buford, J. B. Akin, G. M. Eddington, R. M. Yankee Jr., R. E. Naylor. **Second Row (L to R):** Bobby Lofton, Frank Giles, Walter Reed Capps, Phelps Montgomery, Jimmy Fristoe, Bob Harlin, John Oden, David Pointer. **Third Row (L to R):** Bob Sims, Remón Lavin, Horace Waters Harvey, Leroy Lord, Dan Roberts Jr., Billy Cobb, Norman Brown, Hector Zumbado, Bob Hutcheson. **Fourth Row (L to R):** Gerald Bennett, E. Gale Pewitt, B. C. Phillips. **Bottom Row (L to R):** Owen Alexander, Bob Burnett, Alex Bond, Billy Jordan, William Butts, Robert Allen Smith, Thomas Helton, James W. King.

1951 Senior Class and Faculty

Top Row (Left to Right): Mr. J. B. Akin, Mr. P. H. Wade Jr., Mr. R. B. Jackson, Mr. Jonas S. Coverdale, Mr. Paul Redick, Mr. John Bragg, Mr. R. E. Naylor. **Second Row (L to R):** Paul Brock Gross, Gene Meacham, Robert A. McKay, William A. Camstra, Jimmy B. King, Wm. Burnett Akin, Brown C. Kinnard, Tommy McCall. **Third Row (L to R):** Edgar Blankenship, John Fox Holland, Earl Beasley Jr., Henry Mustelier, Mike Lavin, Joe Magyar, Harold E. Ashworth, James Leonard Jackson Jr., Curry Hearn Jr. **Fourth Row (L to R):** Herbert A. Crockett, George O. Trabue, James W. Byrd Jr., Marshall W. Doggett III, Thomas W. Tate, William Roland Jenkins, Virgil Carroll Jenkins, Allen E. Herron, Dudley E. Casey Jr. **Bottom Row (L to R):** William Hamlett English, Don Blankenship, Charles E. Buis Jr., Ben E. Waller, Bob Brock Jr., Benny Harris.

A Monument to Education

1952 Senior Class and Faculty

Top Row (Left to Right): Mr. J. B. Akin, Mr. P. H. Wade Jr., Mr. John Bragg, Mr. Jonas S. Coverdale, Mr. Paul Redick, Mr. Coleman Crockett, Mr. R. E. Naylor. **Second Row (L to R):** Thomas L. Still, Jack Dewitt, Bob Duke, Dennis Ford, Billy J. Garrett, George L. Spragins, Jimmy Odum. **Third Row (L to R):** Donald Ashworth, Herbert Schneider, John Edward Gillaspy, James R. Hays, Clifton Hicks, David Jones, Bernard Weinstein. **Bottom Row (L to R):** Robert N. Moore Jr., Jimmy Patterson, Buck Wiley Jr., Joe Woods.

1953 Senior Class and Faculty

Top Row (Left to Right): Mr. R. E. Naylor, Mrs. Joe Sharpe, Mr. C. W. Smithson, Mr. Paul Redick, Mr. J. S. Coverdale, Mr. J. A. Bragg, Mrs. W. Paul Redick, Mr. J. B. Akin. **Second Row (L to R):** Marcus E. Nellums Jr., Sidney M. Ford Jr., Harold Dean Nichols, Elbert Ashworth, Alan Kirshner, J. Thomas Helm, Fred C. Akin, Price Erwin McKee, Robert G. Arnett, Early M. McCann Jr. **Third Row (L to R):** Seymore Gerregano Jr., Albert Whitman, William A. Slaven, Parker F. Wilson Jr., William L. Cannon, W. Everette Bethshare Jr., L. Murry Chumley, Everette G. Comer Jr., John O. Crump. **Fourth Row (L to R):** Robert C. Harrison, Lamar M. Smith, William T. Miller, Charles William Grimes, Charles C. Hudlow, John R. Hooton Jr., Reuben N. Pelot III, Clinton H. Pearson Jr., Bob B. Gleve Jr. **Bottom Row (L to R):** Bill F. Gray, Wendell Meacham, Donald G. Hall, Robert M. Johnson, John S. Johnson, James Wm. Turner, William A. Shoemaker, Burnice Anglin.

1954 Senior Class and Faculty

Top Row (Left to Right): Mr. S. Ralph Brown, Mr. C. W. Smithson, Mr. J. A. Bragg, Mr. Paul Redick, Mr. J. S. Coverdale, Mrs. Paul Redick, Mr. R. E. Naylor, Mr. J. B. Akin, Mrs. Joe Sharpe. **Second Row (L to R):** Fred W. Brown Jr., Donald L. Maloney, Jim Tippens Jr., William Steve Murrey Jr., George R. Wagner, Kenneth Brake Jr., David E. Wood, Robert G. Kirkpatrick, Edmund W. Boice. **Third Row (L to R):** Fred W. Beasley Jr., Michie M. Barber, James M. Thompson, Buford S. Feldman Jr., Richard V. Kennedy Jr., James H. Speake, James William Elkins, Fred Stuart Overton, Robert A. Ryan Jr. **Fourth Row (L to R):** William Percy Fly, Thomas Blair Farned, Fleming W. Smith Jr., James Vance Mangrum, Robert Garrett, Hale L. Meacham, Elliott Baldwin, Bill H. Tanksley, R. Charles Shanlever. **Bottom Row (L to R):** John H. Henderson Jr., Ellis Holt, John Richard Reich, Leonard E. McKeand III, James C. Fennel III, Robert A. Gerregano, James Stephen Scarborough, Hugh T. Ammerman Jr., Frank D. Boensch.

Battle Ground Academy

1955 Senior Class and Faculty

Top Row (Left to Right): Mr. S. Ralph Brown, Mr. Abe Hatcher, Mr. J. A. Bragg, Mr. C. W. Smithson, Mr. Paul Redick, Mr. J. S. Coverdale, Mr. J. B. Akin, Mrs. Paul Redick, Mr. R. E. Naylor, Mr. Cannon R. Mayes
Second Row (L to R): Stanley Forbes Gale, Ronald Cleveland Gasser, Rodney Irvin Wise, Thomas Woodson Wilkes Jr., Ronald Sanders Ligon, Clifton Eugene McPherson Jr., William Earl Cherry, Thomas Alexander Clarkson, James Thomas Frost, William Woodford Claypool Jr. **Third Row (L to R):** James H. Miller Jr., Thomas Burton Cates Jr., Patrick Varney Shaw, James Dobson Johnson, Larry Burton Jr., Billy Cleveland Dotson, Tom Sawyer, Jerry Newton Pollard Jr., Theodore Garellas Mooney. **Fourth Row (L to R):** Armando T. Zayas Perez, John Draughon Sprouse, John Edward Nelson, Fred Pilkerton, Charles Hal Johnson, John Roy Ragan, George Augustus Shwab III, Johnnie Gene Middleton, Russell Benjamin Wilkerson Jr. **Bottom Row (L to R):** William Hugh Wallace, Howard Stanley Jones, John Thuss Terrell, James Irvin Moore, William Dickinson Gayden, Robert Marshall Cameron, William Winder Cambell, Raymond Edward Tarkington, Robert R. Schneider.

A Monument to Education

1956 Senior Class and Faculty

Top Row (Left to Right): Mr. W. Paul Redick, Mr. J. S. Coverdale. **Second Row (L to R):** Mr. S. Ralph Brown, Mr. Ralph Naylor, Mr. C. W. Smithson, Mr. J. B. Akin, Mrs. W. Paul Redick, Mr. J. A. Bragg, Mr. Thomas A. Guiton Jr., Mr. Cannon R. Mayes, Mr. Daly Thompson. **Third Row (L to R):** Kip Gayden, Fulton Greer, Joe Evans, George Dodson, Bill Pope, Bill Chamberlain, Kenneth Cline, Bryan Dement, Randy Sherling, Bill Finney. **Fourth Row (L to R):** Jim Beasley, Bobby Cato, Lawson Breedlove, Otto Galdo, Charlie Yancey, Tom Crichlow, Walter Rasmussen, Pedro Paz, Peter Minton, John Leu. **Fifth Row (L toR):** Carl Stoltz, Walter Speake, Joe Pinkerton, Marion Steele, Jerry Sullivan, Jimmy Wise, Bill Herbert, Bobby Flippen, Steven George, Walter Pyle Jr. **Bottom Row (L to R):** Bill Shanlever, Richard Tippens, Tom McKee, Tommy Brown.

1957 Senior Class and Faculty

Top Row (Left to Right): Mr. Ralph Brown, Mr. Carl W. Smithson, Mr. Ralph E. Naylor, Mr. William J. Bryan, Mr. W. Paul Redick, Mr. J. S. Coverdale, Mr. J. B. Akin, Mr. T. A. Guiton, Mrs. W. Paul Redick, Mr. Daly Thompson, Mr. Cannon Mayes. **Second Row (L to R):** Johnny McMahon, Bobby Street, Vance Akin, Curtis Singleton, Noel Brown, Richard Ashworth, Lewis Steele, David McGavock, Bobby Trousdale, Burton Glover, Russell Farnsworth. **Third Row (L to R):** Emmett Russell, Larry Stumb, Tommy Bragg, Henry Chase, Tony Cobb, Fred Sapp, Larry Putnam, Sam Hardy. **Fourth Row (L to R):** Hervin Romney, Harry Spotts, DeBow Casey, Boxwell Hawkins, Pickslay Cheek, Britt Knox, Bill Anderson, Johnson Terry, Billy Breedlove, Albert Merville. **Bottom Row (L to R):** Howard Smithson, Bob Napier, Moises Behar.

A Monument to Education

1958 Senior Class and Faculty

Top Row (Left to Right): Mr. Ralph Brown, Mr. Keith Stephens, Mr. Ralph E. Naylor, Mr. John A. Bragg, Mrs. W. Paul Redick, Mr. W. Paul Redick, Mr. J. S. Coverdale, Mr. J. B. Akin, Mr. Carl W. Smithson, Mr. Daly Thompson, Mr. G. Jack Ellis, Mr. Cannon Mayes. **Second Row (L to R):** Billy Nichols, Seymour Samuels III, Tom Fuqua, Mike Hudgins, Buck Ramsey, Mickey Crowell, Tony Morrissey, Pete Mefford, Gilbert Smith, Charles Ashworth, Warren York. **Third Row (L to R):** John Griffin, Ralph Williams, Jimmy Burchett, Alfred Campbell, Bill Hughes, John McCord, Tommy Herbert, Tommy Parsley, Jim Burton, Mike Rudd, Jerry Brinkley. **Fourth Row (L to R):** John Colton, Hugh Stuart, Bob Cain, Francis Gaines, Carey Brock, Hal Smith, Billy Stephens, Jack Yeiser. **Bottom Row (L to R):** Tommy Arrendale, Harry Weisger, Larry Dodd, Joe Francis, Mac Gayden, David McIntosh, Johnny Frey, Jimmy Cook, Penn Crockett, Bill Burnett, Tommy Hamilton.

1959 Senior Class and Faculty

Top Row (Left to Right): Mr. Ralph Brown, Mr. Ralph E. Naylor, Mr. Keith Stephens, Mr. G. Jack Ellis, Mrs. W. Paul Redick, Mr. W. Paul Redick, Mr. J. S. Coverdale, Mr. J. B. Akin, Mr. John A. Bragg, Mr. Daly Thompson, Mr. Carl W. Smithson, Mr. Cannon Mayes. **Second Row (L to R):** Bruce Bailey Polston, Barry Brown Polston, Allen Crockett Brown, Thomas Norton Bainbridge, Julies David Kaplan, Joe Donald Nichols, B. Roy Kennedy III, Terry Wendell Smith, Thurston Roach. **Third Row (L to R):** Robert S. Cheek II, Jerry Alfred Cooper, John P. W. Brown VI, Charles Walter Clarkson, Walter Wilson, Joseph J. Stevens, Garth E. Green Jr., John Hall Gillespie. **Fourth Row (L to R):** Robert Donnell Stanford III, James Vaughn Hunt, Richard Edmond Boensch, Houston Oliver Gillespie Jr., Lewis Daniel Scott III, Asa H., Jewell III, Joe Cordell Carr Jr., John Elmo Walker, Sam E. Williamson Jr., James Richard Cole. **Bottom Row (L to R):** Richard Leland Potts, Leslie Romney, Ellis Phillips Malone, Richard Osborne Linsert, Sheldon Lee Heilman, William Shearin Montgomery, Houston Brent, Seth H. Griffin, Edward Eugene Myhand, John Shelley Smith.

A Monument to Education

1960 Senior Class and Faculty

Top Row (Left to Right): Mr. Ralph Brown, Mr. David Wood, Mr. Jimmy French, Mr. John Bennett, Mr. William B. Akin, Mr. Paul Redick, Mrs. Paul Redick, Mr. J. B. Akin, Mr. Ernest McCord, Mr. John Bragg, Mr. Cannon Mayes, Mr. Daly Thompson. **Second Row (L to R):** Mr. Ralph Naylor, Mr. Carl Smithson. **Third Row (L to R):** Bill Rhame, Dick Arnold, Abner Alley, George Worthen, Authur Graff, Bill Brown, John Cunningham, Thomas Fiveash, Jim Payne, Steve Rush, Rod Daniel, Ward Akers. **Fourth Row (L to R):** Harry Gray, Gus Puryear, Tommy Roberts, Toby Parrish, Harry Guffee Jr., Richard Sinclair, Campbell Ridley, Mack Henry, Howard Harlan, Sam Lee, Bill Hughes. **Fifth Row (L to R):** Tommy Leek, John Denny, Larry Beasley, Richard Dixon, Bill Cherry, Rod Cantey, Billy Holden, David Morrissey. **Bottom Row (L to R):** Sam Dunlap, George Woodring, Bob Sewell, Terry Geshke, Buddy Benedict.

1961 Senior Class and Faculty

Top Row (Left to Right): Mr. Jimmy French, Mr. David E. Wood, Mr. William B. Akin, Mr. S. Ralph Brown, Mr. Ralph E. Naylor, Mr. John Bragg, Mr. Paul Redick, Mr. J. B. Akin, Mr. Daly Thompson, Mr. Carl W. Smithson, Mr. Cannon Mayes, Mr. John Bennett, Mr. Billy L. Bradshaw. **Second Row (L to R):** White Hall Morrison, Tom Lawrence, Jimmy Miller, Bunny Huggins, John Adger, Hal Herd, Jeff Bethurum, Bill Smithson, Mike Shinkle, Dickey Jewell, Dick Boles, Mike Kidd. **Third Row (L to R):** Elliot Newman, Olin West, Willis Morgan, Albert Pewitt, Monte Holland, Tuck Woodring, Bob Dunkerley, Nelson Spotts, Steve Harper, Padge Beasley, David Gotwald, Charles Trabue. **Fourth Row (L to R):** Larry Merville, Boyce Magli, Jim Thomasson, Steve Sxorman, Ed Steele, Sonny Clouse, John Woodliff, Bill Jones, Joe Torrence, Spike Akin, Tom Kanaday, Frank Teasley. **Fifth Row (L to R):** Bert Phillips, Larry Brown, John Coleman, Cecil Crowson, Bill Ormes, Tony Holcomb, Leo Crane, King Wade, Mac Peterson, John Wade, Tom Paine, Johnnie Webber. **Bottom Row (L to R):** Tom Leonard, Jack Francis, Gary Anderson Jeff Winningham, Don Hasty, Bill Redick, Paul Guffee.

A Monument to Education

1962 Senior Class and Faculty

Top Row (Left to Right): Mr. Ralph Brown, Mr. Jimmy French, Mr. William Akin, Mr. Ralph Naylor, Mr. John Bragg, Mr. Paul Redick, Mr. J. B. Akin, Mr. Carl Smithson, Mrs. Paul Redick, Mr. Bill Bradshaw, Mr. Daly Thompson. **Second Row (L to R):** Mr. John Oxley, Mr. William Jones, Mr. Bob Knight, Mr. Boardman Stewart. **Third Row (L to R):** Sid Tompkins, Charles Fowler, Tony Johnston, Roy Alley, Doswell Brown, Tom Sinclair, Duke Shackelford. **Fourth Row (L to R):** Billy Caplinger, Larry Beadle, Jay Garrett, Dickie Gillespie, Buster Shull, Tommy Marlin, Steve Jacobson, Bill Johnston, Buzz Turner, Melville Barnes, Jim Blackburn, David Jones, Stanley Horn. **Fifth Row (L to R):** Johnny Jewell, Harry Walters, Mack Dobson, Jimmy Flippen, Jackie Caldwell, Harlan Dobson, John Woodliff, George Lockridge, Charles Beziat, Bill Clarkson. **Sixth Row (L to R):** Ned Plumer, Rogers Hays, George Gifford, Bailey Robinson, Gray Bickley, Steve Stockett, Oscar Noel, Sonny Rodgers, Bobby Foote, Johnny Douglass. **Bottom Row (L to R):** Alvin Ford, Russell Gibbs, Mike Henry, Jon Harville, Barry Pilcher, Evans Givan, Carlton O'Neal, Herbert Bingham, David Everson, Ronnie Noll, David Patterson, Don Heinig, Howard Johnston.

1963 Senior Class and Faculty

Top Row (Left to Right): Mr. Ted A. Beach, Mr. Bill Brown, Mr. Jimmy Gentry, Mr. John Oxley, Mr. Ralph Naylor, Mr. Paul Redick, Mr. J. B. Akin, Mr. Bill L. Bradshaw, Mrs. Paul Redick, Mr. Carl W. Smithson, Mr. Daly Thompson. **Second Row (L to R):** Mr. William Smith, Mr. Jimmy French, Mr. Boardman Stewart, Mr. Donald E. Patterson. **Third Row (L to R):** Dickie Pollard, Johnny Wilson, Frank Pinkerton, Tom Cranwell, Walter Donaldson, Scotty Harris, Bobby Schwarts, Allen Cohen, Horace Johns Jr., David Moran, Donald Henderson, Pete Talmadge, Sandy MacPherson. **Fourth Row (L to R):** Pete Fleming, Roger Milam, Frank Beasley, Granbery Jackson, Robert McMillan, Farris Moore, Barry Pilcher, Bobby Morel, Jim Moon, Keith Caldwell, Bill Ashworth, Bob Power, Berry Lannom. **Fifth Row (L to R):** Johnny Guffee, Ed Kelly, George Paine, Walter Kihm, Frank Stratton, Charles Gilbert, David Broemel, Perry Ozburn, Bill Leek, Ronald Crutcher, Robert Holsen, Graham Fuqua, Robin Barksdale. **Bottom Row (L to R):** Mike Rogers, Chuck Lucas, Winston Grizzard, John Hoffmeister, Richard Penny, Hugh Gracey, Bubbie Beasley, Mike McConnell, Larry Vining, Bobby Parrish, Hayes Fowler, Preston Fowlkes.

A Monument to Education 189

1964 Senior Class and Faculty

Top Row (Left to Right): Mr. Bill Brown, Mr. Jimmy Gentry, Mr. Bill Smith, Mr. Ralph Naylor, Mr. Tony Cobb, Mr. Paul Redick, Mr. John A. Bragg, Mr. J. B. Akin, Mr. Bill Bradshaw, Mr. Boardman Stewart, Mr. Don Patterson, Mr. Daly Thompson. **Second Row (L to R):** Mr. Glenn Hays, Mr. John Oxley, Mr. Jimmy French, Mr. Carl Smithson. **Third Row (L to R):** William Moss, Peter Dorland, Jerry Ross, Frank T. Etscorn, Bill Hubbard, James W. Cady, Tommy Grizzard, Gary S. Ghertner, Gary Peterman, James S. Thompson, Bill Herron, H. N. Kirkpatrick Jr., Dickie Heflin. **Fourth Row (L to R):** James W. Jackson, Bill McKeand, Michael Kinnard, Mike Derryberry, Joseph Iverlett, Jack Wyatt, Phillip G. Hollis, Kenny Ward-Smith, Charles M. Sutherland Jr., John M. Lewis, Edward W. Benz Jr., David Proctor, Robert M. Fleming. **Fifth Row (L to R):** Will Ridley, Sam Clement, Ferrell Gregory, Livingston A. Kelley, Donald M. Steele, W. O. Green, John B. Nicholson, Joseph Baugh, Jerry Porter, Harold Dorris, Brock Estes, William H. Rodgers, Will Cowart. **Bottom Row (L to R):** Bobby Dickson, John Thompson, Allen Patton, Ed Walley, Lloyd Daugherty, Gene Carter, Robert L. Hill, William R. Merns, William Kelly, Jim Nichols.

1965 Senior Class and Faculty

Top Row (Left to Right): Mr. Bill Brown, Mr. Jimmy Gentry, Mr. Bill Smith, Mr. Bill Bradshaw, Mr. Ralph Naylor, Mr. Carl Smithson, Mr. Paul Redick, Mr. John A. Bragg, Mr. J. B. Akin, Mr. Daly Thompson, Mr. Herbert Entrekin, Mr. Boardman Stewart, Mr. Spencer Holt, Mr. Don Patterson. **Second Row (L to R):** Mr. Glen Hays, Mr. Tony Cobb, Mr. Don Allen, Mr. W. G. Campbell. **Third Row (L to R):** Steven Head, Chug Morton, Tommy Lawrence, Jim Short Jr., Gig Robinson, Allen Tanksley, Jim Hamblen, David Kefauver, Tom Robinson, Mick McCoy, Andy Mitchell, Stefan Smith. **Fourth Row (L to R):** Jimmie Ellis, Bert Brown, Paul Clements, Billy Adair, John Gerth, Calvin Houghland, Sam Buchanan, Dan Martin, Roger Jackson, John Kennedy, Jody Bowman, Steve Barnes, George Elder, Doug Johnson. **Fifth Row (L to R):** John Tompkins, Gid Wade, Joe Henry, Don Dickinson, Mike Everhart, Stephen Robertson, Fred Hart, Bob Moore, George Leonard, Kenneth Phelps, Bob Thompson Jack Dryden, Sutton O'Neal, Hays Perry. **Sixth Row (L to R):** Eddie Blackman, Jim Parish, Remigius Shatas, Alex Wade, Steve Plonka, Jimmy Sewell, Jim Bassham, Mike Pearson, Park McMillan, Rascoe Rhea, Ronnie Grimes, Mike Ross, Eddy Woodard, John Robbins. **Bottom Row (L to R):** Carter Chapman, Joe Vaulx Crockett, John Paine, Bill Abernathy, Dicky Gotwald, Richard Hillard, David Whalley, Ed Graham, Jimmy Smith, Cliff Parmer, Fred Horrell, Tom Henderson III, Hugh Hobbs, Joe Holliday.

A Monument to Education

1966 Senior Class and Faculty

Top Row (Left to Right): W. Paul Redick, J. B. Akin, John Bragg. **Second Row (L to R):** David Bissell, Bill Bradshaw, Bill Brown, Bill Cherry, Anthony Cobb, James Gentry, Dan Griffith, Allen Hainge. **Third Row (L to R):** Gary Heidinger, Don Patterson, Mrs. Redick, Ralph Reynolds, Bill Smith, Carl Smithson, Howard Smithson, Daly Thompson. **Fourth Row (L to R):** Vaughn Woods, Leonard McGugin, James Thompson, Ross Crutcher, James Dyer. **Fifth Row (L to R):** Vaughn Allen, Mickey Beadle, Charles Beasley, David Bland, Parkes Brandon, Pat Bray, Dan Brown, Paul Brown, Buddy Calvin, Jerry Carter, Wink Cherry, Bill Crosby, John Gifford. **Sixth Row (L to R):** Larry Grissom, Joe Hanson, Loy Hardcastle, Wirt Harlin, Harmon Hays, Albert Hill, Hugh Howser, Brad Hume, Don Hunter, Bobby Jackson, David Johnson, Larry Kain, Buzz Keith, David Kousser. **Seventh Row (L to R):** Jack Lee, Bryan Long, Garath Matthews, Bill McClanahan, Bobby Patterson, Rick Peterson, Gordon Publow, Clyde Redford, Danny Rodgers, Mark Rogers, Billy Rosson, Mike Rudder, Randy Rudolph, Sam Rutherford. **Bottom Row (L to R):** Hank Seaton, Perry Shields, Reese Smith, William Smith, Rob Sturdivant, Bill Sutherland, Ken Tarkington, Tony Trabue, Felix Treadway, Lee Truitt, George Wallace, Bill White, Ralph Whiteman, Breck Wyatt.

1967 Senior Class and Faculty

Top Row (Left to Right): J. B. Akin, W. Paul Redick, John Bragg. **Second Row (L to R):** Bill Bradshaw, Bill Cherry, Anthony D. Cobb, David Freeman, James C. Gentry, Robert Gentry, Joseph C. Green, Lyle E. Hampton. **Third Row (L to R):** Harold Kennedy, Francois Andre Leprun, Donald E. Patterson, Mrs. Paul Redick, Bill Smith, Ralph D. Reynolds, Carl W. Smithson, Daly Thompson, Terrence H. Wilkinson. **Fourth Row (L to R):** Dickie Arnold, Frank Clement Jr., Jack Milam, Bill Pemberton. **Fifth Row (L to R):** Ralph McCracken. **Sixth Row (L to R):** Robert Akin, Terry Alpaugh, John Baugh, Frank Bell, Bill Booher, Joe Brady, Mike Burton, Newton Cannon, Paul Chrisman, Norman Davis, Percy Dempsy, Don Denbo, Tim Derryberry, Mike Estes, Tom Evans. **Seventh Row (L to R):** Bob Ford, Harry Ford, Lory Ghertner, Art Graham, Walter Green Jr., Mike Greene, Bill Gupton, John Hahn, John Hampton, Marion Hickerson, Mike Hickman, David Jackson, Logan Jackson, Don Johnson. **Eighth Row (L to R):** Mac Johnson, Jerome Karr, Newton King, Eddie Lunn, Bubba McCord, Frank McCoy, Walter Medearis, Mike Mott, Allen Muse, Frank North, Grantland O'Neal, Park Owen, John Sam Ridley, Steve Robinson, Terry Rodgers. **Bottom Row (L to R):** Bilbo Short, Clay Shwab, George Slivey, Bob Smith, Mont Smith, Bob Stamps, Jack Staples, Alex Steele, Bill Swiggart, Jim Swiggart, Jerry Thompson, Bill Utley, Jim Webb, Benny Williams, Frank Witherspoon.

A Monument to Education

1968 Senior Class and Faculty

Top Row (Left to Right): David Byrd, Bill Bradshaw, Bill Cherry, Anthony D. Cobb, J. B. Akin, W. Paul Redick, John Bragg, James C. Gentry, J. Robert Gentry, Joseph C. Green. **Second Row (L to R):** Harold Kennedy, Francois Andre Leprun, William Parsons Jr., Donald E. Patterson, Joe C. Peel, Ralph Reynolds, V. Neil Richardson, Bill Smith, Mrs. W. Paul Redick, Carl W. Smithson, Terrence W. Wilkinson. **Third Row (L to R):** Allen Anderson, John Anderson, Hilton Austin Jr., Thomas Brady. **Fourth Row (L to R):** Stewart Campbell Jr., Stephen Chambers, Russell Little, Fred Hamilton Jr., Jay Siegrist Jr., Patrick Cooper, Lawrence Dale. **Fifth Row (L to R):** Timothy Dempsey, Timmons Derryberry Jr., Thomas Dickinson, David Gerth, James Rader, Philip Duke, Robert Estes, Frederick Faircloth III. **Sixth Row (L to R):** Felix Fly, Christopher Folsom, Richard Furman, Wayne Glasgow Jr., Edward Harris, Donald Hedden. **Seventh Row (L to R):** David Heflin, Stephen Hicks, Douglas Holliday, Stephen Horrell, William Johnson, Thomas Lawrence, Joe Lester, Kelly Lish Jr., William Lloyd, Stephen McClanahan, Philip Martin, William Maxwell, Curtis Miles, Michael Minor, Robert Minor. **Bottom Row (L to R):** John Moran Jr., Glenn Osborne, Martin Ozburn, Gary Powers, Edwin Provost, Michael Rainey, William Ramsey, Henry Roberts, Judson Rogers, Frederick Stephens, Stephen Sutherland, John Turner, Michael Vaughn, Frank Wade, John Wilson, Charles Wolff Jr.

1969 Senior Class and Faculty

Top Row (Left to Right): John W. Kuhlman, Jon Hassey, David Byrd, Danny C. Allen, Bill Cherry, William B. Akin, J. B. Akin, John A. Bragg, James C. Gentry, J. Robert Gentry, Joseph C. Green, Marvin A. Franklin Jr., Rodney H. Rogers. **Second Row (L to R):** Kenneth E. Moore, Harold Kennedy, Mrs. E. C. Duke, Anthony D. Cobb, William V. Parsons Jr., Donald E. Patterson, Ralph D. Reynolds, V. Neil Richardson, Bill Smith, Mrs. J. H. Beasley, Carl W. Smithson, Nancy H. Allen. **Third Row (L to R):** Buddy Allen, Bob Anderson, Rob Anderson, Jere Ellis, Chris Dodson, Bob Selph, Bill Armistead, Tommy Ashcraft, Skip Beadle. **Fourth Row (L to R):** Charley Benz, Dewees Berry, Harry Blackburn, Sam Jack Brantley, Mike Williams, Tim Powers, Denson Buttrey, Bucky Crowell, Steve Dudley, Steve Early. **Fifth Row (L to R):** Bill Fisher, Richard Francis, Harrison Gant, David Gardner, Jim Gentry, Irwin Graham, Bill Haffner, Truman Harper. **Sixth Row (L to R):** Hugh Hasty, Bob Henry, Leonard Herrington, Steve Horn, Josh Huffman, Lee Hume, Mike Isaacson, Richard Katzoff, Dwight Lanier, John Lee, Dick Lewis, Johnny Lucas, Lewis Maddux, William E. McLeod. **Bottom Row (L to R):** Marshall Morgan, Paul Muncy, Drew Oliver, Ken Peercy, Monty Powell, Kirby O. Primm Jr., Eddie Roberts, Mark Scantlebury, John Simpson, Tommy Taylor, Douglas Thompson, Tommy West, John Whiteman, Jim Witherspoon, Bobby Wright.

1970 Senior Class and Faculty

Top Row (Left to Right): Rodney Rogers, John W. Kuhlman, Mrs. J. H. Beasley, Bobby Gentry, Ronald Shelton, J. B. Akin, John A. Bragg, Mrs. Dorothy Lea, Dr. Joseph C. Green, John Herrmann, Bill Cherry, David Byrd, Carlton Flatt. **Second Row (L to R):** Bill Smith, Thomas E. Biggs, Bill Parsons, Mrs. Nancy Cole, John Oxley, William B. Akin, Mrs. Nancy H. Allen, Roy F. Alley, Jimmy Gentry, John Colmore, George Vassallo, Carl Smithson, John C. Shields, Danny C. Allen, Harold Kennedy. **Third Row (L to R):** Robert Atwood, Jim Beesley, Rick Bennett, Buck Berry, Tommy Harwell, Bob McClanahan, Teddy Lee, Douglas Berry, Mike Binkley, Robert Chaffin, Chuck Cook. **Fourth Row (L to R):** Alec Dryden, Ralph Duke, Richard Dunavant, Willie Earls, Paul Budslick, Gary Clement, Steve Faust, Winston Gant, Allen Gentry, Dan Gentry. **Fifth Row (L to R):** John Givens, Steve Glenn, Barry Goodman, Joe Gordon, Nate Greene, Steve Harris, Sam Hollins, Jack Howser. **Sixth Row (L to R):** Brad Hutchison, George Irion, Bo Johnson, Jim King, Jim Livingstone, Gene Lovell, Howell Lynch, Tommy Magli, Roger McCullough, Jerry McGinnis, Tommy McLaughlin, Dan Milam, Tom Miner. **Bottom Row (L to R):** Sterling Minor, Jimmy Moore, Jerry Muntz, Vance Ormes, Tommy Price, Chris Ross, Mark Schwartz, Dowell Smith, Tommy Smith, Bob Smithson, Hanes Sparkman, Dale Stephens, Ed Uthman, Dabney Walt.

1971 Senior Class and Faculty

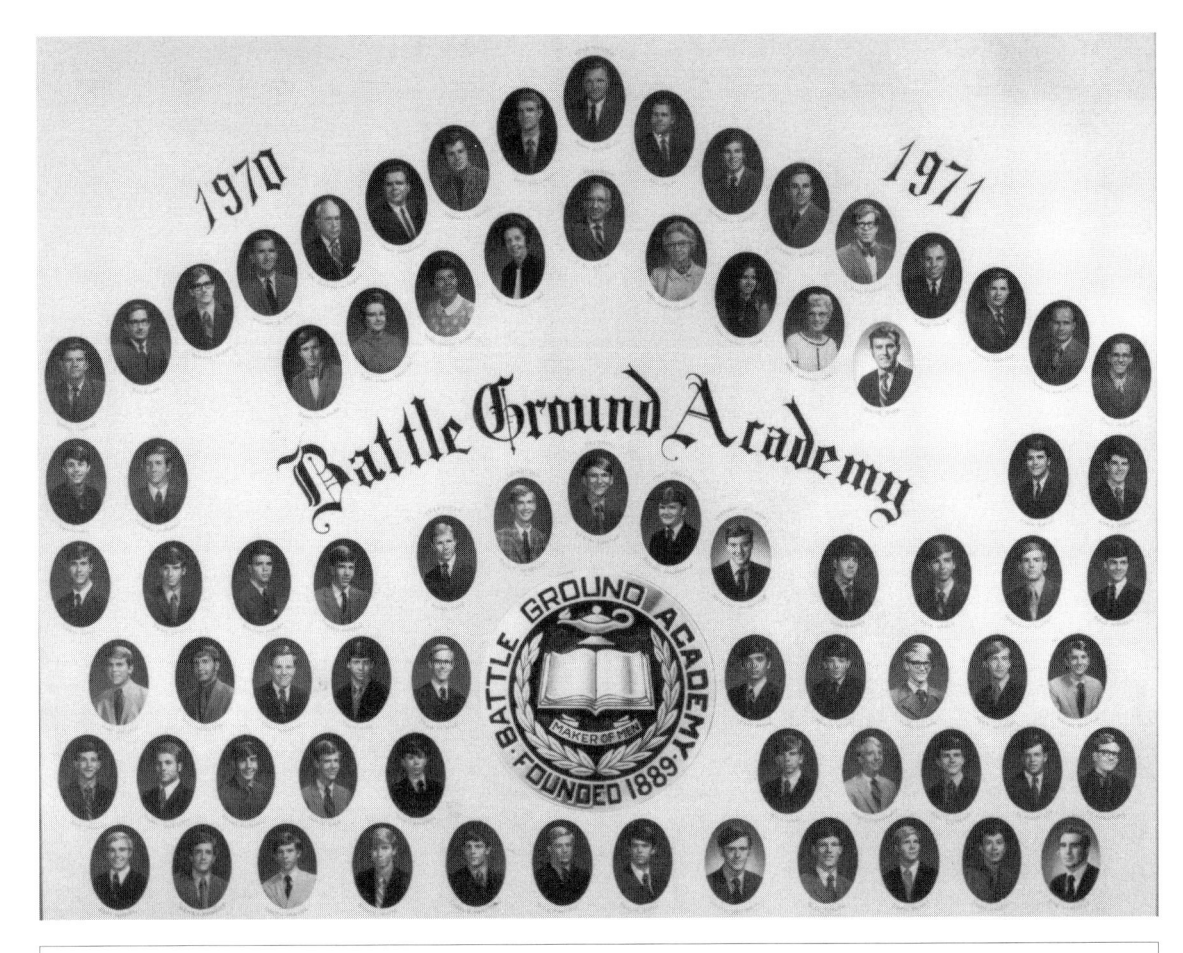

Top Row (Left to Right): Bobby Gentry, Roy Alley, Robert Baker, William B. Akin, Dr. Joseph G. Green, John Herrmann, Thomas E. Biggs, Doy Hollmann, John A. Bragg, Bill Smith, Ronald W. Shelton, Rodney Rogers, Bill Parsons, John Oxley, Jimmy Gentry, John W. Kuhlman, John Ingram. **Second Row (L to R):** John Colmore, Mrs. Hiram Beasley, Mrs. Nancy Allen, Mrs. Matilou Duke, J. B. Akin, Mrs. Mary Cawthon, Mrs. Nancy Cole, Mrs. Dorothy Lea, David Byrd. **Third Row (L to R):** Bram Neil, Turner Snodgrass, John Brown, Webb Powers. **Fourth Row (L to R):** John Hall, John Lykins, Houston Moran, Charlie Haffner Jr., Alan Duke, Billy Anderson, Stack Scoville, Gerard MacDonald, Gordon McDaniels, John Harper, Doug Early, Frederick Funte, Brad Thomason. **Fifth Row (L to R):** Ham Wallace, Bill Wickliffe, John Woodfin, John Boyd, John Ingold, Jeff Payne, Bailey Allen, Mark Coomer, Joey Kesther, Randy Bratton. **Sixth Row (L to R):** Ray Grigsby, Randy Goldstein, Henry Feldhaus, Jamie Dale, Don Cameron, Bill Wall, Scott Sutherland, Bill Tichenor, Lee Morrison, Ed Branding. **Bottom Row (L to R):** Jeff Hoover, Henry Ambrose, Dolph Mayer, Buddy Hume, Charlie Warfield, Rick Philpot, Phillip Rush, Chuck Southall, Bill Smith, John Phipps, John Haley, Bob Armisted.

A Monument to Education

1972 Senior Class and Faculty

Top Row (Left to Right): Henry E. Seaton, John T. Ingram, John Colmore, William B. Akin, Robert C. Baker, John Herrmann, J. B. Akin, John A. Bragg, Gary G. Brock, James R. Pritchard, Ronald W. Shelton, James Hall, Christian B. Niemeyer, B. C. Rauchle. **Second Row (L to R):** Tony E. Chatman, Mrs. Nancy Allen, Luis Leon, James C. Gentry, Mrs. Matilou Duke, Robert Gentry, Robert R. Moore, John W. Kuhlman, Mrs. Norene Beasley, John Oxley, Mrs. Dorothy Lea, James H. Cole, Miss Dorothy Doggett, Doy Hollman. **Third Row (L to R):** B. McLean, Jene Pewitt, W. Reid, S. Wauford, S. Weiland, R. Anderson. **Fourth Row (L to R):** T. Baldridge, J. Lawrence, T. Boyd, B. Cole, S. Bronaugh, B. Fuqua, J. Kinnard, M. Thompson, K. Swann, D. Buntin, J. Nordyke, M. Miller, R. Ball. **Fifth Row (L to R):** M. Beeler, T. Duncan, B. Mott, M. Williams, S. Duke, S. Smith, B. Ogles, M. Brown. **Sixth Row (L to R):** W. Bentley, G. Dale, B. Mitchell, B. Sutton, D. McMillen, B. Moench, S. Scoville, P. Wright, A. Thomas, J. Denbo, William Billington Jr., T. Steele, F. Puryear, L. Grigsby. **Seventh Row (L to R):** W. Berry, D. Cunningham, E. Martin, B. Beard, A. Duley, D. Jackson, P. Porch, T. Stephenson, H. Campbell, J. Harrison, J. Graham, J. Stone, J. Rodgers, J. Haynes. **Bottom Row (L to R):** S. Chaffin, L. Crawford, G. Lott, B. Hickey, C. Gore, C. Harlin, B. Ross, J. Talton, T. Doak, J. Vining, J. McKay, K. Jeter, D. Ozburn, W. Ross, E. Manning.

1973 Senior Class and Faculty

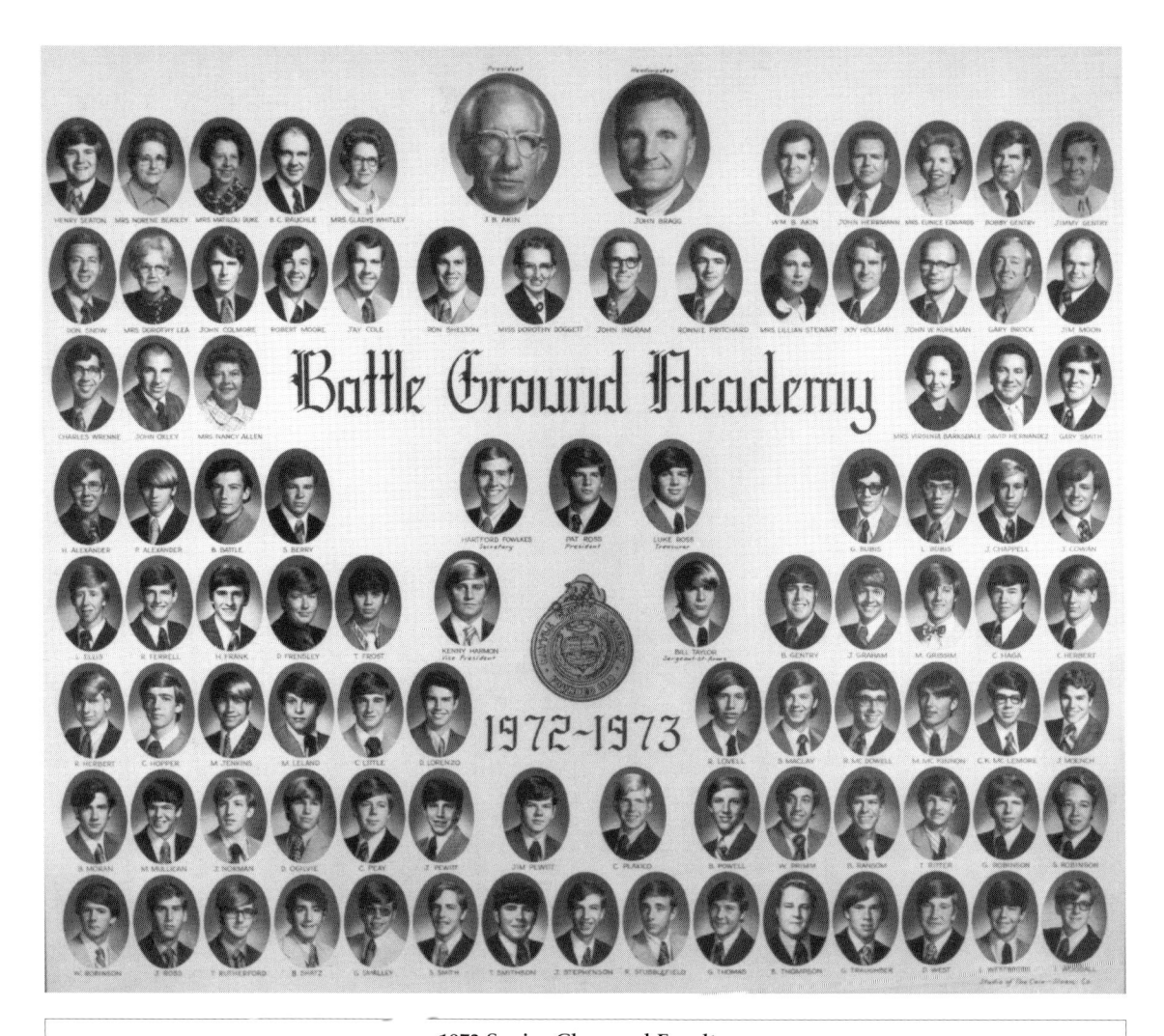

Top Row (Left to Right): Henry Seaton, Mrs. Norene Beasley, Mrs. Matilou Duke, B. C. Rauchle, Mrs. Gladys Whitley, J. B. Akin, John Bragg, Wm. B. Akin, John Herrmann, Mrs. Eunice Edwards, Bobby Gentry, Jimmy Gentry. **Second Row (L to R):** Don Snow, Mrs. Dorothy Lea, John Colmore, Robert Moore, Jay Cole, Ron Shelton, Miss Dorothy Doggett, John Ingram, Ronnie Pritchard, Mrs. Lillian Stewart, Doy Hollman, John W. Kuhlman, Gary Brock, Jim Moon. **Third Row (L to R):** Charles Wrenne, John Oxley, Mrs. Nancy Allen, Mrs. Virginia Barksdale, David Hernandez, Gary Smith. **Fourth Row (L to R):** H. Alexander, P. Alexander, B. Battle, S. Berry, Hartford Fowlkes, Pat Ross, Luke Ross, G. Bubis, L. Bubis, J. Chappell, J. Cowan. **Fifth Row (L to R):** L. Ellis, R. Ferrell, H. Frank, D. Frensley, T. Frost, Kenny Harmon, Bill Taylor, Bob Gentry Jr., J. Graham, M. Grissim, C. Haga, C. Herbert. **Sixth Row (L to R):** R. Herbert, C. Hopper, M. Jenkins, M. Leland, C. Little, D. Lorenzo, R. Lovell, S. Maclay, R. McDowell, Mel McKinnon, C. K. McLemore, J. Moench. **Seventh Row (L to R):** B. Moran, M. Mullican, J. Norman, D. Ogilvie, C. Peay, J. Pewitt, Jim Pewitt, C. Plaxico, B. Powell, W. Primm, B. Ransom, T. Ritter, G. Robinson, S. Robinson. **Bottom Row (L to R):** W. Robinson, J. Ross, T. Rutherford, B. Shatz, G. Smalley, S. Smith, T. Smithson, J. Stephenson, R. Stubblefield, G. Thomas, B. Thompson, G. Traughber Jr., D. West, L. Westbrook, T. Woodall.

A Monument to Education

1974 Senior Class and Faculty

Top Row (Left to Right): Mrs. Dorothy Lea, John Colmore, Mrs. Norene Beasley, Bob Rauchle, J. B. Akin, John Bragg, John Herrmann, Mrs. Eunice Edwards, Bobby Gentry, Miss Dorothy Doggett, Gary Brock. **Second Row (L to R):** Mrs. Linda Allen, John Ingram, Robert Moore, Jay Cole, Don Snow, John Averett, Mrs. Nancy Allen, Don Vick, Ron Pritchard, Mrs. Lillian Stewart, Jimmy Gentry, Mrs. Mitzi Bass, David Hernandez. **Third Row (L to R):** Jimmie Webb, Charles Wrenn, John Oxley, Gary Smith, Larry McElroy, Greg Kinman. **Fourth Row (L to R):** Jerry Creim, Benjie Ernst, Zeb Gentry, Dennis Smithson, Chip Burnette, Mike Lightfoot, Mike Haberman, Johnny Haffner, Greg Harrell. **Fifth Row (L to R):** Steve Head, Randy Herbert, Edward Herndon, Cas Jefferson, Kevin Smith, Andy Ferrell, Steve Justice, Craig Laine, Steve Lawrence, Rusty Longhurst. **Sixth Row (L to R):** Jon McClanless, Terry McCarter, Larry Manofsky, Randy Minor, Phil Moore, Joe Moran, Mark Naftel, Nally Osburn. **Bottom Row (L to R):** Terry Pearson, Brad Rahrer, Julian Scruggs, David Sharber, Drew Shillinglaw, Kerry Stinson, Randy Stratton, Jim Thomas, Crom Tidwell, Earl Vickers, Johnny Walker, Chuck Wells, Jimmy Wilhoite.

BATTLE GROUND ACADEMY

1975 Senior Class and Faculty

Top Row (Left to Right): Charles Wrenn, Jim Webb, Mrs. Lillian Stewart, Don Snow, Gary Smith, B. C. Rauchle, John A. Bragg, Robert Pruitt, Ron Pritchard, Tom Phelps, John Oxley, David McNatt, Larry McElroy. **Second Row (L to R):** Mrs. Dorothy Lea, Doug Langston, Chip Langley, Greg Kinman, John Herrmann, David Hernandez. **Third Row (L to R):** William Hackett, James C. Gentry, Mrs. Marcia Bowen, David Evans, Mrs. Eunice Edwards, Miss Dorothy Doggett, John Colmore, Julian Bibb, Mrs. Mitzi Bass, Mrs. Nancy Allen, Mrs. Linda Allen, J. B. Akin. **Fourth Row (L to R):** John Bartlett, Frank Baugh, Andy Beasley, Bill Warfield, Joe Parkes, Lee Davies, Ken Caldwell, Randy Smotherman, Ricky Caldwell, Rick Clark, Peter Cobb. **Fifth Row (L to R):** Billy Cocke, David Deere, Mike Doody, Ernie Dufton, Robert Elliott, Tim Floyd, Jim Frith, Sam Greene, Greg Gunnells, John Harlin, Roger Hill, MIke Holland, Chuck Isaacs, Tommy Little, David McDowell. **Sixth Row (L to R):** Dennis McDowell, Mike McKinnon, DeWitt, McLaurine, Craig Matthews, Gary Minor, Eddie Moon, Tally Osburn, Tom Parrish, Skip Phipps, Ricky Purcell, Deck Reeks, Terry Richardson, Scott Satterwhite, Steve Scales, Chris Slaymaker. **Bottom Row (L to R):** Mike Smith, Don Smithson, Mac Stone, Mark Stone, Joe Tate, Johnny Taylor, Bill Thomas, Steve Thornton, Pat Wade, Lee Waggoner, Mike Waggoner, Phil Warren, Brad Williams, Tom Wiseman, Greg Woodard.

1976 Senior Class and Faculty

Top Row (Left to Right): Charles Wrenn, Jim Webb, Tom Warren, Lillian Stewart, Don Snow, Gary Smith, B. C. Rauchle, John A. Bragg, Robert Pruitt, Ron Pritchard, Tom Phelps, John Oxley, Burton T. McWhirter, David McNatt. **Second Row (L to R):** Larry McElroy, Mark Llewellyn, Dorothy Lea, Doug Langston, Hiram G. Langley, Greg Kinman. **Third Row (L to R):** John Herrmann, David Hernandez, Jimmy Gentry, David Evans, Eunice Edwards, Dorothy Doggett, John Colmore, Marcia Bowen, Mitzi Bass, Bob Armistead, Linda Allen, J. B. Akin. **Fourth Row (L to R):** Randy Anglin, Mark Barrett, Jack Beasley, David Benson, Chris Biship, Jim Williams, Tim Stewart, Jay Luna, George Stadler, Pat Clarke, Jay Boone, Harold Brewer, Peter Burton, Robert Cain, Harden Caldwell. **Fifth Row (L to R):** Matthew Carden, Bob Cherry, John Collier, Greg Cook, Jim Cook, Ted Darden, Wayne Davis, Paul S. Dickens, David Dunigan, Eric Eckhardt, Dan Elcan, Brad Eskind, Scott Gentry, Gus Grote, Richard Hagan, Buddy Hager, Cy Harper. **Sixth Row (L to R):** Perk Hixon, Mike Hogg, Art Ingman, Robin Ingram, Dale Isaacs, Scot Karr, Mike Keliher, Mike Kinnard, Steve Kinnard, Eddie Knight, George Knox, Binks Lewis, Bill Manofsky, Mickey Martin, Cliff McGown, John B. Moss. **Bottom Row (L to R):** David O'Neil, Jim Parrish, Scott Parrish, George Ragland, Greg Ritter, Todd Robinson, Bob Smith, Jim Smith, Dan Startup, Rudy Steltemeier, Tom Vollmer, Ken Warren, David Wellons, Colley Wells, Wayne Whitt, Russ Willis, Brad Wilson.

1977 Senior Class and Faculty

Top Row (Left to Right): Charles Wrenn, Jim Webb, Tom Warren, Lillian Stewart, Don Snow, Gary Smith, B. C. Rauchle, John A. Bragg, Robert Pruitt, Ron Pritchard, Tom Phelps, John Oxley, Steve Williams, David McNall. **Second Row (L to R):** Larry McElroy, Doug Williams, Dorothy Lea, Doug Langston, Ed Branding, Greg Kinman **Third Row (L to R):** John Herrmann, David Hernandez, Jimmy Gentry, David Evans, Eunice Edwards, Dorothy Doggett, John Colmore, Marcia Bowen, Margaret Ann Reynolds, Pat Welsh, Linda Allen, Erwin Dunlop. **Fourth Row (L to R):** Brett Allen, Wade Baggette, Stephen Bond, Larry Brinton, Henry Buckner, Eddie DeMoss, John Wade, Andy Sharp, Gerry Hood, Greg Brown, Bo Butler, Paul Caplinger, Dan Carmichael, Sean Coughlin, Mark Craig. **Fifth Row (L to R):** Ward DeWitt, Stewart Evers, Bryan Farrell, Rob Fesmire, Fritz Fiedler, Blake Fohl, Henry Geny, Hank Gupton, Richard Hardy, David Harwell, Mark Heldman, Chip Hoffman, Michael Holahan, Ivan Irwin, Tommy Jones, Alton Kelley. **Sixth Row (L to R):** Kurt Koehn, Bob Larkin, Harry Hill McAlister, John McAlister, Tot McCullough, Wayne McGee, Gene Mapes, Albert Menifee, Michael Millis, Jamie Morris, John Moss, Gary Osburn, Paul Peebles, Steve Phillips, Jimmy Pilkerton, George Plaster. **Bottom Row (L to R):** Randy Purcell, Robbie Robeson, Pat Robinson, Tim Robinson, Charlie Rolfe, Jim Sartor, Donnie Smith, Keith Smith, Rusty Stone, John Taylor, Thomas Twitty, James Warren, Randy Westbrook, Tom Wilk, Elliott Williams, Ricky Wood.

A Monument to Education

1978 Senior Class and Faculty

Top Row (Left to Right): Charles Wrenn, Jim Webb, Tom Warren, Lillian Stewart, Don Snow, Gary Smith, John Bragg, Robert Pruitt, Ron Pritchard, Tom Phelps, John Oxley, Doug Langston, Larry McElroy. **Second Row (L to R):** James Holloway, Doug Williams, Dorothy Lea, Ed Branding, Greg Kinman. **Third Row (L to R):** John Herrmann, David Hernandez, David Shaub, David Evans, Eunice Edwards, Dorothy Doggett, John Colmore, Marcia Bowen, Margaret Ann Reynolds, Pat Welsh, Linda Allen, Erwin Dunlop. **Fourth Row (L to R):** Steve Strasinger, Kurt Swensson, Newt Tillman, Ted Walker, David Maloney, Matt King, Craig Wilson, Mark Webb, Alan Isaacs, John Wallace, Jimmy Ward, John White, Donnie Young. **Fifth Row (L to R):** Steve McHugh, Charles Matthews, Scott Milam, Mike Moody, Scott Morris, Doug O'Neil, Bobby Osburn, Terry Paysinger, Tommy Peebles, James Peeler, Bill Puryear, Lee Ragland, Mark Reed, Bobby Rolfe, David Rutherford, Brock Short. **Sixth Row (L to R):** John Elcan, Cracker Ferrell, Don Fisher, Grant Glassford, Russ Goldman, Bobby Hall, Geoff Hartmann, Randy Hill, Ed Honicker, Hank Hymel, Orrin Ingram, Rainey Kirk, Riley Knight, Marc Larson, Joel McAlister, Sidney McAlister. **Bottom Row (L to R):** Jon Alcorn, Cragin Anderson, Mitch Bates, Alan Bostick, Tommy Boyd, Bill Brackney, Ken Browning, John Gain, Bruce Carillon, John Cathey, Joey Cole, Greg Curtis, Art Darden, Campbell Dodd, Ed Douglas, Andy Dunn.

1979 Senior Class and Faculty

Top Row (Left to Right): Linda Allen, Al Bachleda, Marcia Bowen, Steve Dodd, Dorothy Doggett, Eunice Edwards, David Evans, Charles Fryer, Dennis Gibson, David Hernandez, John Herrmann, James Holloway, Greg Kinman, Doug Langston, Ken Lawyer. **Second Row (L to R):** Larry McElroy, John Oxley, Craig Porter, Ron Pritchard, Margaret Ann Reynolds, Barry Sensing, John Patterson, John Bragg, Gary Smith, Don Snow, Lillian Stewart, Tom Warren, Pat Welsh, Doug Williams. **Third Row (L to R):** Charles Wrenn, Craig Cauthen. **Fourth Row (L to R):** John Stover, George Tosh, Alan Treadway, Brad Veeyers, Bill Isaacs, Tommy McArthur, Peter McAlister, Larry Brooks, David Horn, Roger Waynick, Henry Wilson, Bob Wolf, David Woodard. **Fifth Row (L to R):** Jack Norman, Bond Oman, Gary Parkes, Tommy Phillips, Warren Phillips, Ricky Price, Bob Sarratt, Ben Scott, Maurice Scruggs, Don Searcy, Mark Sebastian, Tony Sharber, Brian Smith, David Spaulding, Tommy Stephenson. **Sixth Row (L to R):** John Church, Gary Collier, Tommy Edwards, Jay Garner, Rhea Garrett, David Gilmore, Barry Goss, Greg Grant, John Greer, Jim Gustave, Jay Harrison, Tommy Herbert, Andy Hill, Stephen Hollister, Russell Holloway. **Bottom Row (L to R):** Jeff Adams, Jeff Anderson, Keith Anderson, Steve Bartlett, Travis Bates, Bill Bennett, David Berry, Mike Bervoets, Lee Blank, Anthony Bond, Bick Boyle, Pete Burns, Paul Butts, Stuart Caulkins, Jimmy Charron.

A Monument to Education

1980 Senior Class and Faculty

Top Row (Left to Right): Doug Langston, Larry McElroy, David Martin, Craig Porter, John Rose, Lucas Boyd, John Bragg, Don Snow, Barry Sensing, Doug Williams, Gary Smith, Mike Tanner, Dean Taylor. **Second Row (L to R):** Albert Bachleda, Leslee Dodd, Ward Dickens, Dorothy Doggett, Bobby DuBois, Eunice Edwards, David Hernandez, Jewell Smiley, John Herrmann, Lillian Stewart, Harris Jacobs. **Third Row (L to R):** Carol Leach, Don Vick, Tom Warren. **Fourth Row (L to R):** Margaret Ann Reynolds, David Wilson, Charlie Baugh, Greg Evans, Chip Smith, Joe Chickey, David Butts, Dennis Gibson, Tom Gilman. **Fifth Row (L to R):** Jeanne Reindl, Chris Reynolds, Jeff Rich, Phillip Shackelford, Billy Shea, Chip Skinner, David E. Smith, David H. Smith, Rhonda Trace, Robert Tucker, Van Uselton, Mac Warner, Govan White, Scott White, Jimmy Williams. **Sixth Row (L to R):** David Johnson, Stan Jones, Vince Keene, Bobby Keliher, John Kelley, Scooter Lee, Sandy Ligon, Paige McClain, Tracey McMillan, Danny Maddux, Barry Milam, Russ Morris, Barry Nixon, John Oman, Chris Philbrick. **Seventh Row (L to R):** John Delvaux, Ed Estock, Steve Farrar, Jock Floyd, Jamie Fohl, Flip Fossee, Joey Foxall, Bobby Garrett, David Garrett, Chris Griffin, John Harrison, Bill Hart, Jeff Hoffman, Chase Horton, Jeff Jenkins. **Bottom Row (L to R):** Dale Alden, Jay Allen, David Avery, Philip Bafundo, Raleigh Bates, Dan Becler, Mike Brinton, David Brown, Jeff Burrows, Tony Cameron, Ed Cannon, John Cartwright, Bill Chaffin, Joe Dale, Jeff Darby.

1981 Senior Class and Faculty

Top Row (Left to Right): Albert Bachleda, Richard Cole, Ward Dickens, Dorothy Doggett, Bobby DuBois, Lucas Boyd, John Bragg, Don Snow, Dennis Gibson, Tom Gilman, David Hernandez, Michael Hovan, Harris Jacobs. **Second Row (L to R):** Jody Jones, Vicki Lamb, Doug Langston, Carol Leach, Larry McElroy, David Martin, Buddy Mills, Craig Porter, Margaret Ann Reynolds, John Rose. **Third Row (L to R):** Barry Sensing, Gary Smith, Lillian Stewart, Mike Tanner. **Fourth Row (L to R):** Dean Taylor, Don Vick, Tom Warren, Doug Williams. **Fifth Row (L to R):** Jimmy Stiff, Larry Summarell, Dean Sutherland, Barry Templeton, Steve Moody, Lissa Ring, John T. Johnson, Mike Steele, David Parkes, John Morss, Rob Tudor, John Voss, Jerry Waggoner, Craig Wise. **Sixth Row (L to R):** Rob Little, Tom McHugh, Carter Mays, John Menefee, Bobby Meyer, Tom Mitchell, Chris Nischan, Art Oxley, Bill Perry, Dean Richardson, Will Sanford, Bobby Sebastian, Scott Shepherd, George Shwab, Collins Spaulding. **Seventh Row (L to R):** Alec Estes, Cub Forrest, Scott Frick, Richie Hammond, John Hardebeck, Neal Hixon, Daye Holland, Trey Holt, Stephen Kaludis, Kyle Kinloch, Jason Kinnard, Craig Ladd, Troy Langford, Lance Lannom, Frank Lee. **Bottom Row (L to R):** Rob Abernathy, Billy Alexander, Bill Allen, Bob Anderson, Casey Anderton, Matt Anglin, Kent Bailey, Chris Ball, Buddy Bass, Paul Cole, Ed Crafton, Phillip Crews, Gary Curl, Jim DeMontbreun, Jeff Duckworth.

A Monument to Education

1982 Senior Class and Faculty

Top Row (Left to Right): Jody Jones, Terry Shrock, Judy Cheatham, Don Vick, Robert Walker, Judy Davis, Tom Gilman, David Hernandez, Dennis Gibson, Dorothy Doggett, Barry Sensing, Gary Smith, Lillian Stewart, Jeff Taylor, Thomas Warren. **Second Row (L to R):** Vicki Lamb, Al Bachleda, Lori Freeman, Richard Cole, Charles Comer, Bobby DuBois, Lucas Boyd, John Bragg, Don Snow, Laurel Eason, Doug Langston, Carol Leach, Larry McElroy, David Martin, Gordon Mathis. **Third Row (L to R):** Doug Smith, John Taylor, Leon Stevens, Heren Lee, Michael Hovan, Joel Williams, Beth Wiloughby, Chris Yokom. **Fourth Row (L to R):** Lisa Neal, John Olson, Jeff Phillips, Mark Rembert, Greg Trace, Jeff Williams, John De Leon, Joe Reynolds, Steve Wylie, Randy Uselton, Erwin Ricafort, Missie Savage, Greg Scott, Kyle Seeley. **Fifth Row (L to R):** Matt Johnson, Steve Jones, Ken Julian, Scott Keliher, Doug King, David Kinnard, Eric Lindahl, Leigh McClain, Rob McCullough, Bill Melley, Jim Milliken, Holland Mills, Keith Mitchell, Ellen More. **Sixth Row (L to R):** Marty Crutchfield, Lucy Davies, Lou Ann Day, Sean Patterson, Ronnie Douglas, Donna Draper, Bobby Dyke, Barbara Freeman, John Gholson, Bruce Green, Bo Hagewood, Debby Hardy, Jan Heise, Laurie Hughes, Lori Herman. **Bottom Row (L to R):** Sheila Alley, Andrew Ammons, Michael Bafundo, Grimes Baird, Frank Becker, George Bennett, Kelly Blake, John Blank, Scott Bradford, Todd Brent, DeBow Casey, Jill Cauthen, John Charron, Bill Cherry, Tadd Clarkson.

1983 Senior Class and Faculty

Top Row (Left to Right): Al Bachleda, Judy Cheatham, Richard Cole, Charles Comer, Thomas Warren, Lucas Boyd, John Bragg, Don Snow, David Martin, Laurel Eason, Bobby DuBois, Dorothy Doggett, Judy Davis. **Second Row (L to R):** Jody Jones, Vicki Lamb, Doug Langston, Carol Leach, Larry McElroy, Barry Sensing, Gary Smith, David Hernandez, Jay Gore, Tom Gilman, Dennis Gibson, Lori Freeman. **Third Row (L to R):** Lillian Stewart, Jeff Taylor, Terry Shrock, Gordon Mathis, Robert Walker, Don Vick. **Fourth Row (L to R):** Lain York, Brad Hogg, Preston Crowell, Jeff Davis, Clay Bailey. **Fifth Row (L to R):** Freddy Richardson, Eddie Savage, Richard Sebastian, Scott Sittel, Eric Skinner, Tim Southon, Jeff Steele, Chip Throckmorton, Thad Tolbert, James Tucker, Jim Wall, Boyd Williams, Reese Willis, John Wylie. **Sixth Row (L to R):** Greg Johnson, Mike Johnson, Jennifer Kelso, Rob Kennedy, Kriss Lass, Sandy Lawton, Frank McClure, Chris Meyer, Drew Morris, Kris Niznik, Dave Oxley, Tommy Phillips, Johnny Pratt, Kelly Ricciardi. **Seventh Row (L to R):** Brad Cook, Chris Crutcher, Bill Dickerhoff, Mark Dillard, Charles Dwyer, Deborah Evans, Jeff Freemont, Scott George, Emily Gillig, Leon Helguera, Matt Hicks, Richards Hill, Brandon Holmes, Tommy Holt. **Bottom Row (L to R):** Dillard Adams, Leean Anderson, Thomas Bafundo, Win Barker, Andy Bateman, Kelly Baugh, Lawrence Blank, Lea Boden, Church Bramlett, Darren Briggs, Brett Clark, Becky Clarkson, Lisa Cleveland, Mark Cole.

A Monument to Education

1984 Senior Class and Faculty

Top Row (Left to Right): Sharon Anderson, A. F. Bachleda, Wilson Bates, Charles Comer, Judy Davis, Dr. Lucas Boyd, John A. Bragg, Don Snow, Dorothy Doggett, Bobby DuBois, Laurel Eason, Lori Freeman, Dennis Gibson. **Second Row (L to R):** Tom Gilman, Jay Gore, David Hernandez, Jody Jones, Polly Kinder, Doug Langston, Carol Lea-Mord, Larry McElroy, David Martin, Gordon Mathis. **Third Row (L to R):** Mike Payne, Gloria Robison, Barry Sensing, Terry Shrock, Gary Smith, Lillian Stewart. **Fourth Row (L to R):** Don Vick, Robert Walker, Jay Fahey, John McCullough, Alan Rudolph, Drew Williams, Dr. Tom Warren, Cooper Wood. **Fifth Row (L to R):** Rusty Omer, Ty Ragsdale, Jeff Shaw, Bobby Shell, Carter Simmons, Sterling Smith, Richard Spencer, Bill Stack, Wiley Sullivan, John Waggoner, Sam Walker, Tommy Williams, Rob Wynne. **Sixth Row (L to R):** Jon Holloway, Dana Jaggers, Doug Jeffords, Jennifer Johnson, Ed Kelley, Ashton Lackey, Wilder Lee, Kathy McGee, David McHenry, Andy Maloney, Julian Mays, McNairy Morel, Patrick Nichol. **Seventh Row (L to R):** Anna Gene Chalfant, Bobby Clarkson, Chris Cone, Tom Davis, Jim Elder, John Flaugher, Jim Gilliam, Adam Godmer, Phillip Hanvy, Kevin Hatcher, Mike Hawkins, Kathryn Helsby, Greg Herman. **Bottom Row (L to R):** Hal Abbott, Richard Alley, Jeff Allison, Rodney Barrett, John Boden, Bill Braswell, Charles Brown, Elizabeth Brown, Don Brumit, Felix Bryan, Betsy Burke, Sonia Burton, Scott Cain.

1985 Senior Class and Faculty

Top Row (Left to Right): Sharon Anderson, Judy Davis, Bobby Dubois, Dr. Laurel Eason, Lori Freeman, Tom Gilman, Jay Gore, David Hernandez, Jane Herron, Jody Jones, Polly Kinder, Doug Langston, Carol Lea-Mord.
Second Row (L to R): Larry McElroy, David Martin, Gordon Mathis, Charles Oakes, Patricia Paine, Mike Payne, Gloria Robison, Barry Sensing, Terry Shrock, Don Vick, Robert Walker, Dr. Tom Warren, Travis Wells, Cooper Wood.
Third Row (L to R): John A. Bragg, Dr. Lucas Boyd, Don Snow, Dorothy Doggett. **Fourth Row (L to R):** Carson Sensing, David McNeely, Steve King, Chuck Drayton, J. D. Ryan, Paige Tolbert, Amy Batson, Bethany Bledsoe.
Fifth Row (L to R): Dana Burchett, Curt Campbell, Rick Chapman, Susan Cone, Deanna Courter, Lannie Daniel, Legare Davis, Zack Evans, Pam Gibbs, Tommy Guthrie, Tiffany Hall, Kelly Heithcock, Terri Abbott, Christopher Ban. **Sixth Row (L to R):** Jamie Hoffman, Sean Hoffman, Jen Hood, Johnny Hughes, Hooper Inman, Steve Irwin, Angie Jefferson, William Johnson, Elizabeth Jordan, David Landers, Amy Lawrence, Lelia Lee, Win Maddin, Barry Booker. **Bottom Row (L to R):** Eli Merritt, Frank Molner, Robert Oldham, Lucie Peach, Mark Puryear, Michelle Roussel, Kent Sandidge, Chris Scott, Greg Shaw, Nicholas Shirling, Rob Skinner, Paul Wallace, Tommy Whitehead, Bobby Mattix.

A Monument to Education

1986 Senior Class and Faculty

Top Row (Left to Right): Tom Gilman, Jay Gore, Mike Henson, David Hernandez, Jane Herron, Terry Shrock, Dr. Lucas Boyd, John A. Bragg, Barry Sensing, Gloria Robison, Mike Payne, Patricia Paine, Charles Oakes, Carole Miller. **Second Row (L to R):** Sharon Anderson, Judy Davis, Thomas Delvaux, Dr. Laurel Eason, Greg Ferrell, Dennis Gibson, Gordon Mathis, David Martin, Larry McElroy, Tommy Lee, Carol Lea-Mord, Jody Jones. **Third Row (L to R):** Don Snow, Cooper Wood, Don Vick, Dorothy Doggett, Robert Walker, Dr. Tom Warren, Gary Smith, Doug Langston. **Fourth Row (L to R):** Julie Steltjes, Grant Stockton, Rhonda Turner, Andy Charron, John Jewell, John Davis, Mark Freeman, Stefanie Freeman, Brian Voecks, Roger Walker, Joe Warpool, Lisa Wells. **Fifth Row (L to R):** Brad Jones, Jeff Jones, Mike Keith, Denise Kjellgren, Kenna Lee, Michael Leftwich, Jason MacPherson, John McMahan, Peter Madden, Scott Marshall, Rhonda Menifee, Eric Morrison, Jeremy Much, Michael Nichol, Leya Petty. **Sixth Row (L to R):** Becky Drayton, Will Eason, Gary Eckardt, Lynne Edwards, Adrienne Gehrke, Sherri Goss, Ryan Guest, Tiffy Henry, Kim Hodge, Rob Hollister, Donna Hood, James Jewell, Alice Johnson, Lesley Johnson, Tracy Johnson. **Bottom Row (L to R):** David Alford, Tommy Anderson, Laureen Bastone, Kord Baugh, Jacque Blake, Neil Boddie, Rusty Chism, Stephanie Classem, Anne Cole, Creighton Cook, Doug Cook, Ken Crews, Stacey Dell, Clay Dibrell, Debbie Dimond.

1987 Senior Class and Faculty

Top Row (Left to Right): Charles Oakes, Tommy Lee, Doug Langston, Carole Matthews, Dorothy Doggett, Rebecca Ponder, Greg Ferrell, Thomas Warren, David Martin, Glenda Marshall, Jay Gore, Don Vick, Sharon Anderson, Michael Payne, Doris Webb, David Hernandez. **Second Row (L to R):** Dennis Gibson, Robert Walker, Tom Gilman, Gloria Robison, Gary Smith, Gracie Lawson, Laurel Eason, Cooper Wood, Thomas Delvaux, Jane Herron, Barry Sensing, Bette Ryan, Jody Jones, Phil Jacobs, Michael Farnsworth, Judy Davis. **Third Row (L to R):** Duncan Winter, Jim Dougherty, Carol Lea-Mord, Larry McElroy, Stewart Long, Don Snow. **Fourth Row (L to R):** Nigel Westlake, Frank White, Mitch White, Brad Dennis, Madeline Crosby, Brown Daniel, Tyler Berry IV, Ellen Helm, Matt Ligon, Mike Whitehead, Chris Wood, Michael Wylie. **Fifth Row (L to R):** Tim Moses, Robert Mueller, Chance Noffsinger, Andrew Oldham, Michael Pinto, Lee Pitts, James Ponder, Will Rains, Rondal Richardson, Shane Shetler, Stephanie Shouse, Chris Sittel, Jeff Smithson, Denise Vaughn, Alex Warren, Kristin Warrenfells. **Sixth Row (L to R):** Scott Gordon, Haynes Haddock, Brooke Hardcastle, Jenkins Hardin, Bobby Hash, Charlie Hoffman, Lance Holcomb, Merielle Irvin, Stacy Jackson, George Jones, Mike Lowery, Chris Maxwell, Katie Mays, Vandi McMahon, Drew Moore, Lew Moore. **Bottom Row (L to R):** Roby Adams, Kris Akin, Christopher Batson, Allen Blankenship, Preston Brown, Scott Bryan, Bill Butler, Amy Cherry, Scott Cone, West Cook, Charley Crichton, Patrick Davis, Julikarel Elkin, Stephen Fahey, Lee Ann Foust, Colleen Garvey.

A Monument to Education

213

1988 Senior Class and Faculty

Top Row (Left to Right): Sharon Anderson, Judy Davis, Thomas Delvaux, Dorothy Doggett, James Dougherty, Dr. Laurel Eason, Michael Farnsworth, Greg Ferrell, Dennis Gibson, Tom Gilman, Jay Gore, David Hernandez, Jane Herron, Margaret Hickey, Ann Hines, Gene Jumper. **Second Row (L to R):** Doug Langston, Carol Lea-Mord, Tommy Lee, Stewart Long, Glenda Marshall, David Martin, Carole Matthews, Larry McElroy, Sue Minter, Charles Oakes, Trina Pewitt, Gloria Robison, Bette Ryan, Barry Sensing, Gary Smith Don Vick. **Third Row (L to R):** Don Snow, Robert Walker, Jody Jones, Dr. Tom Warren, Duncan Winter, Cooper Wood. **Fourth Row (L to R):** David Enoch, Jared Hutto, Hardin Daniel, Dr. Lucas Boyd, John A. Bragg, Stan Pope, Wesley Hardin, Chad Jewell. **Fifth Row (L to R):** Scott Ruark, Scott Sanders, Charles Taylor, Georgette Thompson, Woody Trondsen, Suzy Tucker, Jay Formosa, Billy Van Landingham, Steve Wartell, Angie Westbrooks, Brian Williams, Craige Wrenn, Davis Young, Amanda Zeigler. **Sixth Row (L to R):** Merri Justice, Bill Kaludis, Katy Kemp, Jason Kenney, David Lowe, Jennifer Mazalook, Ric McAdams, Chris McCoy, Walker Mock, Brent Moore, Scott Nichol, Kei Pace, Brian Poag, Amy Polk, Dodson Randolph, Allen Roberts. **Seventh Row (L to R):** Briggs Evans, Ricky Felts, Leigh Gillespie, Greg Gilliam Jennifer Gordon, Christi Goss, Brian Gurley, Clint Hart, Jesse Hendricks, Beth Hickman, Edwin Hillenmeyer, Jay Hobbs, Robin Hoffman, Brad Hofstetter, Margaret Hood, Brian Johnson. **Bottom Row (L to R):** Michael Baldree, Simon Bone, Kayron Brewer, Balinda Burton, Ashley Chavers, Leon Chism, Chris Cleveland, Richie Cochran, Nan Conway, Graham Cook, Bryan Cox, Stan Davis, Tom DeJarnette, David Dixon, Andrea Drury, Brooke Edgar.

1989 Senior Class and Faculty

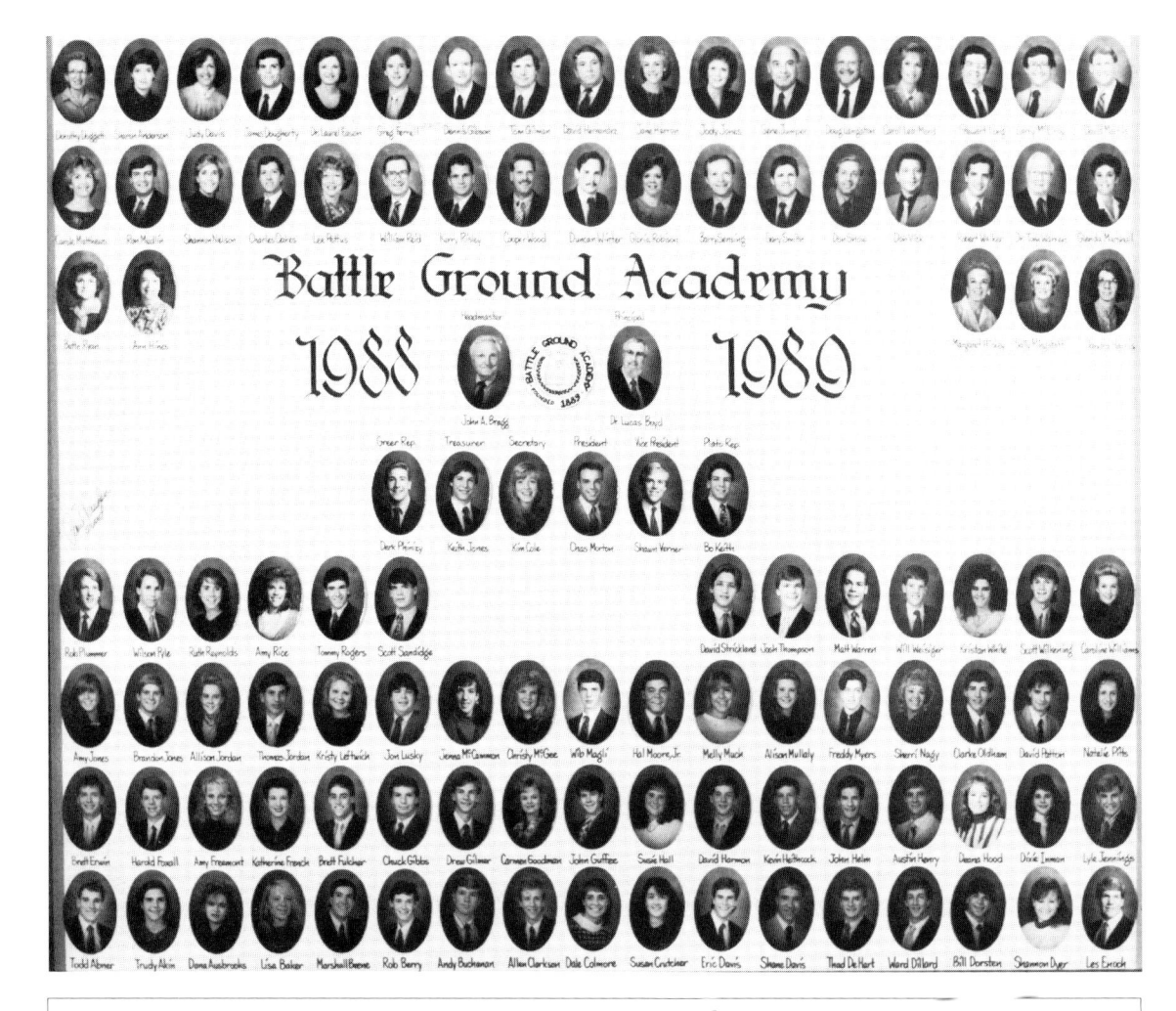

Top Row (Left to Right): Dorothy Doggett, Sharon Anderson, Judy Davis, James Dougherty, Dr. Laurel Eason, Greg Ferrell, Dennis Gibson, Tom Gilman, David Hernandez, Jane Herron, Jody Jones, Gene Jumper, Carol Lea-Mord, Stewart Long, Larry McElroy, David Martin. **Second Row (L to R):** Carole Matthews, Ron Medlin, Shannon Nelson, Charles Oakes, Lee Pettus, William Reid, Kerry Risley, Cooper Wood, Duncan Winter, Gloria Robison, Barry Sensing, Gary Smith, Don Snow, Don Vick, Robert Walker, Dr. Tom Warren, Glenda Marshall. **Third Row (L to R):** Bette Ryan, Ann Hines, Margaret Hickey, Sally Ringstaff, Sandra Harris. **Fourth Row (L to R):** John A. Bragg, Dr. Lucas Boyd. **Fifth Row (L to R):** Derk Phinizy, Keith Jones, Kim Cole, Chas Morton, Shawn Verner, Bo Keith. **Sixth Row (L to R):** Rob Plummer, Wilson Pyle, Ruth Reynolds, Amy Rice, Tommy Rogers, Scott Sandidge, David Strickland, Josh Thompson, Matt Warren, Will Weisiger, Kristan White, Scott Wilkening, Caroline Williams. **Seventh Row (L to R):** Amy Jones, Brandon Jones, Allison Jordan, Thomas Jordan, Kristy Leftwich, Jon Lusky, Jenna McCammon, Christy McGee, Wib Maglie, Hal Moore Jr., Melly Much, Alison Mullaly, Freddy Myers, Sherri Nagy, Clarke Oldham, David Patton, Natalie Pitts. **Eighth Row (L to R):** Brett Erwin, Harold Foxall, Amy Fremont, Katherine French, Brett Fulcher, Chuck Gibbs, Drew Gilmer, Carmen Goodman, John Guffee, Susie Hall, David Harmon, Kevin Heithcock, John Helm, Austin Henry, Deana Hood, Dixie Inman, Lyle Jennings. **Bottom Row (L to R):** Todd Abner, Trudy Akin, Dana Ausbrooks, Lisa Baker, Marshall Beene, Rob Berry, Andy Buchanan, Allen Clarkson, Dale Colmore, Susan Crutcher, Eric Davis, Shane Davis, Thad De Hart, Ward Dillard, Bill Dorsten, Shannon Dyer, Les Enoch.

A Monument to Education

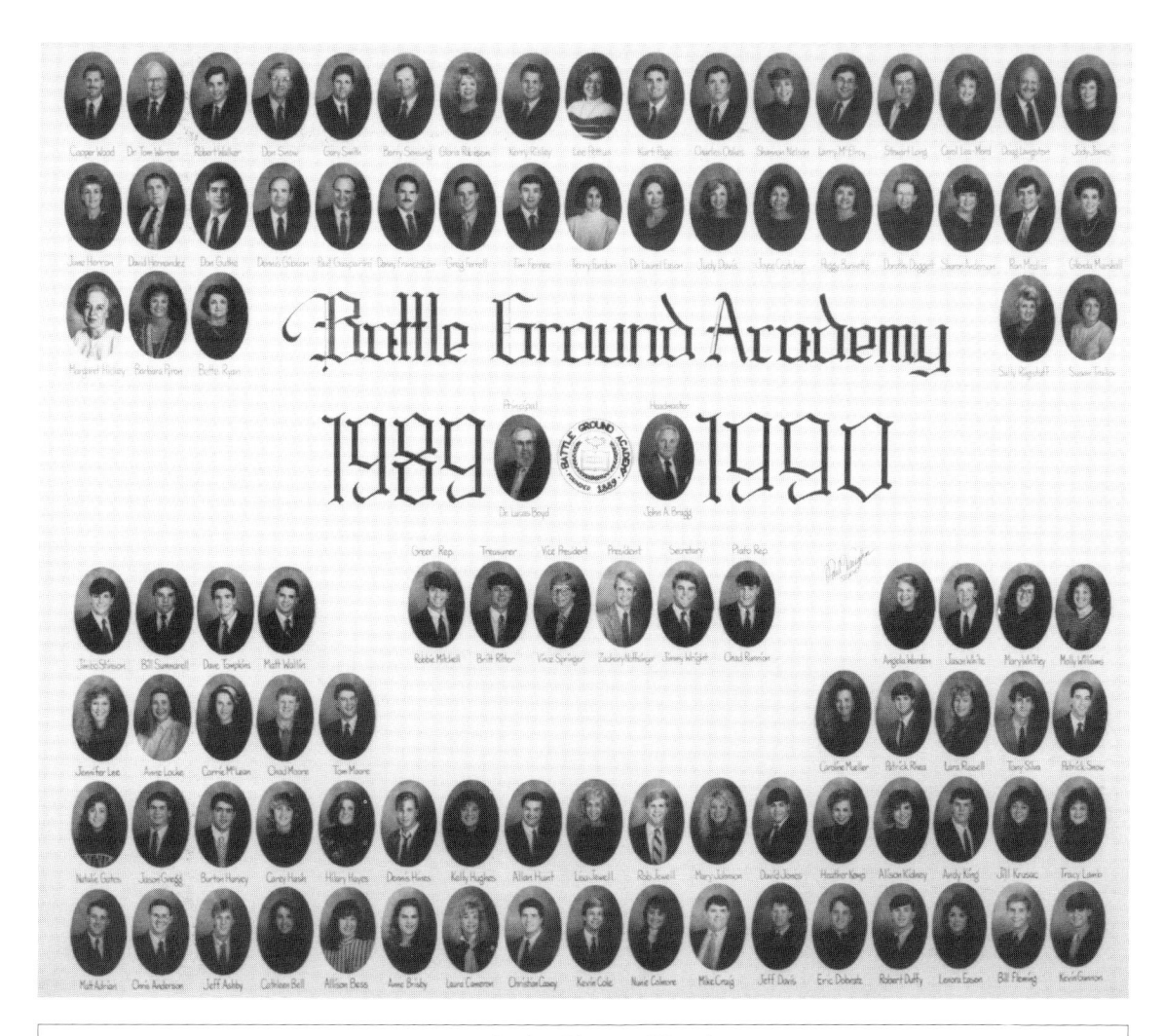

1990 Senior Class and Faculty

Top Row (Left to Right): Cooper Wood, Dr. Tom Warren, Robert Walker, Don Snow, Gary Smith, Barry Sensing, Gloria Robison, Kerry Risley, Lee Pettus, Kurt Page, Charles Oakes, Shannon Nelson, Larry McElroy, Stewart Long, Carol Lea-Mord, Doug Langston, Jody Jones. **Second Row (L to R):** Jane Herron, David Hernandez, Don Guthe, Dennis Gibson, Paul Gasparini, Danny Francescon, Greg Ferrell, Tim Ferree, Terry Fardon, Dr. Laurel Eason, Judy Davis, Joyce Crutcher, Peggy Burnette, Dorothy Doggett, Sharon Anderson, Ron Medlin, Glenda Marshall. **Third Row (L to R):** Margaret Hickey, Barbara Pyron, Bette Ryan, Sally Ringstaff, Susan Trailov. **Fourth Row (L to R):** Dr. Lucas Boyd, John A. Bragg. **Fifth Row (L to R):** Jimbo Stinson, Bill Summarell, Dave Tompkins, Matt Wallin, Robbie Mitchell, Britt Ritter, Vince Springer, Zachary Noffsinger, Jimmy Wright, Chad Runnion, Angela Warden, Jason White, Mary Whitley, Molly Williams. **Sixth Row (L to R):** Jennifer Lee, Anne Locke, Carrie McLeon, Chad Moore, Tom Moore, Caroline Mueller, Patrick Rhea, Lara Russell, Tony Silva, Patrick Snow. **Seventh Row (L to R):** Natalie Gates, Jason Gregg, Burton Harvey, Carey Hash, Hilary Hayes, Dennis Hines, Kelly Hughes, Allan Hunt, Lisa Jewell, Rob Jewell, Mary Johnson, David Jones, Heather Kemp, Alison Kidney, Andy King, Jill Krusac, Tracy Lamb. **Bottom Row (L to R):** Matt Adrian, Chris Anderson, Jeff Ashby, Cathleen Bell, Allison Bess, Anne Brisby, Laura Cameron, Christian Casey, Kevin Cole, Nunie Colmore, Mike Craig, Jeff Davis, Eric Dobratz, Robert Duffy, Lenora Eason, Bill Fleming, Kevin Gannon.

1991 Senior Class and Faculty

Top Row (Left to Right): Sharon Anderson, Tommy Anderson, Ken Atterholt, Peggy Burnette, Joyce Crutcher, Judy Davis, Sandra Davis, Dorothy Doggett, Terry Fardon, Tim Ferree, Greg Ferrell, Danny Francescon, Debbie Gallery, Paul Gasparini, Dennis Gibson, Don Guthe. **Second Row (L to R):** David Hernandez, Jane Herron, Margaret Hickey, Tina Huff, Jody Jones, Doug Langston, Carol Lea-Mord, Stewart Long, Glenda Marshall, Larry McElroy, Ron Medlin, Shannon Nelson, Charles Oakes, Kurt Page, Leigh Pettus, Barbara Pyron. **Third Row (L to R):** Sally Ringstaff, Kerry Risley, Barry Sensing, Gary Smith, Don Snow, Susan Trailov. **Fourth Row (L to R):** Robert Walker, Dr. Tom Warren, Dan Wilson, Cooper Wood. **Fifth Row (L to R):** Dr. Lucas Boyd, Dr. Ron Griffeth. **Sixth Row (L to R):** Beth Anderson, Celia Baxter, Aaron Benward, Kim Christian, Jay Clarkson, Elizabeth Crutcher, Vince Cusomato, Lydia Fan, Cheryl Fite, Lynn Foxalll, Lisa Gates, Anna Gregg, Eleanor Griffith, Scott Grover, Alan Hale. **Seventh Row (L to R):** Melinda Herrington, Mark Hobbs, Candace James, Tim Jefferson Jeff Jordan, Travis Lacey, Chris Miller, Bill Moore, Andy Moore, Mark Mortell, Melissa Neely, Jamie Nichol, Charlie Payne, Frank Prevatt, Charles Plummer, Matthew Ragan. **Bottom Row (L to R):** William Roberts, Lisa Schuur, Camille Sherry, Brad Spencer, John Stovall, Daniel Strickland, Chris Swearingen, Wendy VanLandingham, Kelley Vincent, Walker Vining, Sarah Vollmer, Jenna Werling, Brian Whitaker, Jennifer White, Taylor White, Doug Wilkening.

A Monument to Education

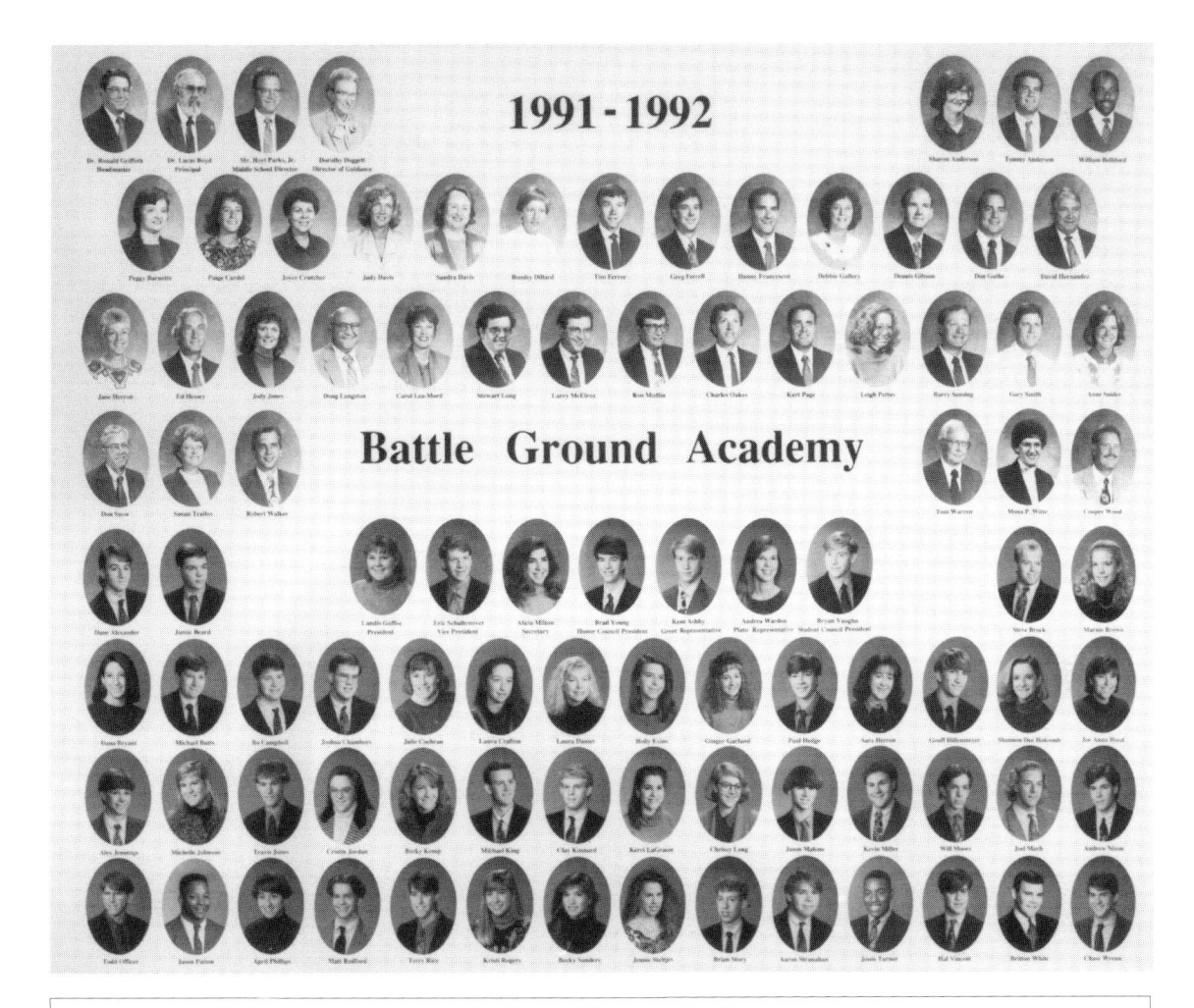

1991-1992 Battle Ground Academy

1992 Senior Class and Faculty

Top Row (Left to Right): Dr. Ronald Griffeth, Dr. Lucas Boyd, Mr. Hoyt Parks Jr., Dorothy Doggett, Sharon Anderson, Tommy Anderson, William Belliford. **Second Row (L to R):** Peggy Burnette, Paige Cardel, Joyce Crutcher, Judy Davis, Sandra Davis, Bondsy Dillard, Tim Ferree, Greg Ferrell, Danny Francescon, Debbie Gallery, Dennis Gibson, Don Guthe, David Hernandez. **Third Row (L to R):** Jane Herron, Ed Hessey, Jody Jones, Doug Langston, Carol Lea-Mord, Stewart Long, Larry McElroy, Ron Medlin, Charles Oakes, Kurt Page, Leigh Pettus, Barry Sensing, Gary Smith, Anne Snider. **Fourth Row (L to R):** Don Snow, Susan Trailov, Robert Walker, Tom Warren, Mona P. Witte, Cooper Wood. **Fifth Row (L to R):** Dane Alexander, Jamie Beard, Landis Guffee, Eric Schultenover, Alicia Milton, Brad Young, Kent Ashby, Andrea Warden, Bryan Vaughn, Steve Brock, Marnie Brown. **Sixth Row (L to R):** Dana Bryant, Michael Butts, Bo Campbell, Joshua Chambers, Julie Cochran, Laura Crafton, Laura Daniel, Holly Evins, Ginger Garland, Paul Hedge, Sara Herron, Geoff Hillenmeyer, Shannon Dee Holcomb, Joe Anna Hood. **Seventh Row (L to R):** Alex Jennings, Michelle Johnson, Travis Jones, Cristin Jordan, Becky Kemp, Michael King, Clay Kinnard, Kerri LaGrasse, Chrissy Long, Jason Malone, Kevin Miller, Will Moore, Joel Much, Andrew Nixon. **Bottom Row (L to R):** Todd Officer, Jason Patton, April Phillips, Matt Redford, Terry Rice, Kristi Rogers, Becky Sanders, Jennie Steltjes, Brian Story, Aaron Stranahan, Jessie Turner, Hal Vincent, Britton White, Chase Wrenn.

1993 Senior Class and Faculty

Top Row (Left to Right): Sharon Anderson, Tommy Anderson, William Belliford, Peggy Burnette, Paige Cardel, Andrew Carter, Joyce Crutcher, Sandra Davis, Bondsy Dillard, Greg Ferrell, Debbie Gallery, Dennis Gibson, Don Guthe, David Hernandez, Jane Herron, Ed Hessey, Jody Jones, Doug Langston, Steve Lape, Carol Lea-Mord, Stewart Long. **Second Row (L to R):** Larry McElroy, Ron Medlin, Tim Moore, Charles Oakes, Kurt Page, Leigh Pettus, Barry Sensing, Gary Smith, Anne Snider, Don Snow, Judy Speulda, Susan Trailov, Robert Walker, Dr. Tim Warren, Mona Witte, Cooper Wood. **Third Row (L to R):** Hoyt Parks Jr., Dr. Ronald H. Griffeth, Michael Franks, Brent Bowman, Donnie Decker, Sara Neff, Hamilton Bowman, Chris Perutelli, Dr. Lucas Boyd, Dorothy Doggett. **Fourth Row (L to R):** Keith Wanzeck, Les Whitley, Brandon Wood. **Fifth Row (L to R):** Murry Kraft, David Lackey, Stacy Lamb, Sarita Lobo, Clark McEwen, Cooper Magli, Jason Miller, Tonja Minter, Andy Moody, Rachel Mosher, Lea Murphy, Ragan Nichols, Mary Plummer, Bill Ritter, Shelley Roberts, Jenny Rodgers, Vall Ross, Jason Shull, Cris Stutts, Amy Sweeney, Will Taylor. **Bottom Row (L to R):** Aaron Anderson, Ben Bolton, Jason Brandon, Travis Burton, Rob Coleman, Rob Coppedge, Mark Cusomato, Bond Dillard, Jennifer Fleming, Steven Fleming George Foy, Tiffy Gillespie, Jeff Goodwin, Sarah Gracey, Steve Greer, Stephen Harvey, Andrew Herrington, Laura Hoos, John Jacobson, Laurie King, Brandon Kinnard.

A Monument to Education

1994 Senior Class and Faculty

Top Row (Left to Right): Sharon Anderson, Tommy Anderson, William Belliford, Peggy Burnette, Doug Cook, Joyce Crutcher, Sandra Davis, Bondsy Dillard, Gretchen Eisenhauer, Greg Ferrell, Debbie Gallery, Dennis Gibson, Don Guthe, David Hernandez, Jane Herron, Ed Hessey. **Second Row (L to R):** Mary Jane Holliday, Jody Jones, Mitchell Karnes, Doug, Langston, Steven Lope, Carol Lea-Mord, Stewart Long, Larry McElroy, Ron Medlin, Tim Moore, Brad Meyers, Charles Oakes, Kurt Page, Leigh Pettus, Barry Sensing, Gary Smith. **Third Row (L to R):** Anne Snider, Don Snow, Judy Speulda, Susan Trailov, Hoyt Parks, Dr. Ron Griffeth, Dr. Lucas Boyd, Dorothy Doggett, Robert Walker, Dr. Tom Warren, Jennifer Williams, Mona Witte. **Fourth Row (L to R):** Will Sharp, Benjamin Stranahan, Kelly Strasser, O. J. Fleming, Brent Jones, Christy Church, Nikki Hines, Jaime Simms, Scott Perkinson, Will Sweeny, Jeffrey Vanlandingham, Carrie White, Scott Womack. **Fifth Row (L to R):** Victoria Martocci, Brad McClanahan, Scott Meece, Jay Moore, Jessica Meyer, Berkeley Nance, Jason Nicoro, Katie Porleji, Andrew Peercy, Seth Pettus, Rachel Pilkinton, Lisa Quillman, Anne Ridley, Jimmy Roberts, Wesley Russell, Sara Schultenover. **Sixth Row (L to R):** Bob Freeman, Michael Garland, Ashley Gentry, Laura Gilmer, Noel Glasgow, Will Graham, Alex Gregg, Rachel Grissom, Rill Harlan, Kevin Herrington, Chris Hillinmeyer, Farrar Hood, Craig Hoover, Currier Howard, Nate Johnson, Brian Jordan. **Bottom Row (L to R):** Kim Armfield, Jim Bass, Bill Beech, Megan Behan, Ashley Burnett, Amanda Christian, Jerry Colley, Erica Cude, Whitney Cunningham, Heather Davis, Jason Durmavont, Chris Edwards, Aaron Ferrell, Fran Fite, Shawne Fitzgerald, Shannon Forbes.

1995 Senior Class and Faculty

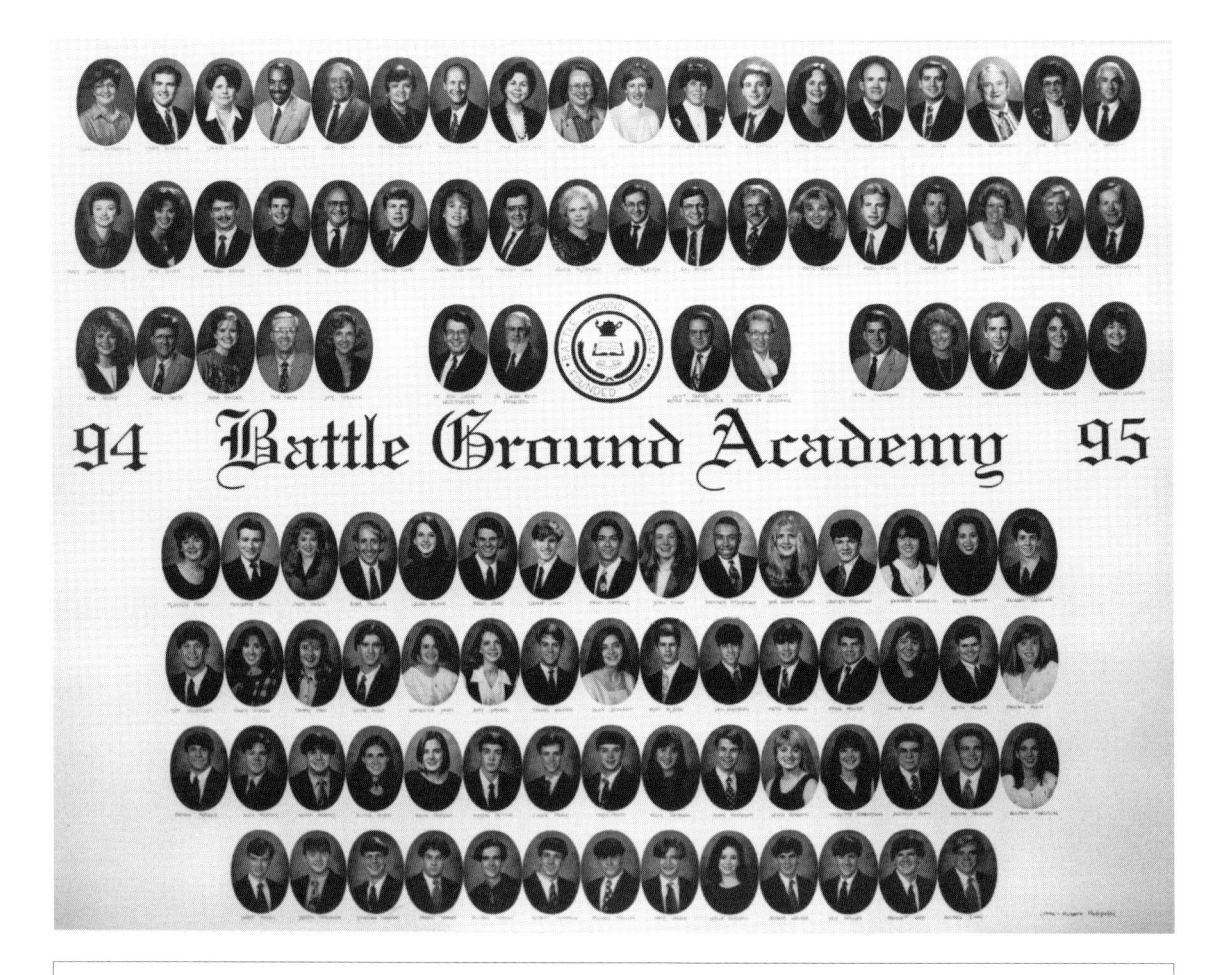

Top Row (Left to Right): Sharon Anderson, Tommy Anderson, Donna Baker, William Belliford, Gary Brock, Peggy Burnette, Matt Callihan, Joyce Crutcher, Sandra Davis, Bondsy Dillard, Gretchen Eisenhauer, Greg Ferrell, Debbie Gallery, Dennis Gibson, Don Guthe, David Hernandez, Jane Herron, Ed Hessey. **Second Row (L to R):** Mary Jane Holliday, Judy Jones, Mitchell Karnes, Kris Klausner, Doug Langston, Steve Lape, Carol Lea-Mord, Stewart Long, Wanda McDonald, Larry McElroy, Ron Medlin, Tim Moore, Beth Morton, Brad Myers, Charles Oakes, Leigh Pettus, Doug Phelps, Barry Sensing. **Third Row (L to R):** Kim Shore, Gary Smith, Anne Snider, Don Snow, Judy Speulda, Dr. Ron Griffeth, Dr. Lucas Boyd, Hoyt Parks Jr., Dorothy Doggett, Peter Thurmond, Susan Trailov, Robert Walker, Susan White, Jennifer Williams. **Fourth Row (L to R):** McKenzie Baker, Benjamin Ball, Cindi Beech, Adam Beeler, Laura Blake, Brad Camp, Wayne Creel, Brad Cumming, Jessi Dunn, Brodney Fitzgerald, Jane Anne Franks, Harvey Freeman, Jennifer Harrell, Kelly Harris, Michael Hassler. **Fifth Row (L to R):** Tutt Hightower, Haley Hinson, Tammy Hood, Kevin Hunt, Katherine Jones, Amy Joyner, Daniel Kinder, Alice Leonard, Matt McAfee, Josh Masters, Seth Maxwell, Eran Miller, Holly Miller, Keith Miller, Braden Moon. **Sixth Row (L to R):** Bryan Mosher, Alex Murphy, Woods Murphy, Alissa Myer, Kelly Parsons, Aaron Pettus, Chuck Pierce, Trey Pratt, Kelly Rayburn, Adam Reynolds, Leigh Roberts, Suzette Robertson, Andrew Ross, Mason Sellers, Allison Shelton. **Bottom Row (L to R):** Jared Shull, Jarron Springer, Jonathan Swenson, Brent Thomas, Michael Thomas, Robert Thompson, Michael Trailov, Matt Unger, Leslie Varnell, Robert Walker, Joey Wollas, Bennett Wood, Andrew Zinn.

Appendices

A. Articles 223
B. Diploma and Dormitory 226
C. Commencement Day Announcement 227
D. Season Football Pass/Poster 228
E. Advertisement 229
F. Remembrances 230

Appendix A
Articles

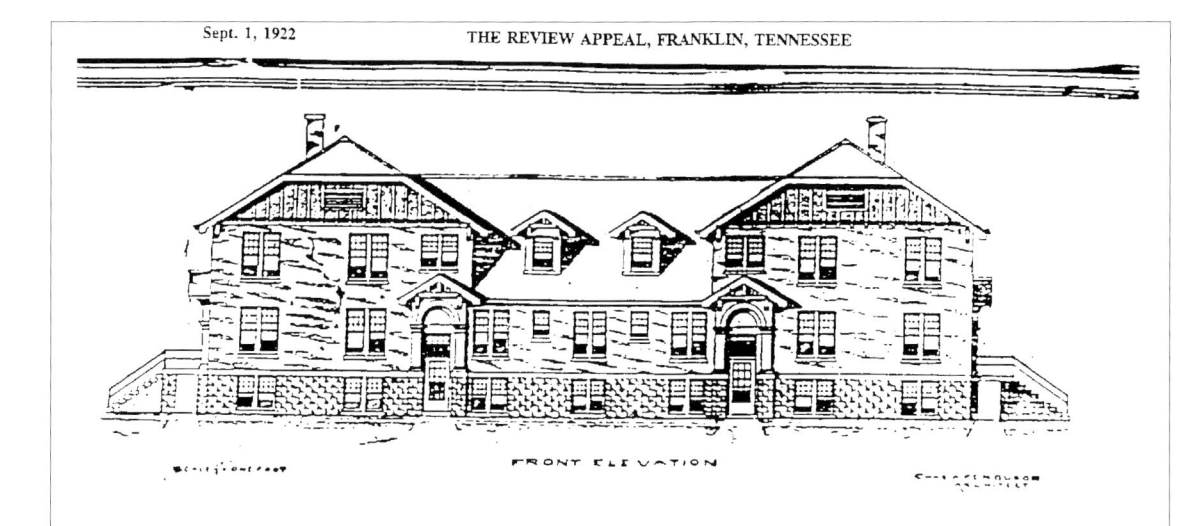

Sept. 1, 1922   THE REVIEW APPEAL, FRANKLIN, TENNESSEE

FRONT ELEVATION

The New Dormitory of the Peoples School
Battle Ground Academy, Franklin, Tenn.

Several new and interesting features distinguish this building from most others of its kind. The dining room, bath rooms and supervising teachers' quarters are all placed in the center, where they will be most easily accessible to every boy. At the same time, they divide each floor into two distinct groups of bedrooms, thus making for increased quiet, orderliness and studiousness. Each bedroom has its table with bookshelves, its closet and its chest of drawers, all solidly built-in and attractively finished. In the bathrooms perfect cleanliness is secured by the tiled floors and hard, smooth, waterproof plaster on all walls and partitions. The absolute straight exterior lines make for the greatest economy of space and construction cost, while at the same time giving the greatest amount of light and air to each room. The building faces east, giving half the day's sunlight to every room.

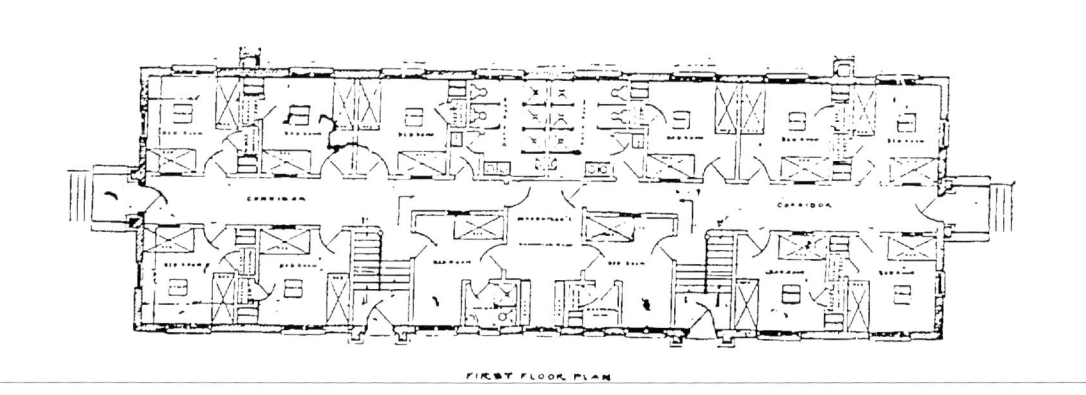

FIRST FLOOR PLAN

Now Is the Time

Compared with other schools, Battle Ground Academy is considered to be more or less conservative. It has many traditions and customs that it will not break unless the most extraordinary circumstances demand it.

Ever since the founding of this fine old institution, there never has been a step taken toward coercing a student into taking military training. It was not deemed wise by the faculty to have the boys learn army tactics.

Now, the situation is different. The faculty has decided to give as much aid as possible in the war effort. No sooner had war been declared than Professor Briggs announced that Battle Ground would do its part toward preparing to meet the aggressor.

Under the leadership of expert militarists, the boys of B.G.A. have been instructed as to the fundamentals of marching, assembling rifles, and executing commands. They have responded well. It is a familiar sight to see an older student explaining some detail to the younger boys, who have not quite grasped the question at hand.

If the hearty response of the boys in regard to their training is typical of the youth of America, we cannot help but win this war.

—from the *Cannon Ball*
March 10, 1912

To Our Friends and Patrons

Battle Ground Academy,
Franklin, Tenn., June 28, 1922

We are under many obligations to you for the generous assistance which has made possible the erection of our new dormitory. It not only will bring enlarged patronage, and thereby enable us to offer larger and better facilities to our students, but the feeling it gives to both teachers and students that they have the backing and confidence of the community will give them new spirit and enthusiasm in their work, and greatly improve the morale of the school.

My teachers are preparing themselves to give better service than ever. Mr. Beasley, who will teach full time next year, is now doing summer work at Emory University with this end in view; and Mr. J. Oren Davis, as soon as the dormitory campaign is over, will resume his work at Peabody.

We all feel that the school has never had a fairer prospect for better work in all lines. We shall appreciate all you can do to bring it the largest and best patronage it has ever had. A good word from you to the right man at the right time will mean more than all we can say for ourselves.

We thank you for saying it, and will do all in our power to make it good.

Sincerely,
R. G. Peoples

—from the *Review Appeal*
Franklin, Tennessee, June 19, 1922

Everbright, Fine Old Home Is Being Razed Here

One of the most historic and finest of Williamson County's old-time colonial homes, "Everbright," built by John D. Bennett in 1840, is being dismantled and its dozens of doors, windows, and hundreds of thousands of bricks will be offered for sale to the general public by H. J. Potts, contractor, who is in charge of razing the structure.

Many gala affairs, attended by the beaux and belles of bygone days, have been in the spacious halls and rooms of this fine old home, and its passing will cause a bit of sadness to scores of the older residents who have enjoyed old-time Southern hospitality within its doors. As bit by bit the razing work is done, one looks and listens for the strains of "The Beautiful Blue Danube," the master waltz of all the ages, to come floating thru the air as in days of yore. "Everbright" was built on a high hill just off the Jackson Highway, south of Franklin. The woodwork was entirely of yellow poplar and the walls are four thicknesses of brick. It is estimated that some 300,000 bricks will be obtained by those in charge of razing the two-story house. An addition, the eastern wing, was built by Mrs. R. L. C. Bostick a number of years after the Bennett main structure was erected.

On two occasions "Everbright" was used as a school by students of Battle Ground Academy when the main building was lost by fire—once under the Mooney administration and once when R. G. Peoples was headmaster.

—from the *Review Appeal*
January 16, 1936

BGA Bell Has Unique History

In removing the tower from the gymnasium at Battle Ground Academy after it was struck by lightning, a very handsome bell inscribed in Spanish was also removed. It will be recalled doubtless by many that the bell was a gift from Col. John Parke, a former resident of Franklin (the son of the late Dr. Parke), who is a distinguished retired army officer of whom Franklin is justly proud, residing now at Portland, Oregon.

The Bell was sent by Colonel Parke from the Philippine Islands as a gift to Battle Ground Academy when the gymnasium was erected and should be a source of pride to every citizen of Williamson County. It will, no doubt, be reinstalled at BGA and its clear tones be used to call many youths for years to come to the historic BGA walls of learning.

—from the *Review Appeal*
July 23, 1925

Appendix B
Diploma and Dormitory

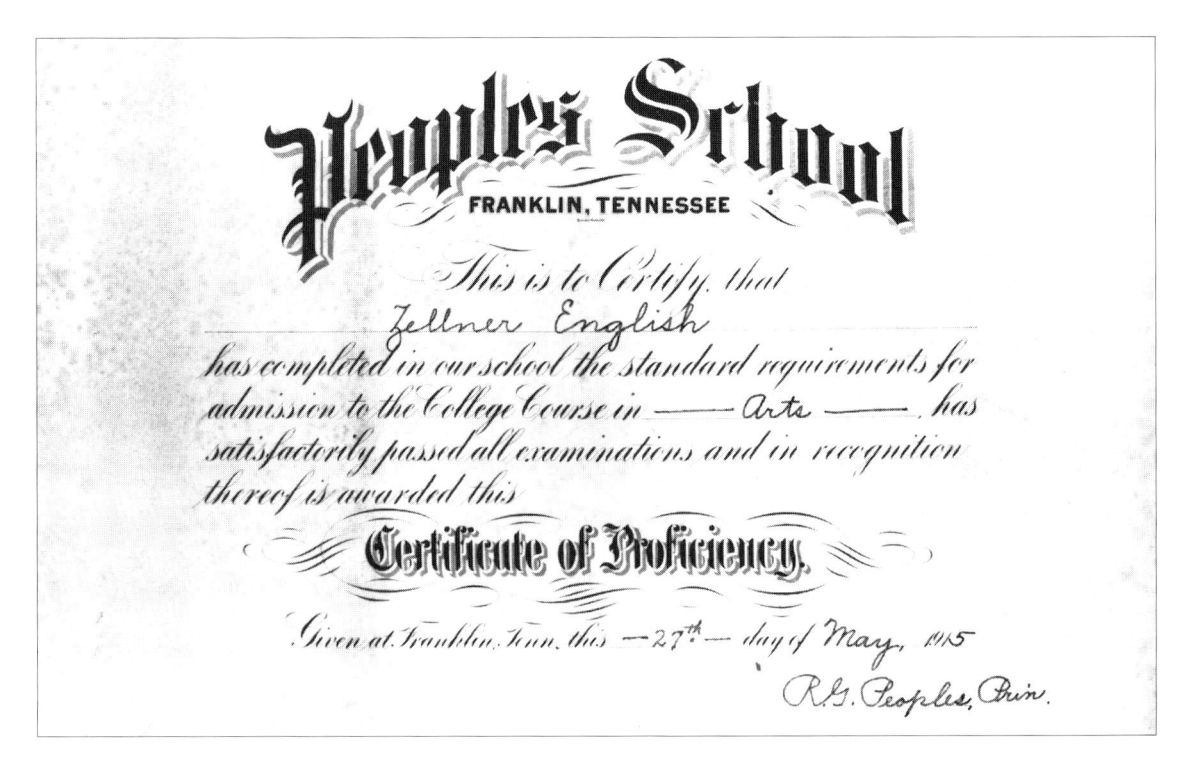

Appendix C
Commencement Day Announcement

Commencement Day
Battle Ground Academy
June 1, 1922

PROGRAM

INVOCATION .... Rev. R. H. Hodgous

MUSIC

ADDRESS .... Rev. F. F. Shannon, D. D.

MUSIC

DELIVERY OF CERTIFICATES TO GRADUATES

CLASS ROLL

Jas H. Bowman, Jr.
George Nichol Britt
Evelyn Guffey Buford
Mary McEwen Floof
Gusto Jordan
John F. Joyce

Elizabeth Matthews
M. T. Menohorn
Sarah Elizabeth Neely
Daniel Hilary Roberts
Mabel Smith
Susie Caro Sugg

Appendix D
SEASON FOOTBALL PASS/POSTER

FOOT BALL

$2 SEASON TICKET $2

HOME GAMES

Oct. 9	Hume-Fogg	Nov. 6	Wallace
Oct. 23	Goodlettsville	Nov. 13	B. & H.
Nov. 20	C. M. A.		

BATTLE GROUND ACADEMY

B. G. A. Yells

1. B. G. A. Rah, rah,
B. G. A. rah, rah,
B. G. A. hurrah!
B. G. A. hurrah!
Hurrah, hurrah,
B. G. A. rah,
B. G. A. ray,
B. G. A., B. G. A.,
She's O. K.

Appendix E

Advertisement

The Review-Appeal, Franklin, Tennessee   THURSDAY, May 24, 1928

"Let's Count Our Blessings"

We think that one of the greatest blessings we can count is the fact that Franklin and Williamson County possess

THE BATTLE GROUND ACADEMY

While we are looking for new enterprises in our community, and should have them, let's don't overlook the greatest factory that we, or any other community has, and that is

"THE MAKING OF MEN OUT OF BOYS"

We Think that The Greatest Factory is the Battle Ground Academy

We know that the Battle Ground Academy with its present faculty is second to no school in the country. We believe that the opportunity of sending boys to Battle Ground Academy and having them associated with the present faculty, is a privilege that any parent should appreciate and one that all who have the opportunity, should take advantage of.

The faculty at Battle Ground Academy, is superior to most faculties, equal to any and second to none. The physical equipment is ample and well kept.

With absolutely no reservations, we believe that Prof. Geo. I. Briggs, the principal of Battle Ground Academy, is the foremost man in his line in the country, and Williamson County and Franklin are glad to claim him not only as a native but as a resident of our community. We believe that Prof. Geo. I. Briggs is the greatest asset that Williamson County and Franklin has had in a generation, and while we believe that many of our people feel and realize this, we do not believe that our county is supporting this school to the fullest.

Let's Do It: Prof. Briggs has associated with him a wonderfully effective faculty, not only as to scholarly attainments and effective teaching ability, but effective in their ability to carry the right ideas and ideals to the student. The association of your boy with these people will leave an impression on his life that will be a wonderful benefit.

The Faculty:

PROF. GEO. I. BRIGGS, Principal	A. B. Southwestern University
GLENN M. EDDINGTON	A. M. Davidson College
JAMES BUFORD	A. B. Princeton University
JAMES M. FARRELL	A. B. Davidson College
REV. CHAS. E. HAWKINS	A. B. Vanderbilt University
R. W. HUGHES	Peabody College
MRS. PRYOR LILLIE	Curry School of Expression
MRS. MARY B. GIBSON	Matron and House Mother

Let's get this school filled to overflowing the coming year.

Let's tell your neighbor and write to your friends at a distance, and let's get them to send their boys back to Franklin. You Will Be Doing Your Friend a Favor.

The First Bank & Trust Company, FRANKLIN, TENNESSEE.

Resources more Than $296,000.00

Appendix F
Remembrances

This beautiful blue and silver bus was the first ever owned by BGA.

Emma "Mama" Haynes, BGA housemother, 1938–1960.

Endnotes

Chapter One: The Battle of Franklin

1. James Lee McDonough and Thomas L. Connelly, *Five Tragic Hours* (Knoxville: The University of Tennessee Press, 1983).
2. Thomas L. Connelly, *Autumn of Glory: The Army of Tennessee, 1862–1865* (Baton Rouge: n.p., 1971): 490.
3. Phillip Thomas Tucker, "The First Missouri Brigade at the Battle of Franklin." *The Brigadier*, Newsletter of the Franklin Memorial Association vol. 3, no. 1 (Spring/Summer/Fall 1993).
4. McDonough and Connelly, *Five Tragic Hours*.
5. *Great Battles of the Civil War* (New York: Gallery Books, 1988): 507–513.
6. McDonough and Connelly, *Five Tragic Hours*.
7. David R. Logsdon (comp.), *Eyewitnesses at the Battle of Franklin* (Nashville: Kettle Mills Press, 1991).
8. *Great Battles of the Civil War*.
9. Ibid.
10. Tucker, *Brigadier*.
11. Logsdon, *Eyewitnesses at the Battle of Franklin*.
12. McDonough and Connelly, *Five Tragic Hours*.
13. Logsdon, *Eyewitnesses at the Battle of Franklin*.
14. Williamson County Historical Society, vol. 21, p. 11.
15. Logsdon, *Eyewitnesses at the Battle of Franklin*.
16. Ibid.
17. Ibid.
18. McDonough and Connelly, *Five Tragic Hours*.
19. Logsdon, *Eyewitnesses at the Battle of Franklin*.
20. McDonough and Connelly, *Five Tragic Hours*.
21. Logsdon, *Eyewitnesses at the Battle of Franklin*.

22. Ibid.
23. Ibid.
24. Sue Berry and Martha Fuqua (comp.), *Homespun Tales* (Franklin: Territorial Press, 1989).
25. Virginia Bowman, *Historic Williamson County* (Franklin: Territorial Press, 1971): 128.

Chapter Two: We Baptize Today—BGA

26. Mary Trim Anderson, Williamson County Historical Society, vol. 7, p. 44.
27. Virginia Bowman, *Historic Williamson County*.
28. Ibid.
29. Ibid.

Chapter Three: Wall and Mooney School

30. Will Ward, "When Old Men Were Young," *The American Indian* (March 1930): 6.

Chapter Four: Mooney Moves—Peoples Arrives

31. Virginia Bowman, *Historic Williamson County*.

Chapter Twelve: Jubilation Celebration

32. Cris Perkins, *One Hundred Years Of BGA Football* (Franklin: Hillsboro Press, 1994).
33. Ibid.
34. Ibid.

Index

Photo page numbers are in bold type.

A

Abbott, Hal, 113, **209**
Abbott, Terri, **210**
Abercrombie, Eugene, **170**
Abernathy, Bill, **190**
Abernathy, Bob, **206**
Abner, Todd, **214**
Adair, Billy, **190**
Adams, Dillard, **208**
Adams, Jeff, **204**
Adams, John, 13
Adams, Roby, **212**
Adger, John, **186**
Adrian, Matt, **215**
Agee, Ivy Jr., **166**
Akers, Ward, **185**
Akin, Kris, **212**
Akin, Frank T., **173**
Akin, Fred C., **178**
Akin, J. B., 77, **79**, 82, 85, 87, **88**, 89, 95, 98, **99**, 100, 108, **151**, 168–201
Akin, James, **157**, **162**
Akin, Jimmy, **163**
Akin, Kernan Jr., **161**
Akin, R. V., **154**
Akin, Robert, 97, **192**
Akin, Robert Millard, **152**
Akin, Spike, **186**
Akin, Trudy, **214**
Akin, Vance, **182**
Akin, William Burnett "Bunny," 100, **176**, **185–187**, **194–198**
Alcorn, John, **203**
Alden, Dale, **205**
Alexander, Billy, **206**
Alexander, Dane, **217**
Alexander, Dave, **160**
Alexander, Ferrell Jr., **170**
Alexander, Guy, **158**
Alexander, H., **198**
Alexander, Owen, **175**
Alexander, P., **198**
Alexander, T. H., **169**
Alford, David, **211**
Allen, Bailey, **196**
Allen, Bill, **206**
Allen, Bob, **163**
Allen, Brett, **202**
Allen, Danny C., 100, **194–195**
Allen, Don, **190**
Allen, Jay, **205**
Allen, Linda, 104, 108, **199–204**
Allen, Nancy H., **194–200**
Allen, Vaughh, **191**
Alley, Abner, **185**
Alley, Abner Wryland, **153**
Alley, Richard, **209**
Alley, Roy, **159**, **187**
Alley, Roy F., **195–196**
Alley, Sheila, 110, **207**
Allison, Jeff, **209**
Alpaugh, Terry, **192**
Ambrose, Henry, **196**
Amis, John E., **134**
Ammerman, Hugh T. Jr., **179**
Ammons, Andrew, **207**
Anastas, Robert, 115
Anderson, Aaron, **218**
Anderson, Allen, 96, **96**, **193**
Anderson, Beth, **216**
Anderson, Bill, **182**
Anderson, Billy, **196**
Anderson, Bob, **194**, **206**
Anderson, Chris, **215**
Anderson, Cragin, **203**
Anderson, Edgar B., **135–136**
Anderson, Elbridge E., **146**
Anderson, Gary, **186**
Anderson, Gordon, **166**
Anderson, Helen, **138**
Anderson, Holmes, **131**
Anderson, J. H., **132**, **138**
Anderson, Jack, **144**
Anderson, Jeff, **105**, **106**, **204**
Anderson, Joe, **151**
Anderson, John, **193**
Anderson, Keith, **204**
Anderson, Leean, 108
Anderson, M. J., **129**
Anderson, R., **197**
Anderson, Rachel, **148**
Anderson, Rob, **194**
Anderson, Sharon, 116, **209–220**
Anderson, Tommy, **211**, **216– 220**
Anderton, Casey, **206**
Andrews, Capers, **162**
Anglin, Burnice, **178**
Anglin, Matt, **206**
Anglin, Randy, **201**
Armfield, Kim, **219**
Armistead, Bill, **194**
Armistead, Bob, **210**
Armistead, G. H. Jr., **133**
Armistead, George H. Sr., 42
Armistead, Graham, **144**
Armistead, Hunter, **167**
Armistead, Louise, **140**
Armistead, L. H., **138**
Armistead, Leonard H. Jr., **165**
Armistead, Parkes, **136**
Armisted, Bob, **196**
Army of Tennessee, 5–6, 9, 14
Arnett, Robert G., **178**
Arnold, Dick, **185**
Arnold, Dickie, **192**
Arrendale, Tommy, **183**
Ashby, Jeff, **214**
Ashby, Kent, **217**
Ashcraft, Tommy, **194**
Ashland City High School, 99
Ashworth, Bill, **188**
Ashworth, Billy, **163**
Ashworth, Charles, **183**
Ashworth, Donald, **177**
Ashworth, Elbert, **178**
Ashworth, Harold E., **176**
Ashworth, Henry, **153**
Ashworth, Jeddie, **154**
Askew, Peter, **165**
Atterholt, Ken, **216**
Atwood, Robert, **195**
Ausbrooks, Dana, **214**
Austin, Hilton Jr., **193**
Austin, William G., **155**
Averett, John, **199**
Avery, David, **205**
Aydelott, Frank, **131**

B

Baasham, Jim, **190**
Bachelda, Albert, **204–209**
Bafundo, Michael, **207**
Bafundo, Philip, **205**
Bafundo, Thomas, **208**
Baggette, Wade, **202**
Bailey, Clay, **207**
Bailey, Kent, **206**
Bainbridge, Thomas Norton, **184**
Baird, Grimes, **207**
Baker, Bill, **162**
Baker, Donna, **220**
Baker, Lisa, **214**
Baker, McKenzie, **220**
Baker, Robert C., **196–197**
Baldree, Michael, **213**
Baldridge, T., **197**
Baldwin, Elliot, **179**
Bales, Everett H., **150**
Ball, Benjamin, **220**
Ball, Chris, 106, **206**
Ball, Edgar, **157**
Ball, R., **197**
Ban, Christopher, **210**
Barber, Michie M., **179**
Barker, Win, **208**
Barksdale, Robin, **188**
Barksdale, Virginia, **198**
Barnett, A., **132**
Barnes, Melville, **187**
Barnes, Steve, **190**
Barney, James E., **174**
Barnhill, W. R., **129**
Barnott, Allen, 44
Barrett, Mark, 104, **105**, **201**
Barrett, Rodney, 112, **209**
Barrier, C. W., **136–137**
Bartlett, John, **200**
Bartlett, Steve, **204**
Bass, Buddy, **206**
Bass, Francis A., **167**
Bass, Jim, **219**
Bass, Mitzi, **199–201**
Bastone, Gina, 110
Basone, Laureen, **211**
Bate, William B., 23
Bateman, Andy, **208**
Bateman, C. H., **135–136**
Bates, Mitch, **203**
Bates, Raleigh, **205**
Bates, Travis, **204**
Bates, Wilson, **209**
Batson, Amy, **210**
Batson, Christoper, **212**
Battle, B., **198**
Battle Ground Breeze, 54, **55**

233

Battle of Franklin, 5, 17, 20–21, 23
Baugh, Charlie, 205
Baugh, Frank, 200
Baugh, Harriette M., 144
Baugh, John, 191
Baugh, Joseph, 189
Baugh, Joseph B., 20
Baugh, Kelly, 110, 208
Baugh, Kord, 211
Bauman, Albert, 163
Baxter, Celia, 202
Baylor School, Chattanooga, Tennessee, 62, 79
Beach, Ted A., 92, 188
Beadle, Larry, 187
Beadle, Mickey, 191
Beadle, Skip, 194
Beaman, Barbara, 91
Beard, B., 197
Beard, Jamie, 217
Beasley, A. W., 147
Beasley, Andy, 200
Beasley, Anne, 54, 56
Beasley, Bubbie, 188
Beasley, Charles, 191
Beasley, Craig, 139
Beasley, Earl, 176
Beasley, Emily, 138
Beasley, Frank, 188
Beasley, Fred W. Jr., 179
Beasley, Hartwell, 157
Beasley, Mrs. Hiram, 196
Beasley, Mrs. J. H., 195
Beasley, Jack, 201
Beasley, Jim, 181
Beasley, John S., 173
Beasley, Larry, 185
Beasley, Norene, 197–199
Beasley, Padge, 186
Beasley, Sarah Anne, 149
Beasley, Turman O., 141
Beasley, Wallis, 168
Beasley, Wilburn, 140
Becker, Billy, 166
Becker, Frank, 207
Beech, Bill, 219
Beech, Cindi, 220
Beeler, Adam, 220
Beeler, Dan, 205
Beeler, M., 197
Beene, Marshall, 214
Beesley, Jim, 191
Behan, Megan, 219
Behar, Moises, 181
Bell Buckle Lion's Bowl, 112
Bell, Cathleen, 215
Bell, Frank, 192
Bell, R. H., 137
Belliford, William, 121
Benedict, Buddy, 91, 185
Bennett, Alma Carter, 152
Bennett, Bill, 204
Bennett, George, 207
Bennett, Gerald, 174
Bennett, James Kilpatrick, 173
Bennett, Jim, 164
Bennett, John, 185–186
Bennett, John D., 43
Bennett, Rick, 195
Benson, David, 105, 201
Bentley, W., 197
Benward, Aaron, 216
Benz, Charley, 194
Benz, Edward W. Jr., 94, 189

Berry, Buck, 195
Berry, C. R., 20
Berry, David, 204
Berry, Dewees, 194
Berry, Douglas, 195
Berry, Rob, 214
Berry, S., 198
Berry, Tyler IV, 212
Berry, Tyler III, 79, 174
Berry, W., 197
Bervoets, Mike, 204
Bess, Allison, 215
Bethshare, W. Everette Jr., 178
Bethurum, Jeff, 186
Beziat, Charles, 187
Bibb, Julian, 200
Bibb, Lewis, 165
Bickley, Gray, 187
Bickley, J. M., 133
Big Harpeth River, 66
Biggs, Thomas E., 195–196
Billington, R. W., 34, 130
Billington, Wallace, 33
Billington, William, 165
Billington, William Jr., 197
Bingham, Herbert, 187
Binkley, Mike, 195
Biship, Chris, 187
Bissell, David, 191
Black, Bill, 167
Black, Bob, 163
Black, Nela Ree, 148
Blackburn, Clem, 171
Blackburn, Gideon, 18
Blackburn, Harry, 97, 194
Blackburn, Jim, 187
Blackman, Eddie, 190
Blake, David, 44, 131
Blake, Jacque, 211
Blake, Kelly, 207
Blake, Laura, 220
Blake, Tom, 44
Bland, David, 191
Blank, John, 207
Blank, Lawrence, 110, 208
Blank, Lee, 204
Blankenship, Allen, 212
Blankenship, Cordell, 174
Blankenship, Don, 176
Blankenship, Edgar, 176
Bledsoe, Bethany, 210
Blythe, Floyd, 44
Blythe, Shelton, 168
Boaz, Lowell, 148
Boaz, Lula Mai, 150
Boddie, Neil, 211
Boden, John, 209
Boden, Lea, 208
Boensch, Frank D., 179
Boensch, Richard Edmond, 184
Boice, Edmund W., 179
Boles, Dick, 186
Bolton, Ben, 218
Bolton High School, Memphis, Tennessee, 104
Bolton, Patti, 34, 130
Bond, Alex, 174
Bond, Anthony, 204
Bond, Leonard P., 142
Bond, Mattie, 151
Bond, Stephen, 201
Bond, Thomas, 150
Bone, Simon, 213
Booher, Bill, 192

Booker, Barry, 114, 210
Boone, Jay, 201
Borders, Tildon Pete, 159
Bostic, Alan, 203
Bostic, Rebecca, 43
Bostic, Richard, 43
Boswell, Wilbur, 159
Bourland, William, 27
Bowen, Marcia, 108, 200–204
Bowman, Brent, 218
Bowman, Hamilton, 218
Bowman, Jody, 190
Bowman, Joe, 147
Bowman, Kirk, 146
Boyd, John, 196
Boyd, Lucas A., 109, 205–211, 213–220
Boyd, T., 197
Boyd, Tommy, 203
Boyle, Bick, 204
Brackney, Bill, 203
Bradford, Bob, 171
Bradford, Scott, 207
Bradshaw, Bill L., 100, 186–193
Brady, Joe, 192
Brady, Thomas, 193
Bragg, John A., 88, 99, 100, 107–109, 115–117, 176–215
Brake, Kenneth Jr., 179
Bramlett, Church, 208
Branch, Rufus, 168
Branding, Ed, 196, 202–203
Brandon, Jason, 218
Brandon, Parkes, 191
Brantley, Sam Jack, 194
Braswell, Bill, 209
Bratton, Bob, 163–164
Bratton, Johnny, 159
Bratton, Randy, 196
Braun, C. B., 132
Bray, Pat, 94, 191
Breedlove, Billy, 182
Breedlove, Lawson, 181
Breese, Dorothy, 142
Breining, Herald, 150
Brent, Houston, 184
Brent, Todd, 207
Brevard, Mary, 141
Brevard, Minnie, 145
Brewer, Harold, 201
Brewer, Kayron, 213
Brick Week, 70
Bridges, M. S., 38
Briggs, Darren, 208
Briggs, George I., 58–59, 60, 62–63, 68, 71–72, 74, 77–78, 80, 130, 144, 151–153, 155–169
Briggs, George I. Gymnasium, 79
Briggs, Otie, 154
Brinkley, Jerry, 183
Brinton, Larry, 202
Brinton, Mike, 205
Brisby, Anne, 215
Britt, James, 151
Britt, Nichol, 147
Brittain, Leonard Jr., 164
Brittain, William, 171
Brock, Bob Jr., 176
Brock, Carey, 183
Brock, David, 188
Brock, Gary G., 197–220
Brock, Steve, 217
Bronaugh, S., 197
Brooks, Larry, 204

Brown, Allen Crockett, 184
Brown, Ben, 131
Brown, Bert, 190
Brown, Bill, 92, 100, 185, 188–191
Brown, C. H., 138
Brown, Charles, 115, 209
Brown, Dan, 191
Brown, David, 205
Brown, Doswell, 187
Brown, Elizabeth, 209
Brown, Enoch, 135
Brown, Enoch Sr., 42
Brown, Fred W. Jr., 179
Brown, George, 157–158
Brown, Greg, 202
Brown, Jimmy, 160
Brown, John, 196
Brown, John P. W. VI, 184
Brown, Larry, 186
Brown, M., 197
Brown, Marnie, 217
Brown, Noel, 182
Brown, Norman, 175
Brown, Paul, 191
Brown, Preston, 212
Brown, Ralph, 90, 91
Brown, S. Ralph, 179–187
Brown, Samuel A. Jr., 174
Brown, Sandy, 167
Brown, Tommy, 181
Brown, Walter, 157
Brown, William Henry, 55, 55
Browne, James G., 149
Browning, Ken, 203
Bruce, Frances, 154
Brumit, Don, 209
Bryan, Eugene, 158
Bryan, Felix, 209
Bryan, Harry Jr., 161
Bryan, Scott, 212
Bryan, William J., 182
Bryant, Burgess Orr, 152
Bryant, Dane, 217
Bryant, W. A., 158–161
Bryson, Dick, 167
Bubis, Gil, 102, 103, 198
Bubis, Larry, 102, 103, 198
Buchanan, Andy, 214
Buchanan, Carroll E., 135–136, 138
Buchanan, Felix G., 161
Buchanan, Gerald, 34, 129
Buchanan, Sam, 190
Buchman, Leslie, 159
Buckley, Ted, 161
Buckner, Henry, 202
Budslick, Paul, 195
Buford, Evelyn, 147
Buford, Farrell, 130
Buford, Frances Gordon, 145
Buford, G. R., 162–166, 171–175
Buford, Gaston, 150
Buford, James Leslie, 144, 153
Buford, Mrs. James, 88
Buford, L. W., 42
Buford, R. M., 129
Buis, Charles E. Jr., 176
Buntin, D., 197
Burchard, John, 34, 130
Burchett, Dane, 210
Burchett, Jimmy, 183
Burchett, Stacy, 110–111
Burke, Betsy, 209
Burke, Russell, 149
Burke, Vance, 159

Burnett, Ashley, **219**
Burnett, Bill, **183**
Burnett, Bob, **175**
Burnette, Chip, **199**
Burnette, Peggy, **215–220**
Burns, C. S., **157–158**
Burns, Pete, **204**
Burris, George W., **27**
Burris, L. C., **27**
Burrow, Dick, **171**
Burrow, Jeff, **205**
Burton, Balinda, **213**
Burton, Jim, **183**
Burton, Larry Jr., **180**
Burton, Mike, **192**
Burton, Peter, **201**
Burton, Sonia, **209**
Burton, Travis, **218**
Butler, Bill, **212**
Butler, Bo, **202**
Butter Bowl, Pulaski, Tennessee, 87, **104**, 112–113
Buttrey, Denson, **194**
Butts, David, **205**
Butts, Michael, **217**
Butts, Paul, **204**
Butts, Paul Thomas, **173**
Butts, William, **175**
Byrd, David, **193–196**
Byrd, James W. Jr., **176**
Byron, Charles E. III, **79**, **174**

C

Cady, James W., **189**
Cain, Bob, **183**
Cain, Jim, **201**
Cain, Robert, **201**
Cain, Scott, **209**
Caldwell, Harden, **201**
Caldwell, Jackie, **187**
Caldwell, Keith, **188**
Caldwell, Ken, **200**
Caldwell, Ricky, **200**
Callihan, Matt, **220**
Calvin, Buddy, **191**
Cameron, Don, **196**
Cameron, Laura, **215**
Cameron, Robert Marshall, **180**
Cameron, Tony, **205**
Camp, Brad, **220**
Campbell, Alfred, **183**
Campbell, Andrew, 18–19
Campbell, Archie, 98
Campbell, Bo, **217**
Campbell, Brother, **96**, 96–97
Campbell, Curt, **210**
Campbell, E. B., 42
Campbell, Florence, 54
Campbell, H., **197**
Campbell, James H., **146**
Campbell, Patrick, 18–19
Campbell School, 18–19
Campbell, Stewart, **149**
Campbell, Stewart Jr., **193**
Campbell, W. G., **190**
Campbell, William Winder, **180**
Camp Hy Lake, Queback, Tennessee, 81, **84**, 85, 88
Camstra, William A., **176**
Cannon Ball, 54, 60, 64, **66**, 68, 70, 77, 123
Cannon, Brown, **168**
Cannon, Buck, **164**
Cannon, Ed, **205**
Cannon, Henry, **161**
Cannon, Newton, 43, **192**
Cannon, William L., **178**
Cannon, William Perkins, **130**
Cantey, Rod, **185**
Caplinger, Billy, **187**
Caplinger, Paul, **202**
Capps, Walter Reed, **175**
Caradja, Princess Catherine, 92
Cardel, Paige, **217–218**
Carden, Matthew, **201**
Carillon, Bruce, **203**
Carl, O. B. Jr., **152**
Carmichael, Dan, **202**
Carnton Mansion, 15
Carothers, Elizabeth, **154**
Carothers, J. C., 42
Carr, Joe Cordell Jr., **184**
Carruth, Weldon, **164**
Carter, Andrew, **218**
Carter, Bobby, **173**
Carter, Edward M., **135**
Carter, Fountain Branch, 7, 9, 13–14
Carter, Francis, 14
Carter, Gene, **189**
Carter, Howard R., **135**
Carter, Jerry, **191**
Carter, John C., 12
Carter, Moscow, 7, 14–15, 19, 24
Carter, Rowell, **156**
Carter, Tod, 14, **15**
Cartwright, John, **106**, **205**
Carvajal, Felix, **170**
Cascade High School, 121
Casey, Christian, **215**
Casey, DeBow, **182**, **207**
Casey, Dudley E. Jr., **176**
Castle Heights Academy, Lebanon, Tennessee, 62, 79, 81
Cates, Thomas Burton Jr., **180**
Cathey, John, **203**
Cato, Bobby, **181**
Caton, James, **167**
Caton, Welch, **159**
Catron, Stephen D., **155**
Caudle, Fitzgerald R., **134**
Caudle, Irene, **133**
Caulkins, Stuart, **204**
Cauthen, Bill, **207**
Cauthen, Craig, **220**
Cave, Bill, **158**
Cawthon, Mary, **196**
Cayce, E. B. Jr., 42
Centennial, The, 119–120
Centre College, 25
Chaffin, Bill, **205**
Chaffin, Robert, **195**
Chaffin, S., **197**
Chalfant, Anna Gene, **209**
Chalfant, Lean, **110**
Chamberlain, Bill, **181**
Chambers, Joshua, **217**
Chambers, Stephen, **96**, **193**
Channell, Hugh, 44
Channell, P. V., 42
Chapman, Jimmy, **165**
Chapman, Ric, 114, **210**
Chapman, Robert, **174**
Chappell, J., **198**
Charron, Andy, **211**
Charron, Jimmy, **106**, **204**
Charron, John, **207**
Chase, Henry, **182**
Chatman, Tony E., **197**
Chattanooga Christian High School, 121
Chavers, Ashley, **213**
Cheairs, N. F., 33
Cheatham, Benjamin F., 8–9
Cheatham, Judy, **207– 208**
Cheek, Pickslay, **182**
Cheek, Robert S. II, **184**
Cherokee Indians, 27
Cherry, Amy, **212**
Cherry, Bill, **97**, **185**, **191–195**, **207**
Cherry, Bob, **201**
Cherry, William Earl, **180**
Cherry, Wink, **191**
Chickasaw Indian Nation, 26
Chickey, Joe, **205**
Chism, Leon, **213**
Chism, Rusty, **211**
Chriesman, Mary, **136**
Chrisman, Paul, **192**
Christian, Amanda, **219**
Christian, Kim, **216**
Chumley, L. Murry, **178**
Church, Christy, **219**
Church, Jack, **162**, **174**
Church, Jerry, 98
Church, John, **204**
Church, John T., **155**
Clark, Brett, **208**
Clark, Rick, **200**
Clarke, Pat, **201**
Clarkson, Allen, **214**
Clarkson, Becky, **208**
Clarkson, Bill, **187**
Clarkson, Bobby, **209**
Clarkson, Charles Walter, **184**
Clarkson, Jay, **216**
Clarkson, Tadd, **207**
Clarkson, Thomas Alexander, **180**
Clarksville High School, 104
Clary, Lawson, **138**
Classem, Stephanie, **211**
Clay, Helen, **144**
Claypool, William Woodford Jr., **180**
Clayton, John, **158**
Cleburne, Patrick, 9, 11–12
Cleland, William, **171**
Clement, Frank Jr., **192**
Clement, Gary, **195**
Clement, Sam, **189**
Clements, Paul, **190**
Cleveland, Chris, **213**
Cleveland, Lisa, **208**
Cliffe, Stephen G., **155**
Cline, Kenneth, **181**
Clouse, Sonny, **186**
Cobb, Anthony D., **191–194**
Cobb, Billy, **79**, **175**
Cobb, Peter, **200**
Cobb, Tony, 100, **182**, **189–190**
Cobb, Vinson, **172**
Cochran, Richie, **203**
Cochran, Julie, **217**
Cocke, Billy, **200**
Cody, Elizabeth, **138**
Cody, Ernest, **159**
Cody, J. C., **136**
Cody, Josh, 50
Cohen, Allen, 94, **188**
Cole, Anne, **210**
Cole, B., **197**
Cole, Edward, **157**
Cole, James H., **197**
Cole, James Richard, **184**
Cole, Jay, **198–199**
Cole, Joey, **203**
Cole, Kevin, **215**
Cole, Kim, **214**
Cole, Mark, **208**
Cole, Nancy, **195–196**
Cole, Paul, **206**
Cole, Richard, **206–208**
Coleman, John, **186**
Coleman, Rob, **218**
Colley, Jerry, **219**
Collier, Annie Levi, **143**
Collier, E. Anderson, **143**
Collier, Gary, **204**
Collier, John, **201**
Colmore, Dale, **214**
Colmore, John, 108, **195–203**
Colmore, Nunie, **215**
Colton, Jesse, **169**
Colton, John, **183**
Columbia Military Academy, 64, 79
Comer, Charles, **207–209**
Comer, Everette G. Jr., **178**
Compton, Samuel H., **150**
Cone, Chris, 115, **209**
Cone, Scott, **212**
Cone, Susan, **210**
Conway, Nan, **203**
Cook, Billy, **79**, **170**, **174**
Cook, Brad, **208**
Cook, Church, **195**
Cook, Creighton, **211**
Cook, Crockett, **163**
Cook, Doug, **211**, **219**
Cook, Graham, **213**
Cook, Greg, **201**
Cook, Jim, **201**
Cook, Jimmy, **183**
Cook, Marshall, **142**
Cook, Mary Jane, **110**
Cook, West, **212**
Cooke, Clarence, **158**
Cooke, J. Lem Jr., **143**
Cooke, Rebecca, **148**
Coombs, Francis, **167**
Coomer, Mark, **196**
Cooper, James R., **174**
Cooper, Jerry Alfred, **184**
Cooper, John, **156**
Cooper, Lawrence, **165**
Cooper, Patrick, **193**
Coppedge, Rob, **218**
Cortner, Clark, **159**
Cotton, Annie, **138**
Cotton, Haynes, **140**, **143**
Cotton, Katie, **136**
Cotton, Mattie P., **136**
Cotton, Rodger, **171**
Cotton, T. H., **144**
Cotton, Walter P., **149**
Coughlin, Shean, **202**
Courter, Deanna, **210**
Courtney, Andrew, 27
Courtney, Richard, **168**
Courtney, Robin, **171**
Courtney, W. W., **132**
Courtney, Wirt Jr., **166**
Coverdale Hall, 86
Coverdale, Jonas S., 81, **82**, 84–85, 88, **176–184**
Covington, J. C., **138**
Covington, Powell, **167**
Cowan, J., **198**

Cowart, Will, 189
Cowie, Laddie, 163
Cox, Bryan, 213
Cox, Jacob D., 7
Cox, N. N., 20
Crafton, Ed, 206
Crafton, Laura, 217
Craig, Burt, 163
Craig, Mark, 202
Craig, Mike, 215
Crane, Leo, 186
Cranwell, Tom, 188
Crawford, L., 197
Creel, Wayne, 220
Creim, Jerry, 199
Crenshaw, Bob, 79
Crews, Ken, 211
Crews, Phillip, 206
Crichlow, Tom, 181
Crichton, Charley, 212
Crockett, Coleman, 177
Crockett, Herbert, 146
Crockett, Herbert A., 176
Crockett, Hilary R. Jr., 148
Crockett, Joe Vaulx, 190
Crockett, Joseph Parkes, 143
Crockett, Louisa, 145
Crockett, Mary J., 152
Crockett, Penn, 183
Crosby, Bill, 191
Crosby, Madeline, 212
Crow, T. D., 32
Crowell, Bucky, 194
Crowell, Mickey, 183
Crowell, Preston, 207
Crowson, Cecil, 186
Crump, John O., 178
Crutcher, Chris, 208
Crutcher, Elizabeth, 216
Crutcher, Joyce, 215–220
Crutcher, Ronald, 188
Crutcher, Ross, 191
Crutcher, Susan, 214
Crutchfield, Marty, 207
Cude, Erica, 219
Culbreath, Bill, 162
Cumberland College/ University, 25, 81
Cumberland Museum, 105
Cumming, Brad, 220
Cuneo, John, 156
Cunningham, D., 197
Cunningham, John, 185
Cunningham, Whitney, 219
Curd, Brice, 38
Curl, Gary, 106, 206
Curry, G. T., 159
Curtis, Greg, 203
Cusomato, Mark, 218
Cusomato, Vince, 216

D

Dabbs, Bill, 168
Dabbs, Charley, 172
Dale, G., 197
Dale, Jamie, 196
Dale, Joe, 205
Dale, Lawrence, 193
Daniel, Brown, 212
Daniel, Hardin, 213
Daniel, Lannie, 210
Daniel, Laura, 217
Daniel, Mary Sue, 152
Daniel, Rod, 185
Daniel, Sinclair, 169
Daniel, William, 158
Daniels, Agnes, 137
Darby, Jeff, 205
Darden, Art, 203
Darden, Ted, 201
Darlington School, 79
Darnell, Arminta, 133
Darnell, Leonard D., 44, 133
Daugherty, Lloyd, 189
Davenport, Jim, 106
Davidson College, 76
Davidson, William W., 155–157
Davies, Frank Jr., 168
Davies, Lee, 200
Davies, Lucy, 207
Davis, D. C., 132
Davis, Earl, 142
Davis, Elva, 34, 130
Davis, Eric, 214
Davis, Fannie Loo, 133
Davis, Frank, 158
Davis, George E., 171
Davis, Gus A., 135
Davis, Heather, 219
Davis, Helen, 146
Davis, J. O., 57, 146–147
Davis, J. O., Jr., 148–149
Davis, Jeff, 208, 215
Davis, Jefferson, 5, 21–22
Davis, John, 114, 211
Davis, Judy, 116, 208–217
Davis, Legare, 210
Davis, Margaret Owen, 149
Davis, Marion, 135
Davis, Mary, 138
Davis, Norman, 192
Davis, Orren, 136
Davis, Patrick, 212
Davis, Phil, 169
Davis, Sam Literary Society, 52
Davis, Sandra, 118, 216–220
Davis, Shane, 214
Davis, Stan, 213
Davis, Ted, 167
Davis, Tom, 209
Davis, Wayne, 105, 201
Day, Lou Ann, 207
DeBrohun, Leon J., 169
Decker, Donnie, 218
Deere, David, 200
Deerfield-Windsor School, Albany, Georgia, 117
De Hart, Thad, 214
DeJarnette, Tom, 213
De Leon, John, 207
Dell, Stacey, 211
Delvaux, John, 205
Delvaux, Thomas, 211–213
Dement, Bryan, 181
DeMontbreun, Jim, 206
DeMoss, Eddie, 202
Dempsey, Timothy, 193
Dempsy, Percy, 192
Denbo, Don, 96–97, 192
Denbo, J., 197
Denham, Marie, 132
Denham, R. H., 132
Dennis, Brad, 212
Denny, John, 185
Dent, W. T., 51, 132, 139,–142
Denton, Mary Farr, 144
Derryberry, Mike, 189
Derryberry, Tim, 192
Derryberry, Timmons Jr., 193
Deschamps, Julio, 165
Dewitt, Jack, 188
DeWitt, Ward, 202
Dibrell, Clay, 211
Dickens, Paul S., 201
Dickens, Ward, 205–206
Dickerhoff, Bill, 208
Dickinson, Bobby, 189
Dickinson, Don, 190
Dickinson, Thomas, 193
Dillard, Bond, 218
Dillard, Bondsy, 217–220
Dillard, Jerry W., 173
Dillard, Mark, 113, 208
Dillard, Ward, 214
Dimond, Debbie, 211
Dinges, Billy, 170
Dixon, David, 213
Dixon, Richard, 185
Dobson, Harlan, 187
Dobson, Mack, 187
Doak, Bill, 173
Doak, T., 197
Dobratz, Eric, 215
Dodd, Campbell, 203
Dodd, Larry, 183
Dodd, Leslee, 205
Dodd, Steve, 204
Dodson, Chris, 194
Dodson, George, 181
Dodson, S. D., 129
Doggett, Dorothy, 102, 108, 116, 122, 197–220
Doggett, Marshall W. III, 176
Donaldson, Lawrence, 151
Donaldson, Walter, 92, 188
Donelson, Frank, 167
Doody, Mike, 200
Dorland, Peter, 189
Dorris, Harold, 189
Dorsten, Bill, 214
Dotson, Billy Cleveland, 180
Dougherty, James, 212–214
Douglas, Ed, 203
Douglas, Ned, 168
Douglas, Ronnie, 207
Douglass, Johnny, 187
Downum, C. E., 138
Doyel, Richard Otis, 169
Dozier, Marguerite, 138
Dozier, Thaniel P., 142
Draper, Donna, 207
Drayton, Becky, 110, 211
Drayton, Chuck, 210
Driskill, Red, 164
Drury, Andrea, 213
Dryden, Alec, 195
Dryden, Jack, 190
DuBois, Bobby, 205–210
Duckworth, Jeff, 206
Dudley, Steve, 194
Duffy, Robert, 215
Dufton, Ernie, 200
Duke, Alan, 196
Duke, Bob, 177
Duke, Mrs. E. C., 194
Duke, Mattie Lou, 100
Duke, Mrs. Matilou, 196–198
Duke, Phillip, 193
Duke, Ralph, 195
Duke, S., 197
Dulaney, Charles, 174
Dulaney, Robert, 174
Duley, A., 197
Dunavant, Richard, 195
Dunbar, S. C., 136
Duncan, T., 197
Dunigan, David, 201
Dunkerley, Bob, 186
Dunlap, Sam, 185
Dunlop, Erwin, 202–203
Dunn, Andy, 203
Dunn, Jessi, 220
Durmavont, Jason, 219
Durrett, John, 159
Dwyer, Charles, 208
Dyer, Shannon, 214
Dyke, Bobby, 207
Dykes, Bill, 171
Dysart, Kelly, 157
Dysart, Mattie Logan, 152

E

Earls, Willie, 195
Early, Doug, 196
Early, Irvine B., 134
Early, Steve, 194
Early, Vance, 143
Easley, Cherry, 168
Eason, Laurel, 116, 207–215
Eason, Lenora, 215
Eason, Will, 211
East, James, 164
Eckardt, Gary, 211
Eckhardt, Eric, 201
Eddington, Glenn M., 76, 77, 81, 152–153, 155–175
Eddington, Glenn Jr., 174
Edgar, Brooke, 213
Edmondson, Ernest, 157
Edmondson, Hugh J., 139
Edwards, Chris, 219
Edwards, Eunice, 198–205
Edwards, Harold, 157
Edwards, Kermit Holland Harold, 158
Edwards, Lynne, 211
Edwards, Tommy, 204
Eggert, Edwin O., 174
Eggleston, Edmund W., 143
Eggleston, J. C., 42
Eggleston, Joe C., 174
Eggleston, Joseph C. Jr., 149
Eisenhauer, Gretchen, 219–220
Elam, E. H., 139
Elcan, Dan, 201
Elcan, John, 203
Elder, George, 190
Elder, Jim, 209
Elkin, Julikarel, 212
Elkins, James William, 179
Ellett, Shelly, 163
Ellis, G. Jack, 183–184
Ellis, Jere, 194
Ellis, Jimmie, 190
Ellis, L., 198
Elliot, T. H., 136
Elliott, Robert, 200
English, Alfred, 144
English, Core, 171
English, Wm. Hamlett, 176
English, Zellner, 140
Enoch, David, 213
Enoch, Les, 214
Entrekin, Herbert, 190
Ernst, Benjie, 199
Ervin, Bert, 157

Ervin, Neil, **160**
Erwin, Brett, **214**
Eskind, Brad, **201**
Estes, Alec, **206**
Estes, Brock, **189**
Estes, Mike, **192**
Estes, Robert, 97, **193**
Estock, Ed, **205**
Etscorn, Frank T., **189**
Eudailey, William, **162**
Evans, Briggs, **213**
Evans, David, 108, **200–204**
Evans, Deborah, **208**
Evans, Greg, **205**
Evans, Joe, **181**
Evans, Tom, **192**
Evans, Zack, **210**
Everbright Mansion, **42**, 43
Everhart, Mike, **190**
Evers, Stewart, **202**
Everson, David, **187**
Evins, Frank, **160**
Evins, Holly, **217**
Ewell, Justin, **148**
Ewell, W. T., **174**
Ewin, William W., **139**
Ewing, A. H., **42**
Ewing, Alex Jr., **151**
Ewing, Rebekah Lyle, **144**

F

Fahey, Jay, **209**
Fahey, Stephen, **212**
Faircloth, Frederick III, **193**
Fan, Lydia, **216**
Fant, A. C., **150**
Fardon, Terry, **215–216**
Farned, Thomas Blair, **179**
Farnsworth, Martha Elizabeth, **153**
Farnsworth, Michael, **212–213**
Farnsworth, Russell, **182**
Farrar, Steve, **205**
Farrell, Bryan, **202**
Farrell, J. M., **153**
Father Ryan High School, 90, 105
Faulkner, Vernon, 156, **157**
Faust, Steve, **195**
Faw, Elizabeth, **145**
Faw, Kernan, **136**
Faw, Margaret W., **137**
Faw, Ruth, **141**
Faw, Sarah, **148**
Faw, W. W., **42**
Feldhaus, Henry, **196**
Feldman, Buford S. Jr., **179**
Fellowship of Christian Athletes, 101
Felts, Ricky, **213**
Fennell, Ben Jr., **170**
Fennell, James C. III, **179**
Ferree, Tim, **215–217**
Ferrell, Aaron, **219**
Ferrell, Andy, **199**
Ferrell, Cracker, **203**
Ferrell, Greg, **211–220**
Ferrell, R., **198**
Fesmire, Rob, 105, **202**
Fiedler, Fritz, **202**
Figuers, Hardin, 9
Finley, States Rights, **174**
Finney, Bill, **181**
Fisher, Bill, **194**
Fisher, Don, **212**
Fisher, J. E., **174**
Fisher, J. H., **42**

Fite, Cheryl, **216**
Fite, Fran, **219**
Fitzgerald, Brodney, **220**
Fitzgerald, Shawne, **219**
Fiveash, Thomas, **185**
Fiveash, Tom, 91
Flanigan, George, **173**
Flatt, Carlton, **195**
Flaugher, John, **209**
Fleming, A. B., **133**
Fleming, Bertha, **131**
Fleming, Bill, **215**
Fleming Hall, **49**, 86, 125
Fleming, Jennie, **146**
Fleming, Jennifer, **218**
Fleming, John D., **166**
Fleming, John West, **166**
Fleming, Mickie, **148**
Fleming, O. J., 119, 121, **219**
Fleming, Pete, **188**
Fleming, Rebekah, **138**
Fleming, Robert M., **189**
Fleming, Samuel M. Jr., 49, **57**, 94, **149**
Fleming, Steven, **218**
Fleming, Swope, **156**
Flemming, Lois, **132**
Flippen, Bobby, **181**
Flippen, Jimmy, **187**
Flippen, T. P., **129**
Floyd, Jock, **205**
Floyd, Tim, **200**
Floyd, Tom T., **162**
Fly, Felix, **193**
Fly, William Percy, **179**
Fohl, Blake, **202**
Fohl, Jamie, **205**
Folsom, Christopher, **193**
Foote, Dr. Robert (Bobby), 116, **187**
Forbes, Shannon, **219**
Ford, Alvin, **187**
Ford, Bob, **192**
Ford, Dan, 156, **157**
Ford, Dennis, **177**
Ford, Harry, 96, **192**
Ford, Sidney M. Jr., **178**
Ford, Turney, 72, **165–167**, 172
Forensic League, 111
Formosa, Jay, **213**
Forrest, Cub, **206**
Forrest, Nathan Bedford, 9, 21
Fossee, Flip, **205**
Foster, Ira, **148**
Foust, Lee Ann, **212**
Fowler, Charles, **187**
Fowler, Hayes, **188**
Fowlkes, H. P., 42, **136**
Fowlkes, Hartford, **198**
Fowlkes, Preston, **188**
Foxall, Harold, **214**
Foxall, Joey, **205**
Foxall, Lynn, **216**
Foy, George, **218**
Francescon, Danny, **215–217**
Francis, Jack, **186**
Francis, Joe, **183**
Francis, Richard, **194**
Frank, H., **198**
Franklin Confederate monument, 17
Franklin Female Institute, 18, 20
Franklin Grammar School, 20
Franklin High School, 99, 112
Franklin, Marvin A. Jr., **194**

Franklin, William Fleming, **153**
Franks, Jane Anne, **220**
Franks, Michael, **218**
Freeman, Barbara, 110, **207**
Freeman, Bob, **219**
Freeman, David, **191**
Freeman, Harvey, **220**
Freeman, Lori, 110, **207–210**
Freeman, Lynn Barrett, **152**
Freeman, Mark, **211**
Freeman, Stefanie, **211**
Freemont, Jeff, **208**
Fremont, Amy, **214**
French Club, 106
French, Jimmy, 100, **185–189**
French, Katherine, **214**
Frensley, D., **198**
Frey, Johnny, **183**
Frick, Scott, **206**
Fristoe, Jimmy, 79, **175**
Fristoe, John, **172**
Frith, Jim, **200**
Frost, James Thomas, **180**
Frost, T., **198**
Fryer, Buddy, 105, **106**
Fryer, Charles, **204**
Fryer, Libby, 95
Fulcher, Brett, **214**
Fuller, Henry, **173**
Funte, Frederick, **196**
Fuqua, B., **197**
Fuqua, Graham, **188**
Fuqua, Tom, **183**
Furman, Richard, **193**

G

Gain, John, **203**
Gaines, Francis, **183**
Galdo, Otto, **181**
Gale, Bill, **167**
Gale, Stanley Forbes, **180**
Gallavin, Leilah, **143**
Gallery, Debbie, **216–220**
Gannaway, J. W., **136**
Gannon, Kevin, **214**
Gant, Ben, **164**
Gant, Harrison, **194**
Gant, Winston, **195**
Gardner, Carl, 56, **139**, **145**
Gardner, David, **194**
Garland, Ginger, **217**
Garland, Michael, **219**
Garner, Jay, **204**
Garner, Robert, **158–159**
Garrett, Billy J., **177**
Garrett, Bob, **170**
Garrett, Bobby, **205**
Garrett, David, **205**
Garrett, Howard H., **174**
Garrett, Jay, **187**
Garrett, Rhea, 106, **204**
Garrett, Robert, **179**
Garvey, Colleen, **212**
Gasparini, Paul, 118, **215–216**
Gasser, Ronald Cleveland, **180**
Gates, Lisa, **216**
Gates, Natalie, **215**
Gatlin, Claud, **172**
Gayden, Kip, **181**
Gayden, Mac, **183**
Gayden, William Dickinson, **180**
Gayle, Stanley, 112
Gehrke, Adrienne, **211**
Gentry, Allen, ix, **195**

Gentry, Ashley, **219**
Gentry, Bob Jr., **198**
Gentry, Cindy, ix
Gentry, Dan, **164**, **195**
Gentry, J. Robert, 97, 100, 108, **171**, **192–199**
Gentry, James C., 92, 95–96, 100, 108, **188–198**, **200–202**
Gentry, Jim, **194**
Gentry, Scott, **201**
Gentry, Steven, **181**
Gentry, Zeb, **199**
Geny, Henry, **202**
George, Scott, **208**
George, Steven, **181**
Georgia Military Academy, 79
German, Dan Jr., **149**
German, Dick Jr., **161**
Gerregano, Robert A., **179**
Gerregano, Seymore Jr., **178**
Gerth, David, **193**
Gerth, John, **190**
Geshke, Terry, 92, **185**
Ghertner, Gary, 94
Ghertner, Gary S., **189**
Ghertner, Lory, **192**
Gholson, John, **207**
Gibbs, Chuck, **214**
Gibbs, Kennedy M., **173**
Gibbs, Kennedy, **150**
Gibbs, Malcolm, **148**
Gibbs, Pam, **210**
Gibbs, Russell, **187**
Gibbs, William M., **143**
Gibson, Dennis, 116, **204–209**, **211–220**
Gibson, Springer M., **155**
Gifford, George, **187**
Gifford, John, **191**
Gilbert, Charles, **188**
Giles, Frank, 79, **175**
Gillaspy, John Edward, **177**
Gillespie, Andrew D. Jr., **155**
Gillespie, Dickie, **187**
Gillespie, Houston Oliver Jr., **184**
Gillespie, John Hall, **184**
Gillespie, Leigh, **213**
Gillespie, Ross, **166**
Gillespie, Tiffy, **218**
Gilliam, Greg, **213**
Gilliam, Jim, **209**
Gillig, Emily, **208**
Gilman, Tom, 116, **205–214**
Gilmer, Drew, **214**
Gilmer, Laura, **219**
Gilmore, David, 106, **204**
Gilmore, James, **154**
Gilmore, W. T., 64, **154**
Gist, S. R., 12
Givan, Evans, **187**
Givens, John, **195**
Glasgow, Noel, **219**
Glasgow, Wayne Jr., **193**
Glassford, Grant, **203**
Glaze, J. W., **136**
Glen Echo, 125
Glenn, Steve, **195**
Gleve, Bob B. Jr., **178**
Glover, Burton, **182**
Godmer, Adam, **209**
Godwin, Emery, **148**
Goforth, J. H., **27**
Goldman, James, **164**
Goldman, Russ, **203**
Goldstein, Randy, **196**

Goodman, Barry, **195**
Goodman, Carmen, **214**
Goodpasture High School, 112, 121
Goodwin, Jeff, **218**
Goodwin, Lewis, **170**
Gorden, William O., **173**
Gordon, Claude, **163**
Gordon, Fielding G., **34**, **129**
Gordon, G. W., 12
Gordon, J. H., 51, **139**
Gordon, Jennifer, **213**
Gordon, Joe, **195**
Gordon, Scott, **212**
Gore, C., **197**
Gore, D. A., **166**
Gore, Jay, **208–213**
Goss, Barry, **204**
Goss, Christi, **213**
Goss, Sherri, **211**
Gotwald, David, **186**
Gotwald, Dickie, **190**
Govantes, Felix, **171**
Gracey, Bob, 57
Gracey, Clarence Bradshaw "Pete," 62, 66, **154**
Gracey, Gene, **166**
Gracey, Hugh, 158, **188**
Gracey, Sarah, **218**
Gracy, Annie Mary, **151**
Graff, Arthur, **185**
Graham, Art, **192**
Graham, Ed, **190**
Graham, Irwin, **194**
Graham, J., **198**
Graham, Jimmy, 102, **197**
Graham, Will, **219**
Grant, Greg, **204**
Grant, Ulysses S., 6
Grantham, Carl Jr., **170**
Grantham, Kenneth, **163**
Gray, Bill F., **178**
Gray, Edwin D. Jr., **169**
Gray, Harry, **185**
Gray, Jesse H., **34**, **130**
Gray, Russell, **131**
Gray, Warren, **154**
Gray, William Francis Jr., **150**
Grayson, Charles, **168**
Grayson, James E., **166**
Graystone Cottage, **73**, 74
Graves, Jimmy, **169**
Green, Bruce, **207**
Green, Curtis, **148**
Green, Garth E. Jr., **184**
Green, Harrison Haywood, **150**
Green, Joe, **141**
Green, John Jr., **170**
Green, John M., **139**
Green, Joseph C., 98, **192–195**
Green, Joseph G., **196**
Green, Lucy, **143**
Green, Marion, **146**
Green, W. O., **189**
Green, Walter, **165**
Green Walter Jr., **192**
Greenback High School, 119
Greene, Mike, **192**
Greene, Nate, **195**
Greene, Sam, **200**
Greene, W. K., **132**
Greer, Fulton, **181**
Greer, Fulton M., **155**
Greer, John, **204**
Greer, Steve, **218**

Greers, the, 60, 66, 95–96, **96**, 106
Gregg, Alex, 119, 121, **219**
Gregg, Anna, **216**
Gregg, Jason, **215**
Gregory, Cleo, **143**
Gregory, Ferrell, **189**
Gregory, Thomas, **154**
Griffeth, Ronald H., ix, 117, **118**, **216–220**
Griffin, Chris, **205**
Griffin, John, **183**
Griffin, Seth H., **184**
Griffith, Dan, **191**
Griffith, Eleanor, **216**
Grigsby, Elizabeth, **144**
Grigsby, L., **197**
Grigsby, Ray, **196**
Grigsby, Susie Lee, **142**
Grimes, Charles Wm., **178**
Grimes, Ronnie, **190**
Grissim, M., **198**
Grissom, Larry, **191**
Grissom, Rachel, **219**
Griswold, Nelson, **172**
Grizzard, Tommy, **189**
Grizzard, Winston, 94, **188**
Groner, Carroll, **172**
Gross, Eddie, **174**
Gross, Paul Brock, **176**
Grote, Gus, **201**
Grover, Scott, **216**
Gryder, Jack, **172**
Guest, Ryan, **211**
Guffee, Harry Jr., **185**
Guffee, Harry Jasper, **155–156**
Guffee, John, **214**
Guffee, Johnny, **188**
Guffee, Landis, **217**
Guffee, Paul, 123, **154**, **186**
Guffee, Paul Award, 123
Guiton, Thomas A. Jr., **181–182**
Gunnells, Greg, 105, **200**
Gupton, Bill, **192**
Gupton, Hank, **202**
Gurley, Brian, **213**
Gustave, Jim, **204**
Guthe, Don, **215–220**
Guthrie, Tommy, **210**

H

Haberman, Mike, **199**
Hackett, William, **200**
Haddock, Haynes, **212**
Haffner, Bill, **194**
Haffner, Campbell, **164**
Haffner, Charles, **158–159**
Haffner, Charlie Jr., **196**
Haffner, Johnny, **199**
Haga, C., **198**
Hagan, Richard, **201**
Hager, Buddy, **201**
Hagewood, Bo, **207**
Hagler, Lewis, **165**
Hagstrom, Bob, **172**
Hahn, John, 97, **192**
Hainge, Allen, **191**
Hale, Alan, **216**
Haley, John, **196**
Hall, Bill, 116
Hall, Bobby, **203**
Hall, Donald G., **178**
Hall, James, **197**
Hall, John, **196**
Hall, Susie, **214**

Hall, Tiffany, 115, **210**
Hamblen, Jim, **190**
Hamilton, Buzzy, **96**, 97
Hamilton, Charles, **168**
Hamilton, Ed, 38
Hamilton, Fred Jr., **193**
Hamilton, Tommy, **183**
Hammond, Richie, **206**
Hampton, Jerry, **131**
Hampton, John, 93, **192**
Hampton, Lyle E., **192**
Hamra, Jerry Farris, **173**
Haney, David, **169**
Hanner, J. P., 18
Hanson, Joe, **191**
Hanvy, Phillip, **209**
Happy Valley High School, 104
Hardcastle, Brooke, **212**
Hardcastle, Loy, **191**
Hardebeck, John, **206**
Hardin, Jenkins, **212**
Hardin, Kim, 110
Hardin, Wesley, **213**
Hardison, Albert W., **142**
Hardison, Allan, **170**
Hardison, I. A., **169**
Hardison, John M., **146**
Hardison, Leroy, **168**
Hardy, Debby, **207**
Hardy, Richard, **202**
Hardy, Sam, **182**
Harlan, Howard, **185**
Harlan, Rill, **219**
Harlin, Alex, **173**
Harlin, Bill, **167**
Harlin, Bob, **175**
Harlin, C., **197**
Harlin, John, **200**
Harlin, Tom, **168**
Harlin, Wirt, **191**
Harmes, R. F., **173**
Harmon, David, **214**
Harmon, Kenny, **198**
Harper, Cy, **201**
Harper, John, **196**
Harper, Steve, **186**
Harper, Truman, **194**
Harpeth Academy, **18–19**
Harpeth River, 7–8, 95
Harpeth Valley Athletic Conference, 115
Harrell, Greg, **199**
Harrell, Jennifer, **220**
Harris, Benny, **176**
Harris, Bob, **169**
Harris, Davis, **171**
Harris, Edward, **193**
Harris, Kelly, **220**
Harris, M. C., **170**
Harris, Richard N., **161**
Harris, Sandra, **214**
Harris, Scottie, **188**
Harris, Steve, **195**
Harrison, J., **197**
Harrison, J. W., 42
Harrison, Jay, **204**
Harrison, John, **205**
Harrison, Robert C., **178**
Hart, Bill, **205**
Hart, Clint, **213**
Hart, Fred, **190**
Hart, John, **139**
Hartman, Geoff, **203**
Harvard University, 126

Harvey, Burton, **215**
Harvey, Horace Waters, **175**
Harvey, Stephen, 122, **218**
Harville, Jon, **187**
Harwell, David, **202**
Harwell, Horace Riggs, **153**
Harwell, Tommy, **195**
Hash, Bobby, **212**
Hash, Carey, **215**
Hassey, Jon, **194**
Hassler, Michael, **220**
Hasty, Don, **186**
Hasty, Hugh, **194**
Hatcher, Abe, **180**
Hatcher, Albert S., **146**
Hatcher, Cynthia, 137, **144**
Hatcher, George A., **135**
Hatcher, Kathryn Alice, **149**
Hatcher, Kevin, **209**
Hatcher, Mark, **164**
Hatcher, Martha, **150**
Hatcher, Willie R., **136**
Haueter, Fred, **135**
Hawkins, Boxwell, **182**
Hawkins, Elizabeth, **154**
Hawkins, Mike, **209**
Hayes, Hilary, **215**
Haynes, Emma, 88
Haynes, J., **197**
Haynes, James, **154**
Hays, Glenn, **189–190**
Hays, Harmon, **191**
Hays, James R., **177**
Hays, Rogers, **187**
Hayworth, Richard, **157**
Head, Stephen, **190**
Head, Steve, **199**
Hearn, Curry Jr., **176**
Hedden, Bill, **170**
Hedden, Bob, **170**
Hedden, Donald, **193**
Hedden, Henry Jr., **166**
Hedge, Paul, **217**
Heflin, David, **193**
Heflin, Dickie, **189**
Heidinger, Gary, **191**
Heilman, Sheldon Lee, **184**
Heinig, Don, **187**
Heise, Jan, **207**
Heithcock, Kevin, **214**
Heithcock, Kelly, **210**
Heldman, Mark, 105, **202**
Helguera, Leon, **208**
Helm, Ellen, **212**
Helm, J. Thomas, **178**
Helm, John, **214**
Helsby, Kathryn, **209**
Helton, Thomas, **175**
Henderson, Donald, **188**
Henderson, J. H., 42
Henderson, John H. Jr., **179**
Henderson, Matt, **172**
Henderson, Tom, 29
Henderson, Tom P. Jr., 62
Henderson, Tom III, **190**
Hendricks, Jesse, **213**
Henry, Austin, **214**
Henry, Billy, **169**
Henry, Bob, **194**
Henry, Gene, **158**
Henry, Joe, **190**
Henry, Mac, **185**
Henry, Mike, **187**
Henry, Parman, **172**

Henry, Tiffy, **211**
Henson, Mike, **211**
Hep Cat, 85
Herbert, Bill, **181**
Herbert, C., **198**
Herbert, R., **198**
Herbert, Randy, **199**
Herbert, Tommy, **106**, **183**, **204**
Herd, Hal, **186**
Herman, Greg, **209**
Herman, Lori, **110**, **207**
Hernandez, Alfredo, **174**
Hernandez, David, 106, 108, 116, 122–123, **198**–**220**
Herndon, Edward, **199**
Herrera, Francisco A., **71**, **163**–**164**
Herrington, Andrew, **218**
Herrington, Kevin, 219
Herrington, Leonard, **194**
Herrington, Melinda, **216**
Herrmann, John, 108, **95**, **196**–**205**
Herron, Allen E., **176**
Herron, Bill, **189**
Herron, Jane, **210**–**220**
Herron, Sara, **217**
Hessey, Ed, **217**–**220**
Hickerson, Allan R., **141**
Hickerson, Marion, **192**
Hickman, Beth, **213**
Hickman, Mike, **192**
Hickey, B., **197**
Hickey, Margaret, **116**, **213**–**216**
Hicks, Clifton, **177**
Hicks, Matt, **208**
Hicks, Stephen, **96**, **193**
Hightower, Tutt, **220**
Hill, Albert, **191**
Hill, Andy, **204**
Hill, Harry, **163**
Hill, Jimmy, **167**
Hill, Kirtley, **174**
Hill, Randy, **203**
Hill, Richard, **208**
Hill, Robert L., **189**
Hill, Roger, **200**
Hillard, Esmond, **161**
Hillard, Richard, **190**
Hillenmeyer, Edwin, **213**
Hillenmeyer, Geoff, **217**
Hillinmeyer, Chris, **219**
Hillsboro Invitational Tournament, 115
Hines, Ann, **213**–**214**
Hines, Dennis, **215**
Hines, Nikki, **219**
Hinkle, Carl, 66, **159**
Hinkle, Jack, **166**
Hinson, Haley, **220**
Hixon, Neal, **206**
Hixon, Perk, **201**
Hobbs, Hugh, **190**
Hobbs, Jay, **213**
Hobbs, Mark, **216**
Hobgood, Jim, **165**
Hodge, Kim, **211**
Hoffman, Charlie, **212**
Hoffman, Chip, **202**
Hoffman, Jamie, **210**
Hoffman, Jeff, **205**
Hoffman, Robin, **213**
Hoffman, Sean, **210**
Hoffmeister, John, **188**
Hofsteter, Brad, **213**
Hoge, William L., **171**

Hogg, Brad, **207**
Hogg, Mike, **201**
Hohenwald High School, 104
Holahan, Michael, **202**
Holcomb, Lance, **212**
Holcomb, Shannon Dee, **217**
Holcomb, Tony, **186**
Holden, Billy, **185**
Holland, Day, **206**
Holland, John Fox, **176**
Holland, Mike, **105**, **200**
Holland, Monte, **186**
Holliday, Douglas, **193**
Holliday, Joe, **190**
Holliday, Joe Jr., **165**
Holliday, Mary Jane, **219**–**220**
Hollins, Sam, **195**
Hollinshead, R. P., **129**
Hollis, Phillip G., **94**, **188**
Hollister, Rob, **211**
Hollister, Stephen, **204**
Hollman, Day, 102
Hollman, Doy, **196**–**198**
Holloway, James, **203**–**204**
Holloway, Jon, **208**
Holloway, Russell, **204**
Holmes, Brandon, **208**
Holsen, Robert, **188**
Holt, Ellis, **179**
Holt, James W., **141**
Holt, Laird, 62, **153**
Holt, Murphy, **148**
Holt, Robert, **145**
Holt, Spencer Jr., **168**, **190**
Holt, Tommy, **208**
Holt, Trey, **206**
Honicker, Ed, **203**
Honor Council, 115
Hood, Deana, **214**
Hood, Donna, **211**
Hood, Farrar, **219**
Hood, Gerry, **202**
Hood, Jen, **210**
Hood, Joe Anna, **217**
Hood, John Bell, 5, **6**, 7, 10, 14
Hood, Margaret, **213**
Hood, Tammy, **220**
Hood, William E., **174**
Hoof, Mary, 54
Hooff, Mary M., **56**, **147**
Hooff, Wm. L. Jr., **149**
Hooper, C., **198**
Hoos, Laura, **218**
Hooton, John R. Jr., **178**
Hoover, Craig, **219**
Hoover, Jeff, **196**
Horkins, Maxwell, 105
Horn, David, **220**
Horn, Stanley, **187**
Horn, Steve, **194**
Horrell, Fred, **190**
Horrell, Stephen, **193**
Horton, Chase, **205**
Horton, H. H., **144**
Horton, Robert R., **146**
Hoskins, John, **165**
Houghland, Calvin, **190**
Houk, James, **158**
House, Elizabeth, **142**
House, Nat, **148**
House, Bill, **204**
House, R. W., **136**
House, S. John, **135**
House, William, 20, 42
Houseal, James E. II, **174**

Houston County High School, 113
Hovan, Michael, **206**–**207**
Howard, Currier, **219**
Howard, Edward, **151**
Howard, Eugene R. Jr., **174**
Howard, John, **166**
Howlett, James H., **141**
Howlett, K. S., **41**–**42**, **146**
Howlett, Maxie Perry, 58, **150**
Howlett, Virginia R., **137**
Howser, Hugh, **191**
Howser, Jack, **195**
Hubbard, Bill, **189**
Huddleston, William, **157**
Hudgens, James Findlay, **150**
Hudgins, Mike, **183**
Hudlow, Charles C., **178**
Huff, Harold, **170**
Huff, Tina, **216**
Huffman, Josh, **194**
Hug, Paul, **159**–**160**
Huggins, Bunny, **186**
Hughes, Bill, **183**, **185**
Hughes, Johnny, 114, **210**
Hughes, Kelly, **215**
Hughes, Laurie, **207**
Hughes, Ralph Montague Jr., **173**
Hughes, Ralph Waldo, **151**–**153**
Hughes, W. J., **138**
Huie, Arthur, **163**
Hume, Bill, **160**
Hume, Brad, **191**
Hume, Buddy, **196**
Hume, James P., **155**
Hume, Lee, **194**
Hume, Mayes Jr., **150**
Hume, William, **161**
Hunt, Allan, **215**
Hunt, James Vaughan, **184**
Hunt, Kevin, **220**
Hunter, Don, **191**
Hunter, Elvis, **158**
Huntland High School, 112
Huntley-Brinkley Show, 95
Hutcheson, Bob, **175**
Hutchison, Brad, **195**
Hutto, Jared, **213**
Hyde, Freeman, **139**
Hymel, Hank, **203**

I

Ingman, Art, **201**
Ingold, John, **196**
Ingram, John T., **196**–**199**
Ingram, M. D., **162**
Ingram, Orrin, **203**
Ingram, Robin, **201**
Inman, Dixie, **214**
Inman, Hooper, **210**
Insight Program, 118
Irion, George, **195**
Irvin, Alice Gertrude, **153**
Irvin, Martha, **151**
Irvin, Merielle, **212**
Irwin, Ivan, **202**
Irwin, Steve, **210**
Isaac Litton High School, Nashville, 91
Isaacs, Alan, **203**
Isaacs, Bill, **204**
Isaacs, Chuck, **200**
Isaacs, Dale, **201**
Isaacs, Jim, **169**
Isaacs, William E., **79**, **174**

Isaacson, Mike, **194**
Iverlett, Joseph, **189**

J

Jackson, Andrew, 27
Jackson, Billy, **169**
Jackson, Bobby, 96, **191**
Jackson, David, **192**
Jackson, Doug, 102, **197**
Jackson, George B., **142**
Jackson, Granbery, **188**
Jackson, James Leonard Jr., **176**
Jackson, James W., **189**
Jackson, Logan, 97, **192**
Jackson, R. B., **176**
Jackson, Roger, **190**
Jackson, Sarah E., **150**
Jackson, Stacy, **212**
Jacobs, Harris, **205**–**206**
Jacobs, Jimmy, **174**
Jacobs, Phil, **212**
Jacobson, John, **218**
Jacobson, Steve, **187**
Jaggers, Dana, **209**
James, Candace, **216**
Jamison, Billy, **163**
Jefferson, Alva, **169**
Jefferson, Angie, **210**
Jefferson, Cas, **199**
Jefferson, Mary Frances, **142**
Jefferson Society, 52
Jefferson, Tim, **216**
Jefferson, Will, **131**
Jeffords, Doug, **209**
Jenkins, Jeff, **205**
Jenkins, M., **198**
Jenkins, Virgil Carroll, **78**, **79**, **176**
Jenkins, William Roland, **78**, **79**, **176**
Jennette, Joe Percy, **174**
Jennings, Alex, **217**
Jennings, Bob, 57
Jennings, James, **106**
Jennings, Lyle, **214**
Jennings, Margaret Frances, **150**
Jennings, Robert, **151**
Jeter, K., **197**
Jewell, Asa H. III, **184**
Jewell, Chad, 115, **213**
Jewell, Dickey, **186**
Jewell, James, **112**, 114, **211**
Jewell, John, **112**, 114, **211**
Jewell, Johnny, 92, **187**
Jewell, Lisa, **215**
Jewell, Rob, **215**
Johns, Horace Jr., **188**
Johnson, Alice, 111, **211**
Johnson, Alma, **147**
Johnson, Bo, **195**
Johnson, Brian, **213**
Johnson, Charles Hal, **180**
Johnson, David, **191**, **205**
Johnson, Don, **192**
Johnson, Doug, **190**
Johnson, Ellis, **167**
Johnson, Gerald L.,
Johnson, Gerald L. "Mama," 79, 79, **174**
Johnson, Greg, **208**
Johnson, James Dobson, **180**
Johnson, Jennifer, **209**
Johnson, John S., **178**
Johnson, John T., **206**
Johnson, Lesley, **211**
Johnson, Mac, **192**

Johnson, Mary, **215**
Johnson, Matt, **207**
Johnson, Michelle, **217**
Johnson, Mike, **208**
Johnson, Nate, **219**
Johnson, Robert M., **178**
Johnson, Tracy, **211**
Johnson, William, **193**, **210**
Johnston, Bill, **187**
Johnston, Howard, **187**
Johnston, James V., **141**
Johnston, Joseph, 5
Johnston, Tony, **187**
Johnston, Wm. H. Jr., **139**
Jones, Amy, **214**
Jones, Bill, **186**
Jones, Brad, 114, **211**
Jones, Brandon, 113, **214**
Jones, Brent, **219**
Jones, Cecil Derwent, **149**
Jones, David, **177**, **187**, **215**
Jones, Edward, **160**
Jones, George, 113, **212**
Jones, Howard Stanley, **180**
Jones, Ira L., **168–169**
Jones, James, **131**, 157
Jones, Jeff, **211**
Jones, Joe, **164**
Jones, Jody, 110, **206–220**
Jones, John Addison Jr., **152**
Jones, Katherine, **220**
Jones, Keith, **214**
Jones, Stan, **205**
Jones, Steve, **207**
Jones, Tommy, **202**
Jones, Travis, **217**
Jones, William, **158**, **187**
Jones, Wm. S. Jr., **155**
Jones, Willis, **140**
Jones, Zack, **106**
Jordan, Albert III, **171**
Jordan, Albert D. Jr., 57, **149**
Jordan, Allison, **214**
Jordan, Billy, **175**
Jordan, Brian, **219**
Jordan, Cristin, **217**
Jordan, Clyde Wm. Jr., **152**
Jordan, Elizabeth, **210**
Jordan, Genie, 56
Jordan, Helen Hogin, **150**
Jordan, Jeff, **216**
Jordan, John Jr., **157**
Jordan, L. W., **139**, 148
Jordan, Nance B., **155**, **161–164**
Jordan, Robert, **140–141**
Jordan, Seval, 54
Jordan, Thomas, **214**
Joyce, John, 55, **147**
Joyner, Amy, **220**
Julian, Ken, **207**
Jumper, Gene, **213–214**
Junior Classical League, 102
Justice, Merri, **213**
Justice, Steve, **199**

K

Kain, Larry, **191**
Kaludis, Bill, **213**
Kaludis, Stephen, **206**
Kanaday, Tom, **186**
Kaplan, Julies David, **184**
Karnes, Mitchell, **219–220**
Karr, Jerome, **192**
Karr, Scott, **201**

Katzoff, Richard, **194**
Kaye, Frank, **168**
Keene, Vince, **205**
Kefauver, David, **190**
Keith, Buzz, **191**
Keith, James, **136**
Keith, Mike, **211**
Keliher, Bobby, **205**
Keliher, Mike, **201**
Keliher, Scott, **207**
Kell, Robert E., **155–160**
Kelley, Alton, **202**
Kelley, Charles, **168**
Kelley, Ed, **209**
Kelley, Fred L., **167**
Kelley, John, **205**
Kelley, Livingston A., **189**
Kelly, Bill, **174**
Kelly, Ed, 94, **188**
Kelly, Edward, **156**
Kelly, William, **189**
Kelson, Jennifer, **208**
Kelton, Bobby, **168**
Kemp, Becky, **217**
Kemp, Heather, **215**
Kemp, Katy, **213**
Keene, Vince, **106**
Kennedy, B. Roy, **184**
Kennedy, D. J., 42
Kennedy, Harold, 90, **192–195**
Kennedy, John, **190**
Kennedy, Phil, **130**
Kennedy, Richard V. Jr., **179**
Kennedy, Rob, **208**
Kenney, Jason, **213**
Kent, Charles M. Jr., **161**
Kessy, W. A., 6
Kesther, Joey, **196**
Key Club, 96, 109
Kidd, Mike, **186**
Kidney, Alison, **215**
Kihm, Walter, **188**
Kinard, Brown C., **139**
Kinder, Daniel, **220**
Kinder, Polly, **209–210**
King, Andy, **215**
King, Billy, **106**
King, Doug, **106**, 207
King, Henderson Jr., **170**
King, Hiram, **172**
King, Jack, **169**
King, James W., **175**
King, Jim, **195**
King, Jimmy J., **176**
King, John M., **161**
King, Laurie, **218**
King, Mack, **164**
King, Mary Elise, **152**
King, Matt, **203**
King, Michael, **217**
King, Newton, **192**
King, Steve, **210**
King, William M., **141**
Kinloch, Kyle, **206**
Kinman, Greg, 108, 116, **199–204**
Kinnard, Amis, **158**
Kinnard, Brandon, **218**
Kinnard, Brown C., **176**
Kinnard, C. H. Sr., 42, 78
Kinnard, Cannon, **172**
Kinnard, Claiborne H. Jr., **155**
Kinnard, Clay, **217**
Kinnard, David, **207**
Kinnard, J., **197**

Kinnard, Jack, **174**
Kinnard, Jason, **206**
Kinnard, Michael, **189**
Kinnard, Mike, **201**
Kinnard, Steve, **201**
Kinnard, Walter T., **174**
Kirk, Rainey, **203**
Kirkland, Chancellor J. H., 46, 60
Kirkpatrick, Bill, **166**
Kirkpatrick, Bubber, **168**
Kirkpatrick, H. N. Jr., **189**
Kirkpatrick, Robert G., **179**
Kirshner, Alan, **178**
Kite, Buddy, **169**
Kittrell, W. H., **138**
Kiwanis Bowl, 112
Kjellgren, Denise, **211**
Klausner, Kris, **220**
Klepper, George, **172**
Klyce, W. H., **133**
Knight, Bob, **187**
Knight, Eddie, **201**
Knight, Riley, **203**
Knox, Britt, **182**
Knox, George, **201**
Koehn, Kurt, **202**
Kousser, David, **191**
Kraft, Murry, **218**
Krusac, Jill, **152**
Kuhlman, John W., **194–198**
Kyle, Frank, 38

L

Lacey, Travis, **216**
Lackey, Ashton, **209**
Lackey, David, **218**
Ladd, Craig, **206**
LaGrasse, Kerri, **217**
Laine, Craig, **199**
Lamb, Stacy, **218**
Lamb, Tracy, **215**
Lamb, Vicki, 112, **206–208**
Lance, Tommy, 79, **173–174**
Landers, David, **210**
Lane, H. H. Jr., **129**
Langford, D. P., **145**
Langford, Troy, **206**
Langley, Chip, **200**
Langley, Hiram G., **210**
Langston, Doug, 108, 116, **200–220**
Lanier, Dwight, **194**
Lannom, Berry, **188**
Lannom, Lance, **206**
Lape, Steve, **218**, 220
Largen, J. W., **165**
Larkin, Bob, **202**
Larson, Mark, **203**
Lass, Kriss, **208**
Lavin, Mike, **176**
Lavin, Remon, **175**
Lawrence, Amy, **210**
Lawrence, J., **197**
Lawrence, Steve, **199**
Lawrence, Thomas, **193**
Lawrence, Tom, **186**
Lawrence, Tommy, **190**
Lawson, Gracie, **212**
Lawton, Sandy, **208**
Lawyer, Ken, **204**
Lea, Dorothy, 108, **195–203**
Lea, Milton, **168**
Leach, Carol, **205–208**
Lea-Mord, Carol, 116, **209–220**
Lee, Frank, **206**

Lee, Heren, **207**
Lee, Jack, **191**
Lee, Jack III, **160–161**
Lee, Jennifer, **215**
Lee, John, **194**
Lee, Kenna, 211
Lee, Lelia, **210**
Lee, Sam, **185**
Lee, Scooter, **205**
Lee, Teddy, **195**
Lee, Tommy, **211–213**
Lee, Wilder, **209**
Leek, Bill, **188**
Leek, Tommy, **185**
Leftwich, Kristy, **214**
Leftwich, Michael, **211**
Leland, M., **198**
Leon, Luis, **197**
Leonard, Alice, **220**
Leonard, George, **190**
Leonard, John Clarence, **152**
Leonard, Tom, **186**
Leprun, Francois Andre, **192–193**
Leslie, Alistair, 106
Lester, Joe, **193**
Leu, John, **181**
Lewis, Binks, **105**, 201
Lewis, Dick, **194**
Lewis, John M., **189**
Liggett, John M., **143**
Light, Bill, **168**
Lightfoot, Mike, **199**
Ligon, Matt, 113, **212**
Ligon, Ronald Sanders, **180**
Ligon, Sandy, **205**
Ligon, Winston, **171**
Lille, Theodore R., **150**
Lillie, Bessie, **142**
Lillie, J. B. Jr., 42
Lillie, James, **170**
Lillie, Mrs. Pryor, 65, 88
Lindahl, Eric, **207**
Linsert, Richard Osborne, **184**
Lipscomb High School, 104
Lipscomb Invitational
   Tournament, 110
Lish, Kelly Jr., **193**
Little, C., **198**
Little, Rob, **206**
Little, Russell, **193**
Little, Tommy, **200**
Livingstone, Jim, **195**
Llewellyn, Mark, **201**
Lloyd, Bobby, 93
Lloyd, William, **193**
Lobb, Archie, **165**
Lobo, Sarita, **218**
Locke, Anne, **215**
Lockhart, Jack Monroe, **153**
Lockridge, George, **187**
Lofton, Bobby, **175**
Lofton, James, **173**
Logan, W. G., **134**
Long, Bryan, **191**
Long, Charles A., 48, **135**
Long, Chrissy, **217**
Long, John F., **149**
Long, Leroy, **175**
Long, Stewart, **212–220**
Longhurst, Rusty, **199**
Lope, Steven, **219**
Lorenzo, Dan, 102, **103**, 198
Lotspeich, Tom, **172**
Lott, G., **197**

Love, Billy, 159, **160**
Lovell, Gene, **195**
Lovell, J. W., **136**
Lovell, R., **198**
Lowe, David, **213**
Lowe, R. E., **137**
Lowery, Mike, **212**
Lucas, Chuck, **188**
Lucas, Johnny, **194**
Lucas, Pete, **163**–**164**
Luna, Irving, **148**
Luna, Jay, **105**, **201**
Lunn, Eddie, **192**
Lunn, Jack, **171**
Lusky, Jon, **214**
Lykins, John, **196**
Lyles, G. A., **172**
Lynch, Howell, **195**
Lyon, James W., **174**
Lyon, William, **154**
Lyons, Tommy, **167**

M

MacDonald, Gerard, **196**
MacPherson, Jason, **211**
MacPherson, Sandy, **188**
Maclay, R., **198**
Madden, Peter, **211**
Maddin, Win, **210**
Maddux, Danny, **205**
Maddux, Lewis, **194**
Magli, Boyce, **186**
Magli, Cooper, **218**
Magli, Tommy, **195**
Maglie, Wib, **214**
Magyar, Joe, **176**
Maiden, Billy, **169**
Mallery, Buford, 38
Mallory, Miss Willie James, **135**
Malone, Ellis Phillips, **184**
Malone, Jason, **217**
Maloney, Andy, **209**
Maloney, David, **203**
Maloney, Donald L., **179**
Mangrum, James Vance, **179**
Manley, Buford, **150**
Manning, E., **197**
Manofsky, Bill, **201**
Manofsky, Larry, **199**
Mapes, Gene, **202**
Marlin, Tommy, **187**
Marlin, William, **158**
Marquess, Jack, **167**
Marshall, Cornelia Estelle, **152**
Marshall, Courtney Kennedy, **57**, **150**
Marshall, Ewing, **140**
Marshall, German, 42
Marshall, Glenda, **212**–**216**
Marshall, Margaret, **144**
Marshall, Scott, **211**
Martin, Dan, **190**
Martin, David, **205**–**214**
Martin, E., **197**
Martin, Jake, **154**
Martin, Mickey, **201**
Martin, Norval, **154**
Martin, Philip, **193**
Martin, Walker, **131**
Martocci, Victoria, **219**
Mason, Edwin, **162**
Masonic Hall, Franklin, 28
Masters, Josh, **220**
Mathis, Gordon, **207**–**211**

Matthews, Carol, **212**–**214**
Matthews, Charles, **203**
Matthews, Craig, **200**
Matthews, Elizabeth, **147**
Matthews, Garath, **191**
Matthews, George I., 42
Matthews, Tom B., **34**, **130**
Mattix, Bobby, **210**
Maury, Edna Porter, **153**
Maxwell, Chris, **212**
Maxwell, Seth, **220**
Maxwell, William, **193**
May, Edward, **160**
Mayer, Dolph, **196**
Mayes, Cannon R., 88, **180**–**186**
Mayes, Wendell, **157**
Mayfield, Becky, **110**
Mays, Allen, **166**
Mays, Carter, **206**
Mays, Julian, **209**
Mays, Katie, **212**
Mays, Seth J., **141**
Mazalook, Jennifer, **213**
McAdams, Rick, **213**
McAfee, Matt, **220**
McAlister, Harry Hill, **202**
McAlister, Joel, **203**
McAlister, John, **202**
McAlister, Peter, **204**
McAlister, Sidney, **203**
McAlpin, Ida, **134**
McAlpin, K., **134**
McAlpine, Frances, **138**
McArthur, Bill, **78**, 79
McArthur, Bobby, **78**, 79
McArthur, Tommy, **204**
McCain, J. R., 58
McCall, Herbert L., **149**
McCall, Nick, **106**
McCall, Tommy, **176**
McCall, Travis, **174**
McCallie School, Chattanooga, Tennessee, 79–80
McCallum, Robert, **151**
McCammon, Jenna, **214**
McCann, Early M. Jr., **178**
McCarter, Terry, **199**
McClain, Leigh, **110**, **207**
McClain, Paige, **107**, **205**
McClanahan, A. E., **132**
McClanahan, Bill, 94, **191**
McClanahan, Bob, **195**
McClanahan, Brad, **219**
McClanahan, Stephen, **193**
McClanless, Jon, **199**
McClure, Frank, **208**
McConnell, Mike, **188**
McCord, Bubba, **192**
McCord, Ernest, **185**
McCord, John, **183**
McCord, William, **171**
McCorkle, D. E., 42
McCoy, Chris, **213**
McCoy, Frank, **192**
McCoy, Mick, **190**
McCracken, Ralph, 96, **192**
McCullough, John, **209**
McCullough, Rob, **207**
McCullough, Roger, **195**
McCullough, Tot, **202**
McCullough, W. A., **138**
McCutcheon, Martha Byrns, **152**
McDaniel, Gordon Jr., **171**
McDaniel, Margaret, **54**, **56**, **146**

McDaniel, Matthew, 55
McDaniel, Matthew F., **145**
McDaniels, Gordon, **196**
McDonald, Wanda, **220**
McDougall, Anna Hall, **144**
McDowell, David, **200**
McDowell, Dennis, **200**
McDowell, R., **198**
McElroy, Larry, 108, **199**–**201**, **211**–**220**
McElveen, George, **167**
McEwen, Clark, **218**
McEwen, John B., 42
McFadden, Eleanor, **145**
McFerrin, Jim A., **20**, **34**, **130**
McGavock, Caroline, 15–16
McGavock, David, **182**
McGavock, John, 15–16
McGavock, William, **151**
McGee, Christy, **214**
McGee, Kathy, **209**
McGee, Sam, 97, 98
McGee, Wayne, **202**
McGinnis, Jerry, **195**
McGlocklin, Clem E. Jr., **155**
McGown, Cliff, **201**
McGugin, Leonard, **191**
McHenry, David, **209**
McHugh, Steve, **203**
McHugh, Tom, **206**
McIntosh, David, **183**
McKay, J., **197**
McKay, Robert A., **176**
McKeand, Bill, **189**
McKeand, Leonard E. III, **179**
McKee, Erwin, 83
McKee, Price Erwin, **178**
McKee, Tom, **181**
McKeel, Richard, **171**
McKinney, Charles, **161**
McKinnon, Mel, **198**
McKinnon, Mike, **200**
McLaughlin, Tommy, **195**
McLaurine, DeWitt, **200**
McLean, B., **197**
McLean, W. H., **137**
McLemore, C. K., **164**, **198**
McLemore, Patti, **154**
McLemore, Robert W., **144**
McLeod, William E., **194**
McLeon, Carrie, **215**
McLish, T. B., 27
McMahan, John, **211**
McMahon, Johnny, **182**
McMahon, Vandi, **212**
McMillan, Park, **190**
McMillan, Robert, **188**
McMillan, Tracey, **205**
McMillen, D., **197**
McMullen, Nathan J., **161**
McNatt, David, **201**–**203**
McNeely, David, **210**
McPherson, Clifton Eugene Jr., **180**
McPherson, Howell W., **150**
McPherson, Josephine, **132**
McWhirter, Burton T., **201**
McWhorter, Martin, **172**
McWilliams, Bouldin, **162**
McWilliams, Jasper H., **166**
Meacham, Gene, **176**
Meacham, Florence, **146**
Meacham, Hale L., **179**
Meacham, Harold Jr., **164**
Meacham, Marshall, **164**

Meacham, Milton, **165**
Meacham, Turner, **147**
Meacham, W. P., **133**
Meacham, Wendell, **178**
Medearis, Walter, **192**
Medlin, Ron, **214**–**220**
Meece, Scott, **219**
Mefford, Pete, **183**
Melley, Bill, **207**
Menefee, John, **206**
Menifee, Albert, **202**
Menifee, Rhonda, **211**
Merns, Wm. R., **189**
Merritt, Eli, **210**
Merville, Albert, **182**
Merville, Larry, **186**
Meyer, Bobby, **206**
Meyer, Chris, **208**
Meyer, Jessica, **219**
Meyers, Brad, **219**
Middle Tennessee State University, 99
Middleton, Johnnie Gene, **180**
Midway Cottage, 73, 74
Milam, Barry, **205**
Milam, Dan, **195**
Milam, Jack, 96–97, **192**
Milam, Roger, **188**
Milam, Scott, **203**
Miles, Curtis, **193**
Miller, Carole, **211**
Miller, Chris, **216**
Miller, Clyde, **158**
Miller, Eran, **220**
Miller, Frank, **154**
Miller, Gus, **160**
Miller, Holly, **220**
Miller, James H. Jr., **180**
Miller, Jason, **218**
Miller, Jimmy, **186**
Miller, Keith, **220**
Miller, Kevin, **217**
Miller, M., **197**
Miller, North, **159**
Miller William T., **178**
Milliken, Jim, **207**
Millington, Fred, **158**
Millis, Michael, **202**
Mills, Buddy, **206**
Mills, Holland, **207**
Mills, J. O., **146**
Milton, Alicia, **217**
Miner, Tom, **195**
Ming, Charles, **172**
Minor, Gary, **200**
Minor, Michael, **193**
Minor, Randy, **199**
Minor, Robert, **193**
Minor, Sterling, **195**
Minter, Tonja, **218**
Minton, Peter, **181**
Mishler, Paul, **163**
Mississippi River, 27
Mitchell, Andy, **190**
Mitchell, B., **197**
Mitchell, Donald, **147**
Mitchell, G. L., **167**
Mitchell, Graham, **163**
Mitchell, Keith, **207**
Mitchell, Robbie, **215**
Mitchell, Tom, **206**
Mitchell, William E., **144**
Mock, Walker, **213**
Moench, B., **197**

Moench, Jay, 102, **103**, **198**
Molner, Frank, **210**
Moncrief, W. C. Jr., **161**
Montague, Bettis, **168**
Montgomery Bell Academy, Nashville, Tennessee, 62, 64, 66, 70
Montgomery, Phelps, **175**
Montgomery, Shannon, **171**
Montgomery, William Shearin, **184**
Moody, Andy, **218**
Moody, Curtis Jr., **160**–**161**
Moody, Mike, **203**
Moody, Steve, **205**
Moon, Braden, **220**
Moon, Eddie, **200**
Moon, Jim, **188**, **198**
Mooney School, 28
Mooney, Theodore Garellas, **180**
Mooney, W. D., 21–22, **23**, **26**, 125
Mooney, W. D. Jr., **33**–**34**
Mooney, Wellborn, 22
Moore, Andy, **216**
Moore, Bill, **216**
Moore, Bob, **190**
Moore, Brent, **213**
Moore, Chad, **215**
Moore, Drew, **212**
Moore, Farris, **188**
Moore, Hal Jr., **214**
Moore, Herman, 44, **131**
Moore, Jack, **161**
Moore, James Irvin, **180**
Moore, Jay, **219**
Moore, Jim, **171**
Moore, Jimmy, **195**
Moore, Kenneth E., **194**
Moore, Lew, **212**
Moore, Phil, **199**
Moore, Richard, **174**
Moore, Robert N. Jr., **177**
Moore, Robert R., **197**–**199**
Moore, Tim, **218**–**220**
Moore, Tom, **215**
Moore, Will, **217**
Moore, William McD., **155**
Moran, B., **198**
Moran, David, **188**
Moran, Gus Jr., **161**
Moran, Houston, **196**
Moran, J. R., **129**
Moran, Joe, **199**
Moran, John Jr., **96**, **193**
Moran, Sam Jr., **171**
More, Ellen, **110**, **207**
Morel, Bobby, 92, **188**
Morel, McNairy, **209**
Morelock, M. M., **132**
Morgan School, 79
Morgan, Marshall, **194**
Morgan, Willis, **186**
Morris, Drew, **208**
Morris, Jamie, **202**
Morris, Russ, **205**
Morris, Scott, **203**
Morris, Will, **44**
Morrissey, David, **185**
Morrissey, Tony, **183**
Morrison, D. W., **137**
Morrison, Eric, **211**
Morrison, Lee, **196**
Morrison, Whitehall, **186**
Morss, John, **205**
Mortell, Mark, **216**
Morton, Beth, **220**

Morton, Chas, 113, **114**, **214**
Moseley, Robert, **158**
Moses, Tim, **212**
Mosher, Bryan, **220**
Mosher, Rachel, **218**
Moss, Bill Jr., **164**
Moss, John, **202**
Moss, John B., **201**
Moss, Mary, **34**, **130**
Moss, William, **189**
Moss, William Henry, **150**
Motlow, J. D. Jr., **160**–**161**
Mott, B., **197**
Mott, Mike, **192**
Mount, G. Eric, **144**
Mu Alpha Theta, 117
Much, Jeremy, **211**
Much, Joel, **217**
Much, Melly, **214**
Mueller, Caroline, **215**
Mueller, Robert, **212**
Mullally, Allison, **214**
Mullens, Will Reese, **163**
Mulley, Theresa, **34**, **129**
Mullican, M., **198**
Muncy, Paul, **194**
Muntz, Jerry, **195**
Murdock, Charles, **165**
Murphy, Alex, **220**
Murphy, Lea, **218**
Murphy, Woods, **220**
Murrey, Steve, **158**
Murrey, William Steve Jr., **179**
Muse, Allen, **192**
Mustelier, Henry, **176**
Myatt, Early, **162**
Myer, Alissa, **220**
Myers, Brad, **220**
Myers, Freddy, **214**

N

Naftel, Mark, **199**
Nagy, Sherri, **214**
Nance, Berkeley, **219**
Nance, John, **106**
Napier, Bob, **182**
Nashville Banner, 66
Nashville Bridge Company, 95
National Football Hall of Fame, 51, 66
Naylor, Ralph F., 82, 85, 88, 100, **171**–**190**
Naylor, Sarah, 59
Neal, Lisa, **207**
Neely, Elizabeth, **147**
Neely, John, **142**
Neely, Leonard, **143**
Neely, Melissa, **216**
Neely, Will, 44, **131**
Neff, Sara, **218**
Neil, Bram, **196**
Nellums, Marcus E. Jr., **178**
Nelson, John Edwards, **180**
Nelson, Shannon, **214**–**216**
Newell, Elizabeth, **144**
Newell, Sam W. Jr., **166**
Newman, Elliot, **186**
Nichol, Jamie, **216**
Nichol, Michael, **211**
Nichol, Patrick, **209**
Nichol, Scott, **213**
Nichols, Billy, **183**
Nichols, H. C., 30
Nichols, Harold Dean, **178**

Nichols, Jim, **189**
Nichols, Joe Donald, **184**
Nichols, Ragan, **218**
Nicholson, Bruce, **168**
Nicholson, John B., **189**
Nicoro, Jason, **219**
Niemeyer, Christian B., **197**
Nischan, Chris, **206**
Nixon, Andrew, **217**
Nixon, Barry, **205**
Nixon, Clarence, **172**
Niznik, Kris, **208**
Noel, Oscar, **187**
Noffsinger, Chance, **212**
Noffsinger, Zachary, **215**
Nolan, Mike, **164**
Nolen, B. T., **34**, **130**
Nolen, Sarah, **151**
Noll, Ronnie, **187**
Noojin, Kenneth, **160**
Nordyke, J., **197**
Norman, J., **198**
Norman, Jack, **204**
North Campus, 124, 125
North, Frank, **163**–**164**, **192**
Notre Dame School, 79
Nunn, J. A., **137**

O

Oakes, Charles, 118, **210**–**220**
Oden, John, **175**
Oden, Marion Jr., **166**
Odum, Jimmy, 79, **177**
Officer, Todd, **217**
Ogilvie, Annie, **142**
Ogilvie, D., **198**
Ogilvie, Paul, **164**
Ogilvie, Walter W. Jr., **174**
Ogles, B., **197**
Oldham, Andrew, **212**
Oldham, Clarke, **214**
Oldham, Robert, **210**
Oliver, Cecil Jr., **169**
Oliver, Drew, **194**
Olson, John, **207**
Oman, Bond, **204**
Oman, John, **205**
Omer, Rusty, **209**
O'Neal, Carlton, **187**
O'Neal, Grantland, **192**
Oneida High School, 119, 121
O'Neil, David, **201**
O'Neil, Doug, **203**
O'Neil, Sutton, 95, **190**
O'Neill, Tip, 116
Orme, Constance, **151**
Orme, W. C., **151**–**152**
Ormes, Bill, **186**
Ormes, Billy, **167**
Ormes, Vance, **195**
Osborne, Glenn, **193**
Osborne, Nathan Jr., **164**
Osborne, Reams, **166**
Osburn, Bobby, **203**
Osburn, Gary, **202**
Osburn, Mack, **165**
Osburn, Nally, **199**
Osburn, Tally, **200**
Overbey, William, **156**
Overby, Beasley, **145**
Overton, Fred Stuart, **179**
Overton High School, Nashville, Tennessee, 102
Overton, John H., **166**

Owen, Frank, **148**
Owen, J. V., **143**, **153**
Owen, Martha Lou, **149**
Owen, Park, **192**
Owen, R. S., 42
Oxley, Art, **206**
Oxley, Dave, **208**
Oxley, John, 92, 100, 104, 108, **187**–**189**, **195**–**204**
Ozburn, D., **197**
Ozburn, Martin, **193**
Ozburn, Perry, **188**

P

Pace, Bryan, **171**
Pace, Harold, **164**
Pace, Kei, **213**
Padgett, L. P. Jr., **139**
Padgett, William L., **135**
Page, Kurt, 119, **215**–**219**
Page, Lela Abernathy, **142**
Paine, George, **188**
Paine, John, **190**
Paine, Patricia, **210**–**211**
Paine, Tom, **186**
Palacio, Joe, **169**
Pannell, W. L., **169**
Parham, Philip, **148**
Parish, Jim, **190**
Parker, Franklin, **172**
Parker, Harold, **139**
Parker, John W., **143**
Parker, Vassar, **154**
Parkes, David, **205**
Parkes, Fred V., **149**
Parkes, Gary, **106**, **204**
Parkes, J. L. Sr., 20, 42
Parkes, Joe, **200**
Parks, Hoyt Jr., **217**–**220**
Parks, Sam, **160**
Parks, Warren Arthur, **157**
Parmer, Cliff, **190**
Parrish, Bert, **168**
Parrish, Bobby, **188**
Parrish, Jim, **201**
Parrish, Scott, **201**
Parrish, Toby, **185**
Parrish, Tom, **200**
Parry, Lucy, **141**
Parsley, Tommy, **183**
Parsons, Kelly, **220**
Parsons, William V. Jr., **193**–**196**
Paschall, A. B., **133**
Paschall, George C. Jr., **150**
Paschall, W. D., **138**
Paterson, John, **165**
Patterson, A. M., **133**
Patterson, Bobby, 95, **191**
Patterson, David, **187**
Patterson, Donald E., 92, 100, **188**–**194**
Patterson, Eugene Jr., **157**
Patterson, John, **204**
Patterson, Jimmy, **177**
Patterson, Sean, **205**
Patton, Allen, **189**
Patton, David, **214**
Patton, Jason, **217**
Patton, Jim Jr., **164**
Paulk, H. J., **133**
Payne, Charlie, **216**
Payne, Jeff, **196**
Payne, Jim, **185**
Payne, Mike, **209**–**212**

Paysinger, Terry, **203**
Paz, Pedro, **181**
Peabody, George College, 76, 82, 85
Peach, Lucy, **210**
Pearson, Buford B., **166**
Pearson, Clinton H., **178**
Pearson, Mike, **190**
Pearson, Terry, **199**
Peay, C., **198**
Peebles, Fred T., **144**
Peebles, J. R., **129**
Peebles, Mac Jr., 78, **170**
Peebles, Paul, **202**
Peebles, Tommy, **203**
Peel, Joe C., **193**
Peeler, James, **203**
Peercy, Andrew, **219**
Peercy, Ken, **194**
Pelot, Reuben N. III, **178**
Pemberton, Bill, 97, **192**
Pennington, Byrom, **154**
Pennington, Wm. C., **173**
Penny, Richard, **188**
Peoples, Greer, **131**
Peoples Hall, 86
Peoples, Hal, 46, 49, **131**
Peoples, James A., 43
Peoples, R. G. "Daddy," **43**, 49, 51, 53, 56, 58, 60, 62, 87, **131**, **133–150**
Peoples, R. H., **132**, **133**, **134**, **135**, **136**, **137**, **138**
Peoples and Tucker School, Springfield, Tennessee, 43
Peoples School, 43–44, 51
Perez, Armando T. Zayas, **180**
Perkins, N. C., 42
Perkins, Sam F., **141**
Perkinson, Scott, 122, **219**
Perrin, Billy, **161**
Perry, Bill, **206**
Perry, Hays, **190**
Perutelli, Chris, **218**
Peterman, Gary, **189**
Peterson, Mac, **186**
Peterson, Rick, **191**
Pettus, Aaron, **220**
Pettus, Leigh, **214–220**
Pettus, Seth, 119, 121, **219**
Petty, Leya, **211**
Pewitt, Albert, **186**
Pewitt, Dudley J., **173**
Pewitt, E. Gale, **175**
Pewitt, Jene, **197**
Pewitt, Jim, **198**
Pewitt, Trina, **213**
Phelps, Charles G. Jr., **169**
Phelps, Doug, **220**
Phelps, Kenneth, 94, **190**
Phelps, Tom, **200–203**
Philbrick, Chris, **205**
Phillips, April, **217**
Phillips, B. C., **175**
Phillips, Bert, **186**
Phillips, Billy, **172**
Phillips, Edmond, **171**
Phillips, Jeff, **207**
Phillips, Steve, **202**
Phillips, Tommy, **204**, **208**
Phillips, Warren, **204**
Philpot, Rick, **196**
Phinizy, Derk, **214**
Phipps, John, **196**
Phipps, Robert, **158**

Phipps, Skip, **200**
Pierce, Chuck, **220**
Pierce, Clarence, **131**
Pierce, Janet, **131**
Pierce, Jessie M., **137**
Pilcher, Barry, **187–188**
Pilkerton, Fred, **180**
Pilkerton, Jimmy, **202**
Pilkington, Rachel, **219**
Pinkerton, Frank, 92, **188**
Pinkerton, Carl, **142**
Pinkerton, Jack, 146, **170**
Pinkerton, Joe, **154**, **181**
Pinkerton, T. O., **171**
Pinkston, Clennie, **168**
Pinto, Michael, **212**
Pioneer Bowl, 112
Pipkin, E. M., **135**
Pitner, William, **160**
Pitts, Elkton, **165**
Pitts, Lee, **212**
Pitts, Natalie, **214**
Plaster, George, **202**
Platos, the, 60, 66–67, 9–96, 106
Plaxico, C., **198**
Plonka, Stephen, 94, **190**
Plumer, Ned, **187**
Plummer, Charles, **216**
Plummer, Mary, **218**
Plummer, Rob, **214**
Poag, Brian, **213**
Poindexter, James E., **164**
Pointer, David, **175**
Pointer, Henry Jr., **136**
Pointer, T. W., **138**
Polk, Amy, **213**
Polk, N. N., **132**
Polk, Sarah G., **144**
Polk, William, **156**
Pollard, Dickie, **188**
Pollard, Jerry Newton Jr., **180**
Pollard, T. G., 34, **129**
Polston, Barry Brown, **184**
Polston, Bruce Bailey, **184**
Ponder, James, **212**
Ponder, Rebecca, **212**
Pope, Alfred, **166**
Pope, Bill, **181**
Pope, Stan, **213**
Porch, P., **197**
Porleji, Katie, **219**
Porter, Craig, 105, **106**, **204–206**
Porter, Jerry, **189**
Porter, Sidney Dale, **166**
Postlethwaite, Willis, **162**
Potts, Richard Leland, **184**
Powell, B., **198**
Powell, Jack, **172**
Powell, Monty, **194**
Power, Bob, **188**
Powers, Gary, **193**
Powers, Tim, **194**
Powers, Webb, **196**
Pratt, Johnny, **208**
Pratt, Trey, **220**
Preuit, Gordon, **172**
Prevatt, Frank, **216**
Price, Milton, **163**
Price, Ricky, 106, **204**
Price, Tommy, **195**
Prichard, Ronnie, 108
Pride, Harvey, **171**
Primm, Kirby, **163**
Primm, Kirby O. Jr., **194**

Primm, W. **198**
Princeton University, 126
Pritchard, James R., **197**
Pritchard, Ronnie, **198–204**
Proctor, David, **189**
Provost, Edwin, **193**
Pruitt, Robert, **200–203**
Publow, Gordon, **191**
Pullen, J. S., **132**
Pullin, Stanley, 44
Purcell, Randy, **202**
Purcell, Ricky, **200**
Purple and Green, 38
Pursell, Joe, **162**
Puryear, Bill, **203**
Puryear, Dan, **171**
Puryear, David, **173**
Puryear, F., **197**
Puryear, Frank, **168**
Puryear, Gus, **185**
Puryear, Mark, 114, **210**
Putnam, Larry, **182**
Pyle, Walter, Jr., **181**
Pyle, Wilson, **214**
Pylon, Barbara, **215–216**

Q

Quadrangle, 119
Quillman, Lisa, **219**
Quizbusters, 94

R

Raburn, J. C., **170**
Rader, James, 96, 97, **193**
Ragan, John Roy, **180**
Ragan, Matthew, **216**
Ragland, George, **201**
Ragland, Lee, **203**
Ragsdale, Sam, **171**
Ragsdale, Ty, **209**
Rahrer, Brad, **199**
Rainey, Michael, **193**
Rains, Will, **212**
Ramsey, Buck, **183**
Ramsey, William, **193**
Randolph, Dodson, **213**
Randolph Macon College, 59
Ransom, B., **198**
Rasmussen, Walter, **181**
Rather, Billy, **172–173**
Rauchle, Bob C., 102, **197–202**
Rayburn, Kelly, **220**
Ream, J. Boudinot, 27
Reams, H. N., **137**
Reams, John G., **135**
Redford, Clyde, **191**
Redford, Irma, **134**
Redford, James P., **173**
Redford, Matt, **217**
Redick, Betsy, 88, 100
Redick, Bill, **186**
Redick, Paul, 81, **82**, 85–86, 88–89, 98–99, 100, 123, **176–193**
Redick, Mrs. Paul, C., 123, **178–188**, **191**, **193**
Redman, Benjamin Rollins, **153–154**
Reed, Mark, **203**
Reeks, Deck, **200**
Reeks, Sam Jr., **170**
Rees, Ernest, 43
Regen, Eugene M., **144**
Regen, John Bell, **153**
Regen, William M., **155–159**
Reich, John Richard, **179**

Reid, G. T., **133**
Reid, H. R., **129**
Reid, W., **197**
Reid, William, **214**
Reindl, Jeanne, 107, **205**
Rembert, Mark, **207**
Reubelt, Grace, 30
Review Appeal, 46
Reynolds, Adam, **220**
Reynolds, Chris, **205**
Reynolds, Ed, **170**
Reynolds, George A., **149**
Reynolds, H. S., **132**
Reynolds, Jack, **169**
Reynolds, Joe, **207**
Reynolds, Margaret Ann, **202–206**
Reynolds, Ralph D., **191–194**
Reynolds, Richard S., **134**
Reynolds, Ruth, **214**
Reynolds, Samuel, 44
Reynolds, Stone, **131**, **167**
Rhame, Bill, **185**
Rhea, Patrick, **215**
Rhea, Rasco, **190**
Rhodes, Cecil Scholarship, 34
Rhyne, J. Morton, **174**
Ricafort, Erwin, **207**
Ricciardi, Kelly, **208**
Rice, Amy, **214**
Rice, Lent, **161**
Rice, Tandy, 105
Rice, Terry, **217**
Rich, Jeff, **205**
Richardson, Dean, **206**
Richardson, Freddy, **208**
Richardson, Oren, **163**
Richardson, Roberta, 54
Richardson, Rondal, **212**
Richardson, Terry, **200**
Richardson, V. Neil, **193–194**
Richardson, Willia Charlotte, **152**
Ridley, Anne, **219**
Ridley, Campbell, **185**
Ridley, John, **164**
Ridley, John Sam, **192**
Ridley, Will, **189**
Riggins, Wilson, **172**
Ring, J. E., **133**
Ring, Lissa, **205**
Ring, N. S., **138**
Ringstaff, Sally, **214–216**
Risley, Kerry, **214–216**
Ritter, Bill, **218**
Ritter, Britt, **215**
Ritter, Greg, **201**
Ritter, T., **198**
Riverdale High School, Murfreesboro, Tennessee, 102
Roach, Thurston, **184**
Robbins, John, **190**
Roberson, Shed, **156**
Roberts, Allen, **213**
Roberts, Dan Jr., **175**
Roberts, Daniel H., **147**
Roberts, E. L., **129**
Roberts, Eddie, **194**
Roberts, Henry, **193**
Roberts, Jimmy, **219**
Roberts, Leigh, **220**
Roberts, Shelley, **218**
Roberts, Susie Lee, 59
Roberts, Tommy, **185**
Roberts, Walter A., 42
Roberts, William, **216**

Robertson, Billy, **164**
Robertson, Jimmy, **171**
Robertson, Stephen, **190**
Robertson, Suzette, **220**
Robeson, Robbie, **202**
Robinson, Bailey, **187**
Robinson, G., **198**
Robinson, Gig, **190**
Robinson, Gloria, 116, 118
Robinson, Pat, **202**
Robinson, S., **198**
Robinson, Steve, 97, 101, **192**
Robinson, Tim, **202**
Robinson, Todd, **201**
Robinson, Tom, **163**, **190**
Robinson, Tommy, 79, **79**, **174**
Robinson, W., **198**
Robison, C. W., **141**
Robison, D. M., **137**, **140–141**
Robison, Gloria, **209–215**
Robison, W. T., **159**, **164–166**
Roddy, Greeley H., **174**
Rodes, Allan Battle, **144**
Rodes, Pattie, **141**
Rodgers, Danny, **191**
Rodgers, J., **197**
Rodgers, Jennie, **218**
Rodgers, Mike, **188**
Rodgers, Sonny, **187**
Rodgers, Terry, **192**
Rogers, Tommy, **214**
Rodgers, William H., **189**
Rogers, Judson, **193**
Rogers, Kristi, **217**
Rogers, Mark, **191**
Rogers, Rodney H., **194–196**
Rolfe, Bobby, **203**
Rolfe, Charlie, **202**
Rolffs, J. H., 42
Romney, Hervin, **182**
Romney, Leslie, **184**
Rooker, H. G., **137**
Roscoe, Edward, **158**
Rose, Billy, **164**
Rose, John, **205–206**
Ross, Andrew, **220**
Ross, Bill, 123, **168**, **197**
Ross, Bill Award, 123
Ross, Chris, **195**
Ross, J., **198**
Ross, Jerry, **189**
Ross, Luke, **198**
Ross, Mike, **190**
Ross, Pat, **198**
Ross, Rufus, **165**
Ross, Val, **218**
Ross, W., **197**
Rosson, Billy, **191**
Roussel, Michelle, **210**
Rozelle, H. B., **137**
Ruark, Scott, **213**
Rucker, M. G., **137**
Rudd, Mike, **183**
Rudder, Mike, **191**
Rudolph, Alan, **209**
Rudolph, Randy, **191**
Rue, Harrison, **162**, **163**
Rue, Waitt, **161**
Runnion, Chad, **215**
Rush, Philip, **196**
Rush, Steve, **185**
Russell, Emmett, **182**
Russell, James, **140**
Russell, Lara, **215**

Russell, Wesley, **219**
Rutherford, David, **203**
Rutherford, Sam, **191**
Rutherford, Sam Jr., **166**
Rutherford, T., **198**
Ryan, Bette, **212–215**
Ryan, J. D., **210**
Ryan, Robert A. Jr., **179**
Ryland, Joe, **131**

S

Saint Andrews School, 79
Samuels, Seymour III, **183**
Sanders, Herbert V. Jr., **174**
Sanders, Becky, **217**
Sanders, Scott, **213**
Sanders, W. A., **132**
Sandidge, Kent, **210**
Sandidge, Scott, **214**
Sands, L. A. Jr., **165**
Sanford, Will, **206**
Sapp, Fred, **182**
Saralegui, Francisco R., **166**
Sarratt, Bob, **204**
Sartor, Jim, **202**
Satterwhite, Scott, **200**
Savage, Eddie, **208**
Savage, Missie, **207**
Savannah High School, 104
Sawyer, Billy, **170**
Sawyer, Edward Jr., **166**
Sawyer, Gordon H., **161**
Sawyer, Herman, **173**
Sawyer, Jimmy, **169**
Sawyer, Robert, **151**
Sawyer, Tom, **180**
Savage, Jim, **169**
Scales, Steve, **200**
Scantlebury, Mark, **194**
Scarborough, James Stephen, **179**
Schmitt, Jack, 79, **174**
Schneider, Herbert, **177**
Schneider, Robert R., **180**
Schofield, John M., 6–8, 14
Schultenover, Eric, **217**
Schultenover, Sara, **219**
Schuur, Lisa, **216**
Schwab, George Augustus III, **180**
Schwarts, Bobby, **188**
Scott, Greg, **207**
Scott, Harold, **174**
Schuler, E. F., 34
Schwartz, Bobby, 92
Schwartz, Mark, **195**
Scott, Agnes College, 58
Scott, Ben, **204**
Scott, Christ, **210**
Scott, Lewis Daniel III, **184**
Scoville, S., **197**
Scoville, Stack, **196**
Scruggs, Cooper, **164**
Scruggs, Julian, **199**
Scruggs, Maurice, **204**
Searcy, Don, 106, **204**
Seaton, Hank, 94, **191**
Seaton, Henry E., 102, **197–198**
Seay, Edward W., **155**
Sebastian, Bobby, **206**
Sebastian, Mark, **204**
Sebastian, Richard, **208**
Sedberry, Clifton, 78, 79
Sedberry, Jimmy, 78, 79
Seeley, Kyle, **207**
Sellers, Mason, **220**

Selph, Bob, **194**
Sensing, Barry, 115, **204–220**
Sensing, Carson, **210**
Sewanee Military Academy, 64, 79, 99
Sewanee University, 25
Seward, D. G., **137**
Seward, Douglas C. Jr., **173**
Seward, Jackson, **139**
Sewell, Bob, **185**
Sewell, Jimmy, **190**
Shackelford, Duke, 92
Shackelford, Phillip, **205**
Shanlever, Bill, **181**
Shanlever, R. Charles, **179**
Shannon, Frances, **142**
Shannon, G. P., **136**
Shannon, James B., **139**
Shannon, Jean Reid, **144**
Shannon, Pope, **143**
Sharber, David, **199**
Sharber, Tony, **204**
Sharp, Andy, **202**
Sharp, Will, **219**
Sharpe, Mrs. Joe, **178–179**
Shatas, Remigius, 94, **190**
Shatz, B., **198**
Shaub, David, **203**
Shaw, Greg, **210**
Shaw, Jeff, **209**
Shaw, Patrick Varney, **180**
Shea, Billy, **205**
Shelby, A. G., **138**
Shelby, O. M., **137**
Shell, Bobby, **199**
Shelton, Allison, **220**
Shelton, Ronald W., **195–198**
Shepherd, Scott, **206**
Sherling, Randy, **181**
Sherman, William T., 8
Sherrill, John, 44, **131**
Sherry, Camille, **216**
Shetler, Shane, **212**
Shields, John C., **195**
Shields, Perry, **191**
Shillinglaw, Drew, **199**
Shinkle, Mike, **186**
Shirling, Nicholas, **210**
Shockley, Andrew G., **174**
Shoemaker, William A., **178**
Shore, Kim, **220**
Short, Bilbo, **192**
Short, Bobby, **169**
Short, Brock, **203**
Short, James Cotton, **152**
Short, James W., **165**
Short, Jesse, 34, 42, **130**
Short, Jim Jr., **190**
Shouse, Stephanie, 111, **212**
Shrock, Terry, **207–211**
Shuler, E. F., **130**
Shull, Buster, 92, **187**
Shull, Jared, **220**
Shull, Jason, **218**
Shull, Wm. H., **161**
Shupe, Anthony P., **171**
Shwab, Clay, **192**
Shwab, George, **206**
Siegrest, Jay Jr., **193**
Sies, Durwood Jr., 123, **165**
Sies, Durwood Award, 123
Sikes, A. T., **136**
Silva, Tony, **215**
Silvey, George, 97

Simmerman, George, **166**
Simmons, Carter, **209**
Simmons, J. B. Jr., **165**
Simms, Jaime, **219**
Simpson, John, **194**
Simpson, Oscar Jr., **170**
Simpson, M. C., **149–150**
Sims, Bob, **175**
Sinclair, Richard, **185**
Sinclair, Tom, **187**
Singleton, Curtis, **182**
Sittell, Chris, **212**
Sittell, Scott, **208**
Skinner, Eric, **208**
Skinner, Chip, **205**
Skinner, Rob, **210**
Slaven, William A., **178**
Slaymaker, Chris, **200**
Slivey, George, **192**
Small, Faxon Jr., **159**
Smalley, G., **198**
Smathers, Jewell, **205**
Smathers, John, **156**
Smith, A. W., **163**
Smith, Bob, **192**, **201**
Smith, Brian, **204**
Smith, Briggs, **141**
Smith, Chip, **205**
Smith, David E., **205**
Smith, David H., **205**
Smith, Donald, **164**
Smith, Donnie, **202**
Smith, Doug, **207**
Smith, Dowell, **195**
Smith, Fleming W. Jr., **179**
Smith, Frank "Red," 38
Smith, Gary, 104, 108, 114, 115, 121, **198–220**
Smith, Gilbert, **183**
Smith, Hal, 87, **183**
Smith, J. C. "Indian," 34, **130**
Smith, J. L., **132**
Smith, James, 148
Smith, Jim, **201**
Smith, Jimmie Jr., **173**
Smith, Jimmy, **190**
Smith, John Shelley, **184**
Smith, Keith, **202**
Smith, Kevin, **199**
Smith, Lamar M., **178**
Smith, Lucien, **131**
Smith, M. M., **137**, **138**
Smith, Marbel, **147**
Smith, Mary Ruth, **146**
Smith, Mike, **200**
Smith, Mont, **192**
Smith, Reese, **191**
Smith, Robert Allen, **175**
Smith, S., **197–198**
Smith, Stefan, **190**
Smith, Sterling, **209**
Smith, Terry Wendell, **184**
Smith, Thomas Benton, 14–15
Smith, Tommy, **195**
Smith, William, 100, **188–196**
Smithson, Bill, **186**
Smithson, Bob, **195**
Smithson, Carl W., 88, 90, 92, **93**, 100, **178**, **180–195**
Smithson, Dennis, **199**
Smithson, Don, **200**
Smithson, Harriet, 54
Smithson, Howard, **182**, **191**
Smithson, J. B., **162**

Smithson, Jeff, **212**
Smithson, Martha, 95
Smithson, T., **198**
Smizer, Booker, 38
Smotherman, Randy, **200**
Smyer, Billy Jr., **170**
Snider, Anne, **217–220**
Snodgrass, Turner, 196
Snow, Don, 108, **198**,–**220**
Snow, Patrick, **215**
Sorrels, O. M., **133**
Southall, Chuck, **196**
South Campus, 124–125
Southern Association for Colleges and Schools, 72
Southon, Tim, **208**
Southwestern Presbyterian University, 22
Southwood, John, **105**
Sowell, J. G., **133**
Spangler, Ralph Jr., 78, **170**
Spanish Club, 106
Sparkman, Hanes, **195**
Spaulding, Collins, **206**
Spaulding, David, **204**
Speake, James H., **179**
Speake, Walter, **181**
Spencer, Brad, **216**
Spencer, Richard, **209**
Speulda, Judy, **218–220**
Spotts, Harry, **182**
Spotts, Nelson, **186**
Spring Hill, Tennessee, 7–8
Springer, Jarron, **220**
Springer, Vince, **215**
Sprouse, John Draughon, **180**
Stack, Bill, **209**
Stadler, George, **201**
Stainback, I. M., **131**
Stalcup, Tyndall, **172**
Stalcup, Wm. J., **173**
Stamps, Bob, **192**
Stanford, Robert Donnell III, **184**
Stanley, Charley, **169**
Stanley, Wells, **163**
Staples, Jack, **192**
Stapp, Andrew, **166**
Stapp, Grady, **163**
Startup, Dan, **201**
Steele, Alex, **192**
Steele, Allen, **160**
Steele, Donald M., **189**
Steele, Ed, **186**
Steele, Edward, **159**
Steele, Elsie, **136**
Steele, Gillis, **138**
Steele, Jeff, **208**
Steele, Lewis, **182**
Steele, Marion, **181**
Steele, Mary Elizabeth, **136**
Steele, Mike, **206**
Steltjes, Jennie, **217**
Steltjes, Julie, **211**
Steltemeier, Rudy, **201**
Stephens, Billy, **183**
Stephens, Dale, **195**
Stephens, Frederick, **193**
Stephens, Keith, **183**
Stephenson, Cowan D., **134**
Stephenson, J., **198**
Stephenson, T., **197**
Stephenson, Tommy, **204**
Stevens, Joseph J., **184**
Stevens, Leon, **207**

Stewart, A. P., 9, 12
Stewart, Boardman, 92, 100, **187–190**
Stewart, Lillian, 108, 116, **198–209**
Stewart, Tim, 104, **105**, **201**
Stiff, Jimmy, 206
Still, John, **162**
Still, Thomas L., **177**
Stinson, Jimbo, **215**
Stinson, Kerry, **199**
Stockett, Steve, **187**
Stockton, Grant, **211**
Stoltz, Carl, **181**
Stone, J., **197**
Stone, James Nolner "Stein," 41
Stone, Mac, **200**
Stone, Mark, **200**
Stone, Rusty, **202**
Story, Brian, **217**
Stovall, John, **216**
Stover, John, **204**
Strahl, O. F., 12–13
Stranahan, Aaron, **217**
Stranahan, Benjamin, **219**
Strasinger, Steve, **203**
Strasser, Kelly, **219**
Stratford High School, 104
Stratton, Frank, **188**
Stratton, Randy, **199**
Street, Bobby, **182**
Strickland, Daniel, **216**
Strickland, David, **214**
Stringer, Jake, **173**
Stuart, Hugh, **183**
Stubblefield, R., **198**
Students Against Drunk Driving, 115
Stumb, Larry, **184**
Sturdivant, Rob, **191**
Stutts, Cris, **218**
Suarez, Orlando, **173**
Sugg, John, **144**
Sugg, Leroy, **163**
Sugg, Susie, 54, **56**, 147
Sugg, W. D., **140**
Sullivan, Jerry, **181**
Sullivan, Wiley, **209**
Summarell, Bill, **215**
Summarell, Larry, **206**
Summers, Gerald, **140**
Summers, Glenn G., **141**
Summers, William D., **152**
Sutherland, Bill, **191**
Sutherland, Charles M. Jr., **189**
Sutherland, Dean, **206**
Sutherland, Scott, **196**
Sutherland, Stephen, **193**
Sutton, B., **197**
Swann, K., **197**
Swearingen, Chris, **216**
Sweeney, Amy, **218**
Sweeney, Leon, **159**
Sweeney, Lionel, **161**
Sweeny, Will, **219**
Swenson, Jonathan, **220**
Swensson, Kurt, **203**
Swiggart, Bill, **192**
Swiggart, Jim, **192**
Sxorman, Steve, **186**

T

Talmadge, Pete, **188**
Talton, J., **197**
Tanksley, Allen, **190**
Tanksley, Bill H., **179**

Tanner, J. Wallace, **135**
Tanner, Mike, **205–206**
Tarkington, Ken, **191**
Tarkington, Raymond Edward, **180**
Tate, Joe, **200**
Tate, Milton, **163–164**
Tate, Sam, **165**
Tate, Thomas W., **176**
Taylor, Bill, **198**
Taylor, Burt F., **143**
Taylor, Charles, **213**
Taylor, Dean, **205–206**
Taylor, Fred Jr., **166–167**
Taylor, J. C., **132**
Taylor, J. C., **132**
Taylor, Jeff, **207–208**
Taylor, John, **202**, 207
Taylor, Johnny, **200**
Taylor, Tommy, **194**
Taylor, Will, **218**
Taylor, Wood, **163**
Teasley, Frank, **186**
Temple University, 51
Templeton, Barry, **206**
Tennessee Female College, 18–19, 21
Tennessee Military Academy, 79
Tennessee River, 6
Tennessee Secondary School Athletic Association, 82, 87
Tennessee Valley Athletic Conference, 87
Terrell, John Thuss, **180**
Terry, George, **172**
Terry, Johnson, **182**
Thomas, A., **197**
Thomas, Albert, **164**
Thomas, Bill, **200**
Thomas, Brent, **220**
Thomas, G., **198**
Thomas, Hamp E., **155–156**
Thomas, Jim, **199**
Thomas, Michael, **220**
Thomas, Spence, **130**
Thomas, Woodlief, **34**, **129**
Thomason, Brad, **196**
Thomasson, Jim, **186**
Thompson, B., **198**
Thompson, Bob, 94, **190**
Thompson, Daly, 51, 88, 98, 100, **135**, **139–142**, **181–192**
Thompson, Douglas, **194**
Thompson, Georgette, **213**
Thompson, Jacob L., **27**
Thompson, James, **191**
Thompson, James M., **179**
Thompson, James S., **189**
Thompson, Jerry, **191**
Thompson, John, 94, **189**
Thompson, Josh, **214**
Thompson, Kenneth, **162**
Thompson, M., **197**
Thompson, Robert, **220**
Thompson, Robert R., **174**
Thompson, Roy, **142**
Thornton, Claude, **57**
Thornton, Steve, **200**
Throckmorton, Chip, **208**
Throop, Ben, **160**
Throop, Willard, **158**
Thurman, Peter, **220**
Thweatt, Harry, **162**
Tichenor, Bill, **196**
Tidwell, Crom, **199**
Tillman, Newt, **203**
Tippens, Bill, **160**

Tippens, Clark, **159**
Tippens, Jim Jr., **179**
Tippens, Richard, **181**
Tobacco Bowl, 97, 104
Tolbert, James M., **162–163**
Tolbert, Paige, **210**
Tolbert, Thad, **208**
Tomlin, Jimmy, **174**
Tompkins, Dave, **215**
Tompkins, John, **190**
Tompkins, Sid, 92, **187**
Torrence, Joe, **186**
Tosh, George, 106, **204**
Trabue, Charles, 91, **186**
Trabue, George O., **176**
Trabue, Tony, **191**
Trace, Greg, **207**
Trace, Rhonda, 107, **110**, **205**
Trailov, Michael, 122, **220**
Trailov, Susan, **215–220**
Training High School, Indianapolis, Indiana, 40
Traughber, G. Jr., **198**
Traughber, Gilliam, 68, **68**, **166**
Treadway, Alan, **204**
Treadway, Felix, **191**
Trezevant, Stanley, **167**
Trousdale, Bobby, **182**
Trondsen, Woody, **213**
Truett, Felix, 55
Truitt, Lee, **191**
Tucker, Frank, **148**
Tucker, James, **208**
Tucker, Margaret Frances, **153**
Tucker, Robert, **205**
Tucker, Suzy, **213**
Tucker, W. H., **151–152**
Tudor, Rob, **206**
Tulloss, Bramlett Jr., **161**
Tulloss, Lucille Temple, **149**
Tulloss, Mary Sam, **150**
Turner, Buzz, **187**
Turner, Carroll Jr., **168**
Turner, Glenn, **160**
Turner, James William, **178**
Turner, Jessie, **217**
Turner, John, **193**
Turner, Rhonda, **211**
Twitty, Thomas, **202**

U

Underwood, John Jr., **168**
Unger, Matt, **220**
United Daughters of the Confederacy, 17
University of Georgia, 117
University of the South, 99
University of Tennessee, 99
Uselton, Randy, 113, **207**
Uselton, Van, **205**
Uthman, Ed, **195**
Utley, Bill, **192**

V

Vaden, John, **157**
Vanderbilt University, 26, 34, 40, 60, 81, 90, 115, 126
VanLandingham, Billy, **213**
VanLandingham, Jeffrey, 119, 121, **219**
VanLandingham, Wendy, **216**
Varnell, Leslie, **220**
Vassalao, George, **195**

Vaughan, Giles, **159**
Vaughn, Bryan, **217**
Vaughn, Denise, **212**
Vaughn, Michael, **193**
Vaughn, V. W., 20
Veeyers, Brad, **204**
Verner, Shawn, **214**
Vick, Don, 112, **199**, **205–214**
Vickers, Earl, **199**
Vincent, Hal, 118, **217**
Vincent, Kelley, **216**
Vining, J., **197**
Vining, Larry, **188**
Vining, Walker, **216**
Voecks, Brian, **211**
Vollmer, Sarah, **216**
Vollmer, Tom, **201**
Voss, John, **206**

W

Wade, Alex, **190**
Wade, Frank, **193**
Wade, John, **186**, **202**
Wade, King, **186**
Wade, P. H. Jr., **170–171**, **174–177**
Wade, Pat, **200**
Waggoner, Jerry, **206**
Waggoner, John, **209**
Waggoner, Lee, **200**
Waggoner, Mike, **200**
Wagner, George R., **179**
Waites, Clay, **167**
Walker, Billy, **172**
Walker, J. O. Jr., **160**
Walker, John Elmo, **184**
Walker, Johnny, **199**
Walker, Marshall, **169**
Walker, N. Y., **167**
Walker, Norvel, **169**
Walker, R. C., **136**
Walker, Robert, 116, **207–220**
Walker, Roger, **211**
Walker, S. B., **139**
Walker, Sam, **209**
Walker, Ted, **203**
Wall and Mooney School, 22–25
Wall, Bill, **196**
Wall, Jim, **208**
Wall, John Brown, 21
Wall, Martha Wilson, 21
Wall, S. V. Jr., **129**
Wall, Simeon Venable, 21, **23**, 125
Wall, T. P., **129**
Wallace, George, **191**
Wallace, Ham, **196**
Wallace, John, **203**
Wallace, Murray, **169**
Wallace, Paul, **210**
Wallace, William Hugh, **180**
Waller, Ben E., **155**
Walley, Ed, **189**
Wallin, Matt, **215**
Walling, Jesse, **163**
Walt, Dabney, **195**
Walters, Harry, **187**
Walton, John, **159**
Wampler, George M., **169**
Wanzeck, Keith, **218**
Ward, Chandler, **167**
Ward, Gene, **168**
Ward, Jimmy, **203**
Ward, William T., 27
Warden, Angela, **215**
Warden, Andrea, **217**

Ward-Smith, Kenny, 94, **189**
Ware, John A., **155**
Warfield, Bill, **200**
Warfield, Charlie, **196**
Warner, Mac, **205**
Warpool, Joe, **211**
Warren, Alex, **212**
Warren, James, **202**
Warren, John, **167**
Warren, Ken, **105**, **201**
Warren, Matt, **214**
Warren, Phil, **200**
Warren, Thomas D., 116, **174**, **201–219**
Warrenfells, Kristin, **212**
Wartell, Steve, **213**
Watkins, A. W., **129**
Watson, Asa Jr., **149**
Wauford, Milton, **169**
Wauford, S., **197**
Waynick, Roger, **204**
Weaver, Bob, **163–164**
Webb, Doris, **212**
Webb, Jim, 108, **192**, **199–203**
Webb, John L., **171**
Webb, Mark, **203**
Webb, Sam G., **148**
Webb, Sawney, 21
Webb School, 21–22
Webber, Johnny, **186**
Weiland, S., **197**
Weinstein, Bernard, **177**
Weisger, Harry, **183**
Weisiger, Will, **214**
Welch, Tom, **158**
Wellons, David, **201**
Wells, Chuck, **199**
Wells, Colley, **201**
Wells, Lisa, **211**
Wells, Travis, **210**
Welsh, Pat, **202–204**
Wemyss, Howlson, **79**, **174**
Wemyss, W. Mac, **161**
Werling, Jenna, **216**
West, D., **198**
West, Olin, **186**
West, Tommy, **194**
Westbrook, L., **198**
Westbrook, Randy, **202**
Westbrooks, Angie, **213**
Westfeldt, F. H., **34**, **129**
Westlake, Nigel, **212**
Westminster College, Fullerton, Missouri, 58
Westover Cottage, **73**, 74, 84, 86
Whalley, David, **190**
Whitaker, Brian, 118, **216**
White, Bill, **191**
White, Britton, **217**
White, Bruce Thomas, **148**
White, Carrie, **219**
White, Frank, **212**
White, George W., **174**
White, Govan, **205**
White House High School, 112
White, Jason, **215**
White, Jennifer, **216**
White, John, **203**
White, John Lawrence, **156**
White, Kristan, **214**
White, Mitch, **212**
White, Newton, **158**
White, Orville, **167**
White, Orville F., **168–171**

White, Scott, **205**
White, Susan, **220**
White, Taylor, **216**
Whiteman, John, **194**
Whiteman, Ralph, **191**
Whitehead, Mike, **212**
Whitehead, Tommy, **210**
Whitfield, Earl B., **143**
Whitfield, J. D. Jr., **150**
Whitfield, Mary Alise, **149**
Whitfield, Raymond S., **150**
Whitley, Gladys, **198**
Whitley, Les, **218**
Whitley, Mary, **215**
Whitman, Albert, **178**
Whitt, Wayne, **201**
Wickliffe, Bill, **196**
Wikle, Charles W., **149**
Wikle, Roberta, **144**
Wilburn, R. Bridgeforth, **135**
Wildcat Newspaper, 83–84, 92–93
Wiley, Buck Jr., **177**
Wilhoite, Jimmy, **199**
Wilk, Tom, **202**
Wilkening, Doug, **216**
Wilkening, Scott, **214**
Wilkerson, Russell Benjamin Jr., **180**
Wilkes, Thomas Woodson Jr., **180**
Wilkinson, Terrence H., **192**
Wilkinson, Terrence W., **193**
Willey, Willis, **165**
Williams, Benny, **192**
Williams, Boyd, **208**
Williams, Brad, **105**, **200**
Williams, Brian, **213**
Williams, Caroline, **214**
Williams, Doug, **202–206**
Williams, Drew, **209**
Williams, Elliott, **202**
Williams, Fleming Jr., **78**, **170**
Williams, Henry, **168**
Williams, Jeff, **207**
Williams, Jennifer, **219–220**
Williams, Jim, **201**
Williams, Jimmy, **205**
Williams, Joel, **207**
Williams, M., **197**
Williams, Mike, **194**
Williams, Molly, **215**
Williams, Ralph, **183**
Williams, Steve, **202**
Williams, Tommy, **209**
Williams, Wilson C. Jr., **174**
Williamson County Historical Society, 118
Williamson County Public Library, 20, 28
Williamson, Sam E. Jr., **184**
Willingham, Bradford, **143**
Willingham, Calder, **154**
Willis, Reese, **208**
Willis, Russ, **201**
Willoughby, Beth, **110**
Willow Plunge, **77**, 78
Wiloughby, Beth, **207**
Wilson, Alex Jr., **169**
Wilson, Brad, **201**
Wilson, Craig, **203**
Wilson, Dan, **216**
Wilson, David, **205**
Wilson, Henry, **106**, **204**
Wilson, John, **193**
Wilson, Johnny, **188**
Wilson, Joseph, **157**

Wilson, Sonny, **167**
Wilson, Walter, **184**
Winningham, Jeff, **186**
Winstead Hall, 8, 11
Winter, Duncan, **212–214**
Wise, Craig, **106**, **206**
Wise, Jimmy, **181**
Wise, Rodney Irvin, **180**
Wiseman, Tom, **200**
Witherspoon, Frank, **192**
Witherspoon, Jim, **194**
Witte, Mona P., **217–219**
Wolf, Bob, **204**
Wollas, Joey, **220**
Womack, Scott, **219**
Woolf, Charles Jr., **193**
Wood, Bennett, **220**
Wood, Brandon, **218**
Wood, Chris, **212**
Wood, Cooper, **210–218**
Wood, David E., **179**, **185–186**
Wood, R. W. Jr., **171**
Wood, Ricky, **202**
Woodall, T., **198**
Woodall, Thomas, 102
Woodard, David, **204**
Woodard, Greg, **200**
Woodard, James E., **161**
Woodard, Milton, **159**
Woodfin, John, **196**
Woodham, Kelly V., **161**
Woodliff, John, **186–187**
Woodring, George, **185**
Woodring, Tuck, **186**
Woodrow, Millard, 33
Woods, Joe, **177**
Woods, Vaughn, **191**
Woodward, Eddy, **190**
Worley, Rush, **138**, **147**
Worthen, George, **185**
Wrenn, Charles, 108, **199–204**
Wrenn, Chase, 118, **217**
Wrenn, Craige, **213**
Wrenn, James, **172**
Wrenne, Charles, **198**, **200**
Wright, Bobby, **194**
Wright, Jimmy, **215**
Wright, P., **197**
Wyatt, Breck, **191**
Wyatt, Jack, **189**
Wylie, John, **208**
Wylie, Michael, **212**
Wylie, Steve, **207**
Wynne, Rob, **209**

Y

Yale University, 126
Yancey, Charlie, **181**
Yankee, R. M. Jr., **175**
Yarbrough, Bobby, **164**
Yeiser, Jack, **183**
Yokom, Chris, **207**
York, Lain, **208**
York, Warren, **183**
Young, Brad, **217**
Young, Donnie, **203**
Young, Davis, **213**
Young Men's Christian Association, 38
Young, Robert O., **141**

Z

Zeigler, Amanda, **213**
Zinn, Andrew, **220**
Zumbado, Hector, **175**